ÉMIGRÉS

Émigrés

FRENCH WORDS THAT
TURNED ENGLISH

Richard Scholar

PRINCETON UNIVERSITY PRESS

PRINCETON & OXFORD

Requests for permission to reproduce material from this work
should be sent to permissions@press.princeton.edu

Published by Princeton University Press
41 William Street, Princeton, New Jersey 08540
6 Oxford Street, Woodstock, Oxfordshire OX20 1TR

press.princeton.edu

Library of Congress Cataloging-in-Publication Data
Names: Scholar, Richard, author.
Title: Émigrés : French words that turned English / Richard Scholar.
Description: 1st. | Princeton : Princeton University Press, 2020. | Includes
bibliographical references and index.
Identifiers: LCCN 2020003918 (print) | LCCN 2020003919 (ebook) | ISBN
9780691190327 (hardback) | ISBN 9780691209586 (ebook)
Subjects: LCSH: English language—Gallicisms. | English language—Foreign
elements—French. | French language—Influence on English.
Classification: LCC PE1582.F8 S36 2020 (print) | LCC PE1582.F8 (ebook) | DDC
422/.441—dc23
LC record available at https://lccn.loc.gov/2020003918
LC ebook record available at https://lccn.loc.gov/2020003919

British Library Cataloging-in-Publication Data is available

Editorial: Ben Tate and Josh Drake
Production Editorial: Natalie Baan
Jacket Design: Layla Mac Rory
Production: Jacquie Poirier
Publicity: Katie Lewis and Alyssa Sanford
Copyeditor: Francis Eaves

Jacket illustration by John Barnett

This book has been composed in Miller

Printed on acid-free paper. ∞

Printed in the United States of America

10 9 8 7 6 5 4 3 2 1

In memoriam

Raissa Landor, Michael McCarthy, and A. D. Nuttall

and for

la jeune génération

CONTENTS

ÉMIGRÉS

Here We Go Round the Mulberry Bush

IT IS WIDELY to be observed that those wishing, at little effort, to lend a certain intrigue to their English conversation season it with a certain *je-ne-sais-quoi* or some other *soupçon* of Gallic garniture. Even the introverted Eeyore, on occasion, reaches for the *mot juste*. Eeyore is the old grey donkey who lives in a corner of a field that is forever England in A. A. Milne's stories about Winnie-the-Pooh and friends. In chapter 6 of *Winnie-the-Pooh*, it is Eeyore's birthday, a fact that his friends have all forgotten. When Pooh Bear chances upon Eeyore and wishes him a good morning, Eeyore doubts that it *is* a good morning, hinting darkly: 'We can't all, and some of us don't. That's all there is to it.' Pooh asks Eeyore to explain. The old grey donkey offers the following list of equivalent words and phrases: 'Gaiety. Song-and-dance. Here we go round the mulberry bush.' A puzzled Pooh asks, 'What mulberry bush is that?', in response to which the donkey merely continues his variations on the theme: ' "Bon-hommy," went on Eeyore gloomily. "French word meaning bonhommy," he explained. "I'm not complaining, but There It Is." [1]

Et voilà: There It Is, indeed, the French word that bursts into flower in the midst of the most English sentence. A word of conspicuously French derivation serves Eeyore's purposes well. It would be too painful for him to name in plain English the simple happiness of being alive that the irrepressible Pooh clearly possesses that morning and which the old grey donkey can't and doesn't, at the best of times, but especially when it is his birthday and They have all Forgotten. Instead, Eeyore names obliquely the capacity for happiness that is denied him, alluding to popular English rhymes that speak of it and producing synonyms that name it. He brilliantly introduces the last of these synonyms, *bon-hommy*, as a French word possessing the meaning of the selfsame word in English. He thereby specifies that meaning as evident to the likes even of Pooh Bear, while using the Frenchness of the word to emphasize its distance from himself, the discontented grey English donkey. His single-word code mixing of French in English at once connects him to, and separates him from, French ways of saying and being.

Eeyore's flourishing of *bon-hommy* is an act of expressive indirection that reveals much about the history of English in its centuries-old relation with French. An equally revealing, if unconscious, act lies at the heart of a story widely told of the forty-third president of the United States of America. George W. Bush was said to have remarked, in July 2002, to his closest ally in international politics, the UK prime minister Tony Blair, that 'the problem with the French is that they don't have a word for entrepreneur'. Whether or not the anecdote is true—and its truth is disputed—matters less, for our purposes, than the fact that it struck a chord with so many people. It circulated at a time of strain in relations between the governments of the three nations, which were taking up different positions in the crisis that eventually saw the UK join the US-led invasion of Iraq in March 2003, opposed by France. The anecdote showed the Anglo-American alliance, in the shape of its leader, revealing—even in the act of denigrating the irksome French—how much the alliance owed to French language and culture. It suggested that many, in the English-speaking world, turn to French much more than they would like to think they do.[2]

We live at a time when the linguistic traffic is, in general, moving much more heavily from English into French than in the contrary direction. After the British empire spread English across the world in the eighteenth and nineteenth centuries, the USA entrenched English as a global lingua franca in the twentieth century, causing the unprecedented amount of lexical borrowing from English that is currently taking place in French and other languages.

This situation ought not to be allowed to conceal a longer and more complex story of linguistic and cultural interaction. Anglophones have borrowed words from French, as Eeyore did consciously and George W. Bush (it seems) did unconsciously, for centuries. More words have entered English from French than from any other modern foreign language. These French words may be said to have 'turned' English in more ways than one. Most have become naturalized. They have done so by means of a process of adoption that is as old as the English language itself, and so thorough that the speaker of English often retains little or no sense of their foreign provenance. It may come as a surprise to many readers, for example, that each of the nouns in the very first sentence of this book—not just *je-ne-sais-quoi*, *soupçon*, and *garniture*, as might be expected, but also *intrigue, conversation*, and *effort*—would have struck seventeenth-century English speakers as a floridly French foreignism. It is a curious fact of linguistic history that while English has fully naturalized many such words, some have over the centuries visibly retained signs of their foreign derivation, eluding translation and resisting naturalization. They may carry traces of their French roots in their pronunciation and spelling. They are often set in italic type to distinguish them from the English surrounding them. They lend English a French twist. They are, we might say, French non-natives in the midst of the language we Anglophones use. For that reason, I propose to use the name for such people that English has (in characteristically magpie fashion) borrowed from French, and to call them *émigrés*.[3]

In this book I explore the varied lives that such émigrés have led. What role, I ask, have they played in the making of modern English? To what extent have they, in their migrations, revealed or changed important aspects of the French linguistic and cultural setting that first shaped them? And what does the study of these words in migration reveal of the fertile but fraught relationship that England and France have long shared, and that now entangles English- and French-speaking cultures all over the world?

In what follows, I argue that émigrés have played an important and largely neglected role in the making of modern English as it is spoken and written in many parts of the Anglophone world today, and has been for centuries. I proceed by drawing together, and then working outwards from, a small cluster of phrases and terms with visibly French roots—*à la mode*, *galanterie*, *naïveté*, *ennui*, and *caprice*—that came to prominence as Charles II and his court, in the period 1660–85, were Frenchifying English language and culture. These are words that retain their émigré status to this day. I explore what meanings and associations they bring with them from French. I place their emergence in Restoration English in the wider context of social and cultural change. I then follow their migration across time and space to examine specific prominent instances over the last three centuries or more in the Anglo-phone cultures of North America, the Caribbean, India, and Ireland, as well as Britain. I draw evidence of the usage and meanings of my chosen words from dictionaries and other lexi-cographical sources. I analyse this evidence alongside instances in literature, film, the visual arts, and music, covering aspects of culture and society that range from opera to ice cream. In this way, I examine how the Anglophone migrations of these words relate to their continuing lives and adventures in French, and I explore in particular what the words mean in—and say about—modern English.

Having taken the Frenchification of Restoration English as my initial focus, I set this development of the language in the wider context of social and cultural change. The two most prominent seventeenth-century English importers of the émi-grés examined in this book—the polymath John Evelyn (1620–1706) and the playwright John Dryden (1631–1700)—trans-ferred into England from France, along with these words, larger-scale cultural ideas and forms: Evelyn proposes that an English equivalent of the Académie française should create a grammar and rhetoric for the English language; Dryden—in his play *Marriage À-la-Mode*—draws freely upon the most suc-cessful modern French dramatic forms even as he satirizes the fashion for Frenchified English among London's social climb-ers of the late seventeenth century.

I pay particularly close attention to episodes in the Anglo-phone migrations of French-derived words when the word in question occurs prominently in the work of artists—writers, of course, but also painters and composers—for whom the use of language is a matter of primary importance. Language, as such artists find it, is no different from what it is for other users of the language. What the artists add to the language they use, however, is an extra edge of consciousness about such matters as the choice of words and their arrangement. I view a word as occurring prominently in the work of these artists when it is sported as the *mot juste* and placed in a position of display, by, for example, being used to name the topic around which an entire work of art is organized, or by figuring in the title of a work.

One example I have mentioned, and to which I return at regular intervals in this book, is Dryden's play *Marriage À-la-Mode* (first published in 1673). Dryden, in that play, satirized French with a forked tongue. He helped the émigré words, whose over-enthusiastic English uses he mocked, to find a lasting place in the language. He explored for his own purposes the questions that such words have always raised about the people who trade in them. These are overwhelmingly questions of identity and affiliation. Who is it that can call upon a word or phrase of foreign derivation in the course of their ordinary linguistic business? Or can understand others who do the same? What do the multilingual transactions of such people say about their place in the social hierarchy, their access to education and culture, and their religious and political loyalties? Dryden's plays ask what such questions mean for the elite of a country, Restoration England, whose society and culture were marked by religious and political conflict.

I examine, in what follows, works of art that return to these questions in quite other times and settings. In his 1971 novel *The Naive and Sentimental Lover*, the English novelist John Le Carré (b. 1931) satirizes the insularity of twentieth-century English middle-class manners by revisiting imaginatively the decisive contribution that the German essayist Friedrich Schiller (1759–1805) made to the meaning of *naive* in 1795, when he paired it with a second foreign word in German, *sentimental*. From the title of her 1809 novel *Ennui* onwards, the Anglo-Irish writer Maria Edgeworth (1768–1849) draws upon the international prestige and analytic power of French language and literary culture in her moral dissection of fashionable life and the state of relations between England and Ireland at the time of their political union. The Canadian novelist George Bowering (b. 1935) exploits the title of his 1987 novel *Caprice* on several levels. The title carries the name of the novel's heroine. It says something about the way in which she manages her predicament. And it is a description of the novel itself, an ingenious remake of the western novel that pits a poetry-loving and bullwhip-toting heroine from Quebec against murderous American outlaws, under the quizzical gaze of two native Indians. It is, in other words, a border-crossing postcolonial Canadian caprice.

Episodes such as these, I suggest, mark in each case a new release of the word's conceptual energies and a remaking of its place in the vocabulary of English. They shed light on the complexity of a process that tends to draw two or more languages and cultures into contact with English: in addition to French, for example, Latin in the making of *à la mode*, Italian in the mixing of *caprice*, and German in the migration of *naive*. They show how that contact between languages and cultures exposes situations of inequality even as it creates new migrant forms of lucidity and expression. And they reveal the particular contradictions that come about as these new forms encounter the entrenched cultures of Anglophone insularity and isolationism.

Such contradictions beset the long history of the English reception of French émigré words. These words inspire admiration in some Anglophones, revulsion in others, and ambivalence in most. They can be reactivated in ways that occasion extraordinary creativity; they even come, at times, to be synonymous with creativity itself; and yet, at the same time, they remain visibly caught up in a power relation between neighbouring cultures that is never perceived as equal. Their Anglophone migrations are often a matter of apparent indifference to guardians of the French language in metropolitan France. Yet these migrations draw the words into spirals and loops of relational development. At times, these émigrés visibly accompany words that have travelled from English into French, acting as their shadows or secret sharers. They are never the same again for having been abroad.

How, in this context, might we best understand the complex history—the transcultural entanglement and creative possibilities—of French words that have turned English? I offer, by way of an answer, the conjecture that this history is best understood as a specific instance of a wider process of creolization. In so doing, I take forward the work that various scholars have published over the last decade or so on relations between English and French, and between England and France, in medieval Europe. That work has shown how, from the Norman conquest of England in 1066 through the age of Chaucer to the time of Shakespeare, the language the English spoke mingled with French, and how this development divided opinion in an England marked by the experience of colonial domination at the hands of the Normans.[4]

I draw inspiration from this body of work even as I extend its scope by shifting the focus to the early modern period and beyond. I explore a time in which the English, once colonized, turned colonizers; and when the language of an imperial nation slowly spread to the four corners of the globe. This historical development brings me to the concept of creolization. That concept has become important to the study of the Caribbean, as a way of understanding the colonizing process practised by the powers of Europe; but it has yet to be considered for its shaping of cultural relations within Europe over centuries. I aim to help fill that gap in *Émigrés* and, in so doing, to contribute to the development of creolization as a conceptual model. My contribution involves significantly adapting that model to a specific instance of translingual and transcultural mixing, which started in early modern England before spreading to other Anglophone countries, thereby reflecting in miniature the development of English in colonial and postcolonial cultures all over the world.

How, then, is creolization best adapted to account for the specific situation of émigré words in modern, global English? My answer to that question involves bringing the concept, as articulated by Caribbean intellectuals such as Édouard Glissant (1928–2011) and Stuart Hall (1932–2014), into contact with the study of keywords as pioneered by Raymond Williams (1921–88). Williams explored particular English words relating to what, as we will see, he called 'the central processes of our common life'. He put the trajectories through history of these words at the centre of an inquiry marked by a quiet political radicalism. He did so by composing, in his *Keywords* (1976), a vocabulary of modern British culture and society. In *Émigrés*, I maintain Williams's simultaneous focus on language in history and on language as history in the area of culture and society. But I look beyond British English, unlike Williams, and I contend that his vocabulary of culture and society lacks one category of keywords, namely, those of conspicuously foreign derivation. I argue for that category's necessary inclusion in any such vocabulary of modern global English.

I offer the émigrés examined in this book as a handful of examples of what would need to be added. Quite why a particular word first becomes key is often hard to say, of course, but there are various signs that this is happening. It may receive a cluster of definitions in a more or less concerted act of conceptualization. Such conceptualization can be more, or less, harmonious, of course, and it is often the case that a word emerges as key not because it encapsulates a single vision but, rather, because it acts as a visible site of encounter and conflict between different ways of seeing culture and society. *À la mode*, I suggest, both captures the fascination with, and betrays some of the fear that many in the English-speaking world entertain towards, the influence of French culture and society. I devote the first two chapters of this book to exploring *à la mode* because I describe, in these chapters, the historical moment at which not only that phrase, but all of the émigrés that interest me here, settled in English. My particular suggestion about *à la mode* is that, as it entered seventeenth-century English, it provoked debate about what it meant to be English.[5] Key to that debate was the complex English reception of a second émigré, *galanterie*, which denoted a model of elegant cultural and social interaction that France both invented and exported. The mixing of French in Restoration English thus revealed attitudes towards foreign cultures and their mediators at a time when to be French meant, in Britain, nothing more nor less than to be foreign. I argue that most native Britons viewed the foreignness of French as religious in nature, as well as political, and—given the long and continuing history of Franco–British wars—actually or potentially hostile in intent. At the same time, they tended to admire France as possessing a superior culture of elegance and refinement, especially if they had experienced some exposure to it. The result of these contrasting views was an ambivalence that lasts, at least in some parts of British society, to this day.

The essays of Part Two, devoted to *naïveté*, *ennui*, and *caprice*, may each be considered as a distinct exploration of a French émigré. If read together, however, they constitute an experiment in a form of cosmopolitan criticism that focusses on languages in migration and the specificities of their cultural entanglements. These essays are connected by the strands of an argument: that émigrés complete English as a language, as it were, by elegantly recalling its fundamental incompleteness.

They reveal its reliance on the languages that surround it. They refuse, by their unassimilated status and their deviation from the norm, to participate in the illusion that English—and, by extension, any language—could hope to express everything of the world that falls within human experience. They mark out its constitutive problems, even as they create new possibilities, of expression. *Naïveté*, as I construe it, has long enabled its English users to point to one such problem of expression, by placing the innocence of which the word speaks at a distance from their experience. It thereby highlights English ways of saying and being as caught up in an asymmetrical entanglement with a French culture and society viewed as superior. *Ennui*, which reflects that same entanglement, has come to be paired in English with native synonyms such as *boredom*. By remaining a markedly foreign element in such pairings, the French word has retained the capacity to suggest that the experience of which it speaks is itself elusively foreign, that it threatens to invade and exhaust all human activity. The creole hybrids that *ennui* has formed in such pairings inhabit a zone in which not only neighbouring languages, but also art forms, come into contact as they attempt to meet that threat. *Caprice* has thrived in the same contact zone and personifies its deviant creativity. It shows this creativity to be in conflict with the powers of hierarchization, of control and resistance, that accompany its historical manifestations. It thereby acts as a figure for all of the émigrés that appear in this book.

I treat these particular words as points of access into a wider exploration of the processes of translingual and transcultural migration. This, then, is a book about translation and its other. It measures the losses and gains in meaning that accompany the translated word, of course, but above all it illuminates the *untranslated* word in its movement between languages and its powers of cultural transformation. To existing studies I bring an approach that is methodologically innovative, in that it yokes together keywords and creolization, two concepts hitherto unrelated in the scholarship.[6] Once combined with due care and rigour, I contend, these concepts make unique sense of the processes of translingual and transcultural migration, specifically, as these have entangled and enriched English and French language and culture in history. For they show untranslated French words, not only turning English, but making it anew. Insofar as English has been made and made anew by being mixed with migrant words, I argue in what follows, it may be invited to take its place among other creoles. This creolizing process has, by now, long since moved to Anglo-French contact zones all over the world. Yet it first emerged in the long and unequal entanglement of England with its nearest continental European neighbour, the country that so many in England fear to love and love to hate, even as they stand in the corner of a field of thistles and take a turn, in French, around the mulberry bush.

Mixings

French *À la Mode*

à la mode, *adv.*, *adj.*, *n.*, and *prep.*

Origin: A borrowing from French.

—*OXFORD ENGLISH DICTIONARY*

There is likewise a manifest rotation and Circling of words, which goe in and out like the mode and fashion.

—JOHN EVELYN

PERHAPS NO PHRASE captures more succinctly the fascination in the English-speaking world with all things French. *À la mode* features in English both as a conspicuous example of that fascination and as its perfect linguistic vehicle. Riding the crest of wave after wave of French fashion across all areas of culture for the last five hundred years, *à la mode* has repeatedly brought home the perception that fashion is French, that these two go—as it were—hand in (this season's) glove.

That perception is by no means confined to the English-speaking world: from the early eighteenth century, people across continental Europe declared France to have a monopoly on fashionable culture, giving the country a reputation it enjoys all over the world to this day.[1] The English were not alone in borrowing, from the French, their *à la mode*. The Germans got there first: from the 1620s, their language features *alamode* as adjective and adverb, and German works of the same period feature other controversially modish French terms that stand out typographically from the Gothic-script text that surrounds them. Forms of the same phrase also appear in Italian and Dutch in the course of the seventeenth century. The feminine French noun at the heart of the phrase—*mode* ('fashion')—travelled, meanwhile, into all of these languages as well as Spanish, Portuguese, Danish, and Swedish. English can therefore lay claim to a mere share of the global phenomenon that is French *à la mode*.[2]

Yet the English share contains specificities. The most revealing of these may be the peculiar fear and loathing that accompanied the fascination with all things French at a time when, in British culture and society, being French was synonymous with being foreign. Several seventeenth-century English lexicographers record of *Frenchman* that, as Edward Phillips puts it in his dictionary, the term was 'anciently us'd to signify every Foreigner or Outlandish Man'. That perception of foreignness not only defined English attitudes towards France and the French but, as we will see, shaped questions of collective identity central to English culture and society.[3]

I will explore these developments in the company of *à la mode*. Historians of French *à la mode* in English have to consider centuries of relations across the English Channel. Yet they need, also, to explore contact with French in English-speaking cultures and societies in other parts of the world. That history would be incomplete, for example, without the episode in which French *à la mode* travels to North America in the late nineteenth century, finds employment selling ice cream as an accompaniment to apple pie, and meets with such success that to this day, in the United States and Canada, *à la mode* means 'served with ice cream'. North Americans use the phrase on countless occasions every day without registering any residual sense of its Frenchness. Their adoption of *à la mode* is a conspicuous instance of the phrase's wider history of migration and cultural mixing.

That history will be at the heart of both this and the following chapter. It begins in the second half of the seventeenth century, in England, as *à la mode* rose to the height of linguistic fashion in English. As it did so, its three constituent words were rolled into one, and the resulting noun—*alamode*—named, among other things, a light, glossy silk fabric, usually black, used for handkerchiefs, headscarves, hoods, and the like. This sartorial accompaniment was every bit as desirable to the dressier English as ice cream became to pie-eating North Americans: the nineteenth-century historian of England Thomas Macaulay described 'regular exchange of the fleeces of Cotswold for the alamodes of Lyons'.[4] The alamode was a finely wrought, floaty thing of nothing, a conspicuous and ubiquitous fashion accessory, designed to lend to every outfit the elusive seductiveness of the foreign. It thus makes the perfect emblem for *à la mode*. The fascinations it conveys and the fear and loathing it inspires along the way are all held in the folds of its silky fabric.

It is a clear sign that a word is starting to fascinate arbiters of linguistic fashion when they, like guests at a *soirée*, find an occasion to sport the latest accessory. They often do this, for example, by placing the word in the title of a work and lending it the status of a topic around which an entire discourse can be organized. This is precisely what happened to *à la mode* in the second half of the seventeenth century in England. English translators of France's leading comic dramatist, Molière, led

the way: in his play, *The Damoiselles À la Mode* (1667), Richard
Flecknoe gathered together elements from three of Molière's
comedies under a fashionably Frenchified title; while Tom
Rawlins translated Molière's *Le Cocu imaginaire* (1660) as *Tom
Essence: or, The Modish Wife* (1677).[5] More prominently still,
England's poet laureate, John Dryden, wrote *Marriage À-la-
Mode* (1673), a comedy featuring a rich woman-about-town,
Melantha, who—in the hope of making it at court—learns each
day new French words with which to season her conversation.
Dryden's fellow playwright George Etherege (c. 1636–c. 1692)
then satirized Melantha's fictional male counterpart, the
Frenchified fop, in *The Man of Mode, or, Sir Fopling Flutter*
(1676). Dryden's *Marriage À-la-Mode* and Etherege's *Man of
Mode* were immediate successes and, as we shall see, have established themselves since as classics of Restoration drama
with continuing afterlives on stage and screen as well as on the
page. They bear eloquent witness to the modalities of French *à
la mode* and the moods it provoked in late seventeenth-century
England.

The Restoration Moment

The new fashion for French *à la mode* in late seventeenth-
century England coincides with the period, known as the Restoration (1660–85), when Charles II of England—after spending many of the Civil War and Commonwealth years in exile in
France along with many displaced English royalists—returned
to England in 1660 and 'restored' its Stuart monarchy. Charles
II, a cousin of Louis XIV of France, brought a highly Frenchified court culture back to England. There was, of course, nothing new about this: if Frenchification may be deemed to include Normanization, as early modern commentators certainly
thought it could, then Frenchification had reached English

culture and society in waves since at least 1066. The Restoration constituted, nonetheless, a high-water mark.

The accession, in 1603, of James VI of Scotland (1566–1625) to the throne of the kingdom of England and its incorporated Principality of Wales—and, with it, the Kingdom of Ireland—considerably strengthened the links of the three kingdoms with France. French was widely spoken at the court of James. James's son, Charles I (1600–49), married a French Catholic princess, Henrietta Maria (1609–69), a daughter of Henri IV of France. Henrietta Maria moved to England in 1625 and brought with her many aspects of contemporary French courtly culture. The Civil War in England, which culminated in the execution of Charles I in 1649, saw the children of Charles and Henrietta Maria exiled in France. Charles II, after his return to England at the Restoration, never dispelled the suspicion among some of his subjects that he included adherence to Catholicism among his Frenchified manners. But exposure to French language and culture cut across confessional lines as well as the social hierarchy of early modern England. Puritan as well as royalist families evacuated their children to France during the years of Civil War in England. The foreign travel of wealthy and privileged English men and women enabled not only them, but also less socially privileged members of their entourage, to become conversant in modern foreign languages, particularly French, and *au fait* with French manners. Foreign trade required English people of varying social conditions, such as sailors, merchants, and diplomats, to learn other tongues: this was a time—so different from our own—when few people born outside the three kingdoms could speak or understand English.[6]

Foreign settlers in the British isles were exceptions to that rule. Many French visited or settled in England, Wales, Scotland, and Ireland during the seventeenth century. They crossed the Channel and the Irish Sea to find work as merchants, domestic servants, chefs, and tailors. Political exiles from the court of Louis XIV, among them the writer Charles de Saint-Evremond (1613–1703), joined them. Many French settlers were Protestants. England had, since the Reformation, been receiving Protestants escaping persecution from countries across Catholic Europe. The Huguenot (French Protestant) community grew substantially at the end of the Restoration period, after Louis XIV signalled a policy of increased intolerance towards Huguenots in France by revoking, in 1685, the Edict of Nantes of 1598, through which his predecessor Henry IV had instituted freedom of conscience, full civil rights, and a wide degree of freedom of cult for Huguenots. Somewhere between fifty and seventy thousand French Huguenots are estimated to have sought refuge in England at that time alone, and around a further ten thousand in Ireland. Fewer travelled to Scotland.[7]

The two groups of people just identified—Francophiles in England, Wales, Scotland, and Ireland and the French living in those realms—brought French fashions to bear on all aspects of Restoration culture, including the English language, which continued to receive wave upon wave of French foreign borrowings. Surfing in on the crest of one such wave was *à la mode*, of course, and it was joined by many other such émigrés. Dryden's female Francomaniac Melantha, having 'drain'd all the French Plays and Romances' of their words, needs more if she is to continue sporting glamorous foreign linguistic accessories in the right company. She orders her serving woman, Philotis, to furnish her with fresh supplies. Philotis is a fictional equivalent of the low-born servants who acquired working knowledge of foreign languages in the entourage of their masters and mistresses. She knows more French than Melantha and, in Act 3 Scene 1 of *Marriage À-la-Mode*, she provides her mistress with a list that runs as follows: *sottises, figure, naive* and *naiveté,*

*foible, chagrin, grimace, embarrasse, double entendre, équi-
voque, éclaircissement, suite, bévue, façon, penchant, coup
d'étourdi*, and *ridicule*. To that list Melantha will add, in the
following scenes, *caprice*.[8]

These words amount to nothing more than a drop in the
ocean of the French-derived words found in *Marriage À-la-
Mode*. That ocean can seem bottomless, because it is on occasions difficult to be certain which of the words are the newly
arrived French foreignisms, and which are erstwhile borrowings now absorbed into English. The first conversation that
Melantha has with the man she will eventually marry, Palamede, illustrates the point. Palamede, who knows of her *penchant* for French, immediately flirts with Melantha by telling
her he looks for her favour (in love) to 'render' him 'accom-
plished'. He introduces into his English syntaxical structures,
as well as lexical choices, from French. Melantha replies in
kind: 'A Gentleman, Sir, that understands the *Grand mond* so
well, who has ha[u]nted the best conversations, and who (in
short) has voyag'd, may pretend to the good graces of any Lady.'
Palamede then comments on Melantha's reply in an aside as
follows: 'Hay day! *Grand mond! conversation! voyag'd!* and
good graces! I find my Mistris is one of those that run mad in
new French words.'[9]

Palamede singles out, in Melantha's sentence, words whose
status as French seems clearly marked by their remaining either unadapted to their new English linguistic environment (as
in the case of *grand mond*) or half adapted (as in the case of
good graces, for example, a literal translation of the French
bonnes grâces). By contrast, the inclusion of *conversation* and
voyag'd in Palamede's aside is surprising to my twenty-first-
century ear, because both words have by now been fully adapted
to English pronunciation and usage. The same observations
might be made of Philotis's list of French borrowings: some of

its items (such as *éclaircissement*) remain unadapted in English, others (such as *naïveté*) strike me as falling somewhere in the middle of the spectrum, and others still (such as *ridicule*) have been wholly adapted. The first audiences and readers of *Marriage À-la-Mode* may have pronounced these words in a variety of ways depending on their level of acquaintance with French, their attitude towards it and other foreign languages, and other sociolinguistic considerations. While concrete evidence about early modern English pronunciation is scarce, we can infer from Palamede's qualification of all these words as 'new' and 'French' that he was to pronounce them in an unnaturalized way on stage, since otherwise his satirical aside would make no sense to the audience. The comic inference for all to draw from Melantha and Palamede's exchange was clear. English was folding French in the ambivalent embrace of a new *à la mode* marriage.

Some of the new arrivals from France were clearly perceived to be more *à la mode* than others. Melantha hopes that fashionable Palamede, with his contacts abroad, will bring home to her everything that is, as she puts it, 'fine, I mean all that's delicate, and *bien tourné*'. There were modes within modes. That this is so is amply demonstrated by Sir Fopling Flutter, in Etherege's *The Man of Mode*, a play that offers us—among other things—a useful means of cross-checking Melantha's list of new French words. Unlike Melantha, Sir Fopling has no need to gather his fashionable language from books or other people, being reported at the beginning of the play to be 'lately arrived piping hot from Paris'. When he makes his first and much awaited appearance on stage, it is in a swirl of modish French trappings, linguistic as well as sartorial.[10]

These trappings confirm their wearer as the extravagant flutter of a Frenchified fopling that his name promises. However, in his use of gallicisms, Sir Fopling in fact differs only in degree from his peers. He and other characters in *The Man of Mode* use as many French-derived words as are found in *Marriage À-la-Mode*. Some of these émigrés—*embarras* being one such—occur in both plays. Others that do so include *billet doux, doux yeux, éclaircissement, fierté, galanterie, galèche, grand ballet*, and *intrigue*. These gallicisms amount to a veritable ABC of flirting, trysting, and other courtly comings-and-goings, including the latest carriage from France in which to do all of the above in style, the *calèche* (which travels into seventeenth-century English as *galèche* or *gallesh*).

The obsession with gallicisms that Melantha and Sir Fopling indulge offers a precious snapshot of a precise moment in the unfolding and inexorable process of language change whereby successive imports of French words have entered modern English. This is the Restoration moment. French was all the rage among the British aristocracy and the rising middle classes who affected aristocratic manners. The works of Dryden and Etherege show that moment of language contact and change taking place within the context of social hierarchy. 'A Town-Lady, without any relation to the Court', Melantha mixes new French words into her English in the hope of being accepted among the nobility and gentry. She seeks to achieve this acceptance by out-courting the court in its setting of fashion. Like her counterpart in Etherege's play, Sir Fopling Flutter, Melantha complains of the 'rudeness of our Court' and presents Frenchification as the best way to improve civility at court.[11] She presents herself, indeed, as the speaking embodiment of that Frenchification. Her story is one of social elevation by marriage to Palamede, a gentleman who—in transactional terms—brings her the place at court she so craves, in return for her dowry. In Etherege's play, by contrast, social hierarchy shapes conflicts over civility among members of the urban nobility and gentry. Sir Fopling, who is already a member of the gentry, overtly mimics French in his English because he thinks that to do so will earn him a place among the London ultrafashionables.

Both plays treat language as part of a wider culture of civility that saw the British import, along with the words to convey them, many French commodities. These included, most palpably, the material consumables of everyday life such as clothing, food and drink, and books. In all three kingdoms, Huguenots and other French settlers were central from the sixteenth century onwards to many professions and trades, including the teaching of French as a foreign language and the book trade, as well as haute cuisine and fashion. Melantha devours her French plays and romances, while Sir Fopling, dressed to the nines in this season's Parisian offerings, celebrates in song the sparklingly restorative powers of the latest French pick-me-up: champagne.[12] Impalpable but equally important French imports included structures of feeling, models of social behaviour, and forms and institutions of cultural activity. Some of these imports are visible within the play-worlds of *Marriage À-la-Mode* and *The Man of Mode*. Etherege's Sir Fopling courts the ladies with a French dance. Dryden's Palamede serenades Melantha with a French song. The ladies and their gallants in both plays do their trysting in parks, gardens, and urban spaces— such as St James's Park (in *The Man of Mode*)—laid out according to French designs.[13]

Some of these social and cultural French imports shaped the very design of English Restoration dramas. Melantha drains French plays and romances of their modish words, for example, only because her creator had found in the same plays and romances the materials with which to construct the fiction that contains her. Dryden devised a double-plotted structure for *Marriage À-la-Mode*. Melantha and Palamede belong to the play's comic plot alongside a second couple, Rhodophil and

Doralice, with the salt provided by the fact that Rhodophil is amorously involved with the woman his friend Palamede is meant to marry—the Francomaniac Melantha—while Palamede plays similarly fast and loose with Rhodophil's witty wife Doralice (fig. 1). The initial dissonance of this situation is eventually dispelled in a comic ending of marriage and reconciliation. The heroic plot of *Marriage À-la-Mode*, meanwhile, tells the story of Leonidas and Palmyra. Separated from their parents at birth and brought up together away from the court, Leonidas is in fact son to the rightful king and his beloved Palmyra is the daughter of the king's usurper, Polydamas. Leonidas, once he knows his true identity, overthrows Polydamas the usurper. He and Palmyra are now free to marry. Marriage is fully *à la mode* by the ending of the play, then, since it resolves both plots. These take place at different (but interrelated) levels of society in the same island setting of Sicily, a sun-soaked proxy for contemporary England, insofar as it is presented as ripe for a Restoration of the true monarchy (in the heroic plot) and in the grip of a Francophilia that is taken to feverish excess by its social climbers (in the comic plot).

In both plots Dryden recycled material from the French literature of his day. He took as his source for the heroic plot the story of Sesostris and Timarete as told in the course of Madeleine de Scudéry's highly successful episodic romance *Artamène, ou le Grand Cyrus*, published first in French in 1649–53 and thereafter in a 1653 English translation (*Artamenes, or The Grand Cyrus*). Sesostris becomes Leonidas in Dryden's play, and Timarete, Palmyra. Melantha, meanwhile, owes her affectation of language and preciousness of romantic sentiment to Magdelon and Cathos, the female leads that Molière sent up in *Les Précieuses ridicules* (*The Conceited Ladies*) of 1659, one of the three plays of his that Richard Flecknoe drew on in *The Damoiselles À la Mode* (1667). The song with which Palamede

Gravelot inv.   G. V.^{der}Gucht Sculp.

FIG. 1. Rhodophil surprises Doralice and Palamede,
in John Dryden's *Marriage À-la-Mode*, Act 5 Scene 1.
Gerard van der Gucht after Hubert-François Gravelot,
illustration to *The Dramatick Works of John Dryden*
(London: Jacob Tonson, 1735), vol. 3, 195. Etching
on paper. Used with the permission of the Provost
and Fellows of The Queen's College, Oxford.

serenades Melantha comes from Molière's *Le Bourgeois Gentil-homme* (*The Cit Turned Gentleman*) of 1670. The mingling, in one play, of Scudéry and Molière, French romance and comedy, was Dryden's doing. In the literary design of his play as much as in the play's themes, then, he made marriage his mode of operation.[14]

In *Marriage À-la-Mode* we see, writ small, the creative processes of mixing and matching, of importation and adaptation, that brought so many elements of French society and culture across the Channel. Dryden, like Etherege, not only reflected the Restoration fashion for French but sought to intervene in that fashion by tracing a middle way between a foppish mimicry of French culture he viewed as servile and an insular rejection of it he viewed as barbarous. In the process, he imported and adapted words and ideas from France, some of which—including the new words that Melantha acquires from her maid—went on to establish themselves as lasting elements in the vocabulary of English.

These processes of mixing and matching did not always come to fruition as successfully as they did in Dryden's play. Throughout the Restoration, for example, Dryden was involved in attempts to translate to Britain that most famous state-sponsored French venture in the institutional management of language and culture, the Académie française. Founded by Richelieu in 1635 on the model of the Accademia della Crusca in Florence, the Académie française comprised forty members (elected for life) whose main task it was to establish and codify French as a language worthy of France's new status as a political and cultural superpower in Europe, and to make the French language eloquent in the service of all arts and sciences. The French state asked its academicians to produce, to that end, a normative French dictionary, grammar, rhetoric, and poetics.

Nearly sixty years later, in 1694, the academicians produced the first dictionary of the Académie française.[15]

Many intellectuals in England wanted to follow suit. The Royal Society, indeed, actively concerned itself, within two years of its foundation (in 1662), with the question of how to improve the English language. A committee of twenty-two members was formed in late 1664. One of the members was Dryden. Earlier that year, in the printed Dedication of his play *The Rival Ladies*, Dryden had made plain his view that the founding of an English Academy after the French model was much needed and would offer him and his fellow writers a 'more certain Measure' of the English language. The undertaking of the committee—as another of its members, John Evelyn, was, years later, to put it in a letter of 1689 to Samuel Pepys— 'crumbl'd away and came to Nothing'.[16]

Dryden revived the idea of an English Academy when, in 1679, he dedicated the published version of his play *Troilus and Cressida* to the Earl of Sunderland. Sunderland had just returned from being the English ambassador in Paris to become Charles II's secretary of state. Dryden urged Sunderland to emulate Richelieu's example in making English a language 'which foreigners may not disdain to learn': 'The genius of the nation seems to call you out, as it were by name, to polish and adorn your native language, and to take from it the reproach of its barbarity.' Dryden made his appeal in vain. By 1693, when addressing his 'Discourse on the Origin and Progress of Satire' to the Earl of Dorset, he was blaming successive governments in England for failing to purify the tongue.[17]

The novelists Daniel Defoe (1660–1731) and Jonathan Swift (1667–1745) were among those leading writers of English in the late seventeenth and early eighteenth centuries who called, after Dryden, for the founding of an Academy after the manner of the French. The idea continued to come to nothing. When a British Academy was eventually founded, in 1902, its aims were conceived differently: to promote historical, philosophical, and philological studies in Britain as a complement to the work of the Royal Society in the natural sciences. The overt linguistic purism and imperialism of Richelieu's Académie française were, by then, no longer in fashion.

Restoration proposals for an English Academy suggest, by contrast, that the period's leading intellectuals and scholars wished not only to see the English language welcome words from the French but to have the entire government of the tongue remodelled on French lines. The most powerful statement of this view came from John Evelyn. A polymath and man of letters, Evelyn was a Fellow of the Royal Society, nominated by Charles II, and a member of the Society's committee for improving the English language. As a young royalist living in self-imposed exile, he had travelled widely in Italy and France in the mid-1640s, meeting and marrying in Paris the daughter of the royalist ambassador Sir Richard Browne, Mary, who counted fluency in French among her many accomplishments. During this period, Evelyn encountered continental European learning and practice in the many areas of human endeavour—including gardening, urban planning, landscape architecture, fashion, trade, writing, and the collecting of books, medals, and other artifacts—that would interest him for the rest of his life. On his return home, he set about improving British society and culture by bringing European ideas to the attention of his compatriots. Helped by Mary, he translated several important works from French, including Nicholas de Bonnefons's *Jardinier françois* (as *The French Gardiner*) in 1658 and Gabriel Naudé's work on building a library in 1661, a year in which he also published an essay on the sartorial fashions of Charles II's Frenchified court.[18]

Evelyn had a wide range of experience and expertise to offer the Royal Society's committee for improving the English language. But he was a busy man. That a record of his contribution to the committee's deliberations has been preserved we owe to his inability to attend the scheduled meetings. In a letter of 20 June 1665 to the committee's chairman, Sir Peter Wyche (1628–c. 1699), Evelyn excuses himself from attending these meetings: he is not available on Tuesday afternoons. He will offer, instead, his thoughts in writing.

He proposes, in essence, that the best contribution to the improvement of English that the committee could make would be that of compiling a dictionary, establishing a grammar, and offering a guide to rhetoric in the language. These were, of course, the chief tasks that had been assigned to the Académie française. Evelyn reveals that he has the French model in mind at the end of his letter. The dictionary that Evelyn proposes is to include, among other things, technical terms, accurate equivalences of weights and measures, foreign terms and phrases, English regionalisms, and those 'Courtly expressions [. . .] in which the French, Italians, and Spanyards have a kind of natural grace and talent'. The dictionary, thus constituted, will provide evidence on the basis of which it will be possible to improve the language by stripping out words and phrases that are obsolete and actively borrowing from foreign languages those that are missing in English. 'For example,' Evelyn observes, 'we have hardly any words that do so fully expresse the French *clinquant, naifaetie, Ennüii, bizarre, concert, façoniere, Chicaneries, Consumme, Emotion, Defer, effort, shocque, entoure, défaute*: or the Italian *Vagezze, garbato, Svelto croopo* [*sic*], etc.' Evelyn pictures English, in its current state, as a merry-go-round of 'words which goe in and out like the mode and fashion'. He argues that the committee of which he is a member needs to manage that inconstant process of language change by producing a dictionary, grammar, and rhetoric for the language. It must consult books, decide which areas in the landscape would benefit from weeding and replanting and which new plants might thrive in these areas, and then ensure that they do.[19]

Evelyn here no longer imagines language as a fashion parade. He views it as a garden, as did his sixteenth-century Franco-Italian predecessors, and as did, also, the constant gardener that Evelyn himself was.[20] The garden of the English language, as Evelyn here conceives it, will be improved by good design and an ambitious programme of transplantation. Evelyn is well aware that there is a politics to transplantation. If the English language is a garden, it is a public garden within the English urban landscape, and it needs to offer a welcoming environment to incoming plants. In order to express that need, Evelyn abruptly introduces a new metaphor into his proposal, which now presents foreign words as people rather than plants: 'Let us therefore (as the Romans did the Greeke) make as many of those do homage, as are like to prove good citizens.' He suggests, here, that English speakers, in their handling of foreign words, should imitate the Roman empire in its treatment of Greek settlers: they should offer rights of citizenship and a warm welcome to those deserving of entry.[21]

The particular foreignisms that Evelyn lists as desirable additions to English did indeed, for the most part, make the journey across the Channel. Only three of his chosen French words—*choc* ('shock'), *façonnier* ('mannered', 'over-refined'), and *entour* ('surrounding')—are nowhere to be seen in the *Oxford English Dictionary* (*OED*). The others, by contrast, are all present and correct in the same dictionary (which lists, in several cases, Evelyn's letter as one example of the word's early usage). They have, indeed, proved themselves to be good citizens of the English-speaking world. They have undergone, like

Melantha's 'new French words', varying degrees of adaptation to their changed linguistic environment. Some—*bizarre, concert, defer, emotion,* and *effort*—have been so wholly adapted to English usage that they have become part of the furniture: it is hard to imagine them as the new arrivals from abroad that Evelyn wished to offer the committee. Others, while achieving and maintaining their currency in English settings, remain only partially adapted to the language—as in the case of *naïveté* and *ennui*—or, indeed, unadapted. Towards the unadapted end of the spectrum are to be found *clinquant* ('glittering', 'spangly'), and *consommé* ('clear soup' and, by figurative extension, 'condensation'). The Italian *svelto* ('slim', 'willowy'), meanwhile, eventually established itself in common English parlance in its French form *svelte*. It seems to have found favour, in other words, by adapting to the English fashion for French elegance.

Cross-Channel Gallantries

The Anglophone characters in plays such as Dryden's *Marriage À-la-Mode* and Etherege's *The Man of Mode* behave in the same way. They import their language of civility from the Continent. The foreign-derived words that Dryden's Royal Society colleague John Evelyn recommended for the enrichment of English were chosen, similarly, to remedy one important respect in which he found the language to be 'infinitely defective': namely, in 'civil Addresses, excuses, and formes'.[22] English lacked the elegant conversational accessories of socially polite and culturally polished interaction, Evelyn felt, and he suggested the civilizing addition of French, Italian, and Spanish words as the remedy. One French word in the field of politeness stands out above others. This is *galanterie*. It denotes the model of elegant social and cultural interaction that seventeenth-century France invented as a national myth and exported elsewhere in Europe, including England, where writers like Dryden and Etherege adopted it as an émigré.[23]

Galanterie combines courtly grace of manner with seductive charm. It is an art which consists of concealing that art. It has Italian precedents, formulated in Renaissance treatises on courtly civility, the most influential on *galanterie* being Baldassare Castiglione's *Il libro del cortegiano* (*The Book of the Courtier*) of 1528. Seventeenth-century French writers disagreed with each other as to whether or not it could be cultivated by those who did not possess it by birthright. Nicolas Faret, who borrowed heavily from Castiglione in a work of 1630, argued that it could. This meritocratic emphasis was crucial to the development of French *galanterie* from the middle of the seventeenth century onwards. The politician Nicolas Fouquet (1615–80), a wealthy member of the professionally trained minor French nobility, gathered around him other minor nobles and bourgeois in support of the monarchist cause during the civil disturbances of the Fronde (1648–53). They were rewarded for their support: Louis XIV's chief minister Cardinal Mazarin (1602–61) made Fouquet minister of finance in 1653, and Fouquet and his circle acquired cultural capital as well as power and wealth. They set about fashioning a social and cultural identity for themselves that would emphasize accomplishments of manner over circumstances of birth. They created, in *galanterie*, the model they needed. Writers of both sexes—such as Madeleine de Scudéry, Molière, and the poet Jean de La Fontaine (1621–95)—portrayed it as an elegant ideal. It became, over the following decades, a modern literary and artistic form in its own right.

The charm of *galanterie* came in various guises. Madeleine de Scudéry, whose romances provided Dryden with plots and Dryden's Melantha with words, claimed that it could be deployed, albeit differently, by both men and women.[24] The advice generally offered to the aspiring male courtier of the period was to acquire that charm in the company of alpha females at court and then to practise it upon them in order to gain their grace and favour. These alpha females would be well placed to put in a good word for their *galant* to the powerful men of their entourage. The calculation for women—who had no prospect of winning direct access to political power in this period—was different. Discreetly attracting and keeping the attention of the alpha males at court constituted a form of social distinction in itself for women, and might also offer them, if the circumstances were right, indirect influence over the male exercise of privilege and power.

The discreet charms of *galanterie* were never far away from frankly sexual forms of behaviour and expression. Quite which favours ladies actually dispensed to their *galants* was a matter of endless interest and gossip. It formed the subject of scandalous publications, such as the *Histoire amoureuse des Gaules* (*The Amorous History of the Gauls*) of 1665 by Bussy-Rabutin, who is mentioned in *The Man of Mode*.[25] Bussy-Rabutin's text joined a well-established tradition of bawdy, indecent, and even obscene writing which became associated with *galanterie* in the seventeenth century.

This meant that there were in effect, as the French cultural historian Alain Viala has shown, two *galanteries*: the decorous and the libertine.[26] La Fontaine, who was as attuned as anyone to the taste of the age, alternated between decorous and libertine *galanterie* in his poetic output. His *Contes et nouvelles* (*Tales*), the first instalment of which was published in 1665, expressed *galanterie* in a libertine mode. The *Contes* sold like hot cakes, but the 1674 collection was censored by the authorities in France, and this surrounded La Fontaine with a whiff of scandal that he found difficult to dispel. His *Fables* (1668) slowly put him back into better odour. They performed *galan-terie* in a decorous mode. Their success was immediate and lasting. La Fontaine used that success, in time, to develop the fable into a remarkably supple and capacious form, capable of smuggling within its flanks a cohort of poetic modes and moods, including even—in the 1694 edition of the *Fables*—two of his 1682 *Contes*. The decorous *Fables* and the licentious *Contes*, then, were two sides of the same coin.

The example of La Fontaine's poetic ouput encapsulates a wider truth about French *galanterie*. Its decorous and libertine modes were not radically opposed, but went together, often hand in hand. This enabled the practitioners of *galanterie* in society and culture to exercise their subtle charms of seduction in varying ways. By the same token, it offered undeniable opportunities to the opponents of *galanterie*, who could—and frequently did—denounce its decorous mode either as a grotesque parade of affectation or as the public face of an indecent libertinism, or, indeed, as both of those things. One person's elegance was another's affectation, in other words, just as one person's civility was another's scurrility.

Galanterie came to feature in seventeenth-century English as a kind of linguistic *consommé* of elegant civility mixed, after the French mode, with seductive appeal. That mixture would by itself have made it controversial as a social and cultural model in the English-speaking world, just as it was in France; but the French provenance of English *galanterie* offered an additional reason for some across the Channel to love and others to loathe it. Some welcomed it as light from an external source; others shunned it as a delusion; still others adapted it, either overtly or covertly, to the environment in which they were operating. All of this comes through in the language. *Galanterie*, in its early modern Anglophone reception, occupies a middling place on the spectrum of adaptation. It settled in two forms, *galanterie* and *gallantry*, marking either end of that spectrum in respect of spelling, pronunciation, and connotation. It met, along the way, with varying degrees of receptivity and resistance.

The enthuasiasts, like their decriers, reveal the currency of the word in Restoration England. Shortly after meeting Palamede, the man she will eventually marry, Dryden's Melantha confides to the audience of *Marriage À-la-Mode*, in her characteristic Franglais, that 'he has the ayre of a gallant *homme*'. An anonymous three-part poem, *Gallantry À-la-Mode* (1674), not only picks up the keywords of Dryden's play, but reworks its central themes, satirizing the decorous and libertine tendencies of London fashionables. Vincent and Dekker describe, in *The Young Gallant's Academy* (also 1674), the everyday rounds of the Frenchified Englishman in London: these include a visit to one of the French establishments where he displays his mastery of the spoken language or—failing that—gathers together 'some fragments of *French* or small parcels of *Italian* to fling about the table'. A gallant of this kind was often called an English *monsieur*—as is the case of the tellingly named lead character, Frenchlove, in James Howard's early Restoration comedy *The English Mounsieur* (1663)—or a *beau*. Sir Fopling decides, meanwhile, to 'have a gallantry with some of our English ladies'. Women in England, not to be outdone by their *beaux*, coveted *galanterie* for themselves: in a 1662 diary entry Samuel Pepys observed of one Lady Batten that 'she would fain be a gallant'.[27]

The *galanterie* to which some Restoration men and women aspired continues to feature in English as a French émigré. The *OED* quotes a 2005 article in the British newspaper *The Observer* claiming that the art of seduction has disappeared from contemporary Britain and asking whether this is because, 'along with the art of galanterie, seduction is considered a sexist con'. Gallants of the United Kingdom, male and female, take note. . . . That same question about *galanterie* remains, meanwhile, the subject of a long-running controversy, chiefly conducted in France, among feminists of differing persuasions who have included Julia Kristeva, Mona Ozouf, and Joan Scott. The controversy has subsequently resurfaced in the context of French responses to the worldwide #MeToo movement and—as Alain Viala has observed—continues to place *galanterie* at the heart of debates in France about French national identity. On both sides of the Channel, then, it seems that *galanterie* maintains to this day its status as a defining and controversial model of Frenchness.[28]

Even as the language of *galanterie* was able to retain its French aura in Restoration English, meeting receptivity and resistance in the process, it was also undergoing processes of adaptation to its new environment. Its most obvious adapted form was the English noun *gallantry*, of course, but there were others: one such was *politeness* (French *politesse*). The English reception of seventeenth-century French *galanterie* also contributed to the development of that quintessentially British character, the gentleman, who is either born or schooled into the 'chivalrous instincts and fine feelings' that define him (as the *OED* puts it). This development explains why, when the French Huguenot and cultural entrepreneur Peter Anthony (Pierre Antoine) Motteux decided to create, in 1692, the first periodical in England, he modelled his publication on the *Mercure galant*—that arbiter of fashionable French *galanterie* since 1672—and chose to call it *The Gentleman's Journal*.[29]

Galanterie in fact found itself variously translated or redescribed. Treated as controversial, the word became a site of conflicting definitions, as writers and other language users sought to establish their own meanings of the word and to discredit the meanings of others in preferring one mode of gallantry to another.

One such controversy took place in two anonymous pamphlets published in 1673. The first was entitled *Remarques on the Humours and Conversation of the Town*. Its anonymous author, stung by the satire of the English country gentleman found in contemporary English theatre, mounts a counterattack on the wits of London, above all on the city's playwrights, in particular for their immoral treatment of women, their belittling of marriage, and their Frenchified manners and language. The rejoinder, *Remarks upon Remarques*, was published in the same year: it identifies as the principal target of the *Remarques* Dryden—whose satirical *Marriage À-la-Mode*, we remember, was in 1673 a recent success in the London theatres—and it defends him and other London wits from the attacks mounted against them.

The author of the *Remarques* makes gallantry central to those attacks. He complains that the 'life of a young Gentleman' in London is 'not only degenerated below the precepts of ancient gallantry and generosity; but beneath that prudence, sobriety, and discretion which ought to be found in all who pretend to man-hood'. He blames the wits and fops of London for debasing the true gallantry of the English country gentleman: it is they, he says, 'who think, that the modish nonsense which they bring from *London*, should be more valued than the civility and agreeableness of rural conversation. But we shall find enough of this sort of Gallantry, in examining the pleasures and entertainments of the Town.' Gallantry of the sort he has in mind and the modish nonsense that dominate London life are, of course, French in provenance: 'As much as we have studied to Ape the *French*,' says the author in a stinging rebuke, 'we have yet only reach'd that perfection as to be ridiculous'.[30]

Another such controversy—about who and what is truly gallant—takes place in Etherege's *Man of Mode*. Sir Fopling Flutter is the main vehicle for this controversy. The first thing the audience is told about him, after his arrival from France has been announced, is that, as young Bellair wryly puts it, 'He thinks himself the pattern of modern gallantry.' Of course he does, we might reflect, since *galanterie* is a fashionable French mode and Sir Fopling mimics fashionable French modes. Yet to mimic *galanterie* is to fall from its graces. Man-about-town Dorimant, rake to the fop that is Flutter, meets Young Bellair's comment about Sir Fopling with a retort: 'He is indeed the pattern of modern foppery.' Dorimant manages here, in one pithy sentence, both to redescribe Flutter's version of gallantry as an excessively Frenchified counterfeit and to leave hanging the suggestion that an authentic form of modern gallantry is to be found elsewhere. Dorimant is not harking back to the old-school version that reactionary members of the older generation, such as Lady Woodvill and Old Bellair, cherish: of chivalric attention paid by knights to ladies in a world where the children of the nobility have dynastic marriages arranged for them. The world, as Dorimant well appreciates, has changed. The 'freedoms of the present', as he calls them, mean that men and women can use their seductive charms on one another to choose their partners and make their way in society. This is modern gallantry in elite London society.[31]

The play explores this form of gallantry in two modes, the decorous and the libertine, each represented by a pair of well-born and fashionable lovers. The (revealingly named) Young Bellair and his beloved Emilia win each other's hands in the decorous mode. They remove the obstacles that the older generation have put in their way and thus add sweetness to the play's well-seasoned comic ending. Dorimant and Harriet, whose witty courtship adds the salt, operate in the libertine mode. We watch the rake dallying with several mistresses before he finds his way to the 'wild, witty, lovesome, beautiful, and young' Harriet.[32]

Dorimant and Harriet end the play on the brink of an uncertain future in which, having given up the freedoms they have variously enjoyed, they will need to find a new mode of living. Modern gallantry in its various modes needs to be carefully handled, as we have seen, if it is not to veer towards the empty social posturing adopted by fops or the sexual manipulation exercised by rakes. Etherege's *Man of Mode* explores all this in its clear-sighted comedy of social manners. It asks whether modern gallantry is truly possible in Restoration Britain, and how it may be used to engineer a happy and stylish ending. It peers beyond its own ending to ask what, besides courting, fashionable Stuart gentlemen and gentlewomen should do with the wit and other talents they possess. It asks, too, how many of these people really possess such talents or, put another way, how many of them in fact resemble Sir Fopling and his female admirers more closely than they do Dorimant and Harriet or Young Bellair and Emilia.

It even finds a way, thanks to Etherege's friend Dryden, of putting these questions, at the last, directly to the audience. Dryden's verse Epilogue to the play, which was most probably spoken by the actress in the role of Harriet, presents the figure of Sir Fopling as central to the play's ability to provoke in its audience—just as Molière's comedies do—a form of laughter that turns back on and includes the audience in its scope. Dryden suggests that characterization is the key to successful satirical implication of this kind. Most playwrights exaggerate foolishness in their characters beyond recognition, making them asses fit only for farce, whereas Etherege depicts altogether more substantial fools:

Something of man must be exposed to view,
That, gallants, they may more resemble you.

Dryden here turns the spotlight on the men in the audience. They, just as much as the Sir Fopling they have been laughing at, may mistake foppery for gallantry. But the women are no less implicated in the fashion for foppery:

Sir Fopling is a fool so nicely writ,
The ladies would mistake him for a wit,
And when he sings, talks loud, and cocks, would cry:
'I vow, methinks, he's pretty company—
So brisk, so gay, so travelled, so refined!'

The speaker of the Epilogue insists that the character of Sir Fopling—admired by the women and curiously resembling their gallants—is drawn from no single person in real life. He is a composite who 'represents ye all', Dryden asserts, before clinching the point:

From each he meets, he culls whate'er he can:
Legion's his name, a people in a man.[33]

Dryden here adds a further and final epithet to those that Sir Fopling Flutter has been accumulating from the title of Etherege's play onwards. Flutter is the man of mode, the pattern of modern foppery, and—most disturbingly for his compatriots—he is a people in a man.

CHAPTER TWO

Modes of English

mode, *n.*

In branch II. < French *mode*, feminine [. . .] < classical
Latin *modus*. [. . .] A prevailing fashion, custom, practice,
or style, *esp.* one characteristic of a particular place or period.
—*OXFORD ENGLISH DICTIONARY*

But *whose* England? *Which* England?
—JOHN LE CARRÉ

FRENCH *À LA MODE*, as it entered
English, called into question English modes of being. In what follows I will be probing the pronounced ambivalence that—as we
saw towards the end of the previous
chapter—the Restoration English,
Sir Fopling's people, showed to-
wards French *à la mode*. This ambivalence had deep roots in
the country's history. The English Restoration moment, with
its fashion for all things French, brought out that ambivalence
as a response to the working out of a question of national
identity.

The people of Britain, starting with the English, had every reason to feel confused about their identity in and after 1660. They were living through a period of unprecedented upheaval. That upheaval had witnessed, in political terms, a constitutional stand-off between Crown and Parliament, Civil War, the execution of the first Charles Stuart, the founding of a republic, and then reversion to monarchic rule under the second Charles Stuart. It had seen continuing religious strife between Protestants, committed to protecting or even deepening the Protestant Reformation in England started under Henry VIII, and Catholics wanting greater liberty or even wishing to put the Reformation into reverse. The political and religious conflicts mentioned above were related in a myriad of ways, of course, the most obvious being that Protestants dominated the English parliament whereas the ruling Stuarts had Catholics within their own family. Charles I had insisted that the children he had with his French Catholic wife, Henrietta Maria, be christened in the Church of England. Many in England suspected their children, however, of harbouring pro-Catholic sympathies. Their son Charles never escaped this suspicion, being seen throughout his reign as either crypto-Catholic or tolerant to a fault, whereas James put an end to all suspicion when he openly converted to the Catholic faith. The opposition that James's Catholicism caused among England's Protestant political elite would come to a head when, shortly after he succeeded Charles II in 1685, James and his Italian second wife produced a Catholic heir to the English throne. English parliamentarians promptly organized the overthrow of James in the so-called Glorious Revolution of 1688, which brought to the throne William III, Prince of Orange, and his wife Mary, James's daughter by his first marriage and a Protestant like her husband.

The Restoration—despite the healing connotations of that name—was nothing more than a further chapter in the continuing story of upheaval. People of all shades of political and religious belief continued to disagree about political and confessional arrangements and what they saw as related questions of society and culture. English Restoration writers, such as those discussed in the previous chapter, explored what cultural forms should define the modern English way of life. What should it sound, look, and feel like to be English? The French fashions of Restoration England altered the terms in which the question of Englishness was put by setting it in the midst of a further question: in what respects—if at all—should being English, in a modern setting, involve imitating the French?

The Imitation Game

The underlying question of imitation met with the same spectrum of responses in early modern England that awaited *galanterie*. These responses ranged from an enthusiastic endorsement of close imitation to its unequivocal and wholesale rejection via all manner of middling positions often characterized by a mixture of overt separation from some aspects of French and Frenchness and covert appropriation of others. Some English writers in this period adopted out-and-out pro- or anti-French positions in respect of one another and as a proxy for a conflict about English identity. This is the case in the controversy noted in the previous chapter, and played out in 1673, between the anonymous anti-French and pro-rural English author of *Remarques on the Humours and Conversation of the Town* and his equally anonymous cosmopolitan and urban respondent in *Remarks upon Remarques*. In other cases, the ambivalence resided within a single English breast, where a fascination with French coexisted with a fear or loathing of its very power to fascinate. At times, this ambivalence was overcome by some act of mastery, whereby the English person appropriated the fetishized French object in order both to avoid being devoured by it and to assume its power. It remained at other times palpably unresolved, as in the case of the fop, whose mimicry of French manners produces a representation that is 'almost the same, *but not quite*', in Homi Bhabha's succinct formulation.[1]

This spectrum of English response towards French and Frenchness—from mimicry to mastery—accompanied the migrations of French words into seventeenth-century English. Mimicry saw the migrant word reproduced in a largely unadapted form in the midst of an English utterance, where it sounded almost the same as in French, but—crucially—not quite. Recall, for example, the *galleshes* of the gallants. Mastery, at its most confrontational, could cause the émigré to be Englished almost—though, again, not quite—beyond recognition. Consider, among many examples, the *hogo* ('high flavour', from *haut goût*) and the *kickshaws* ('Frenchified morsels', from *quelques choses*) of which seventeenth-century English users speak in culinary and associated metaphorical settings. These are migrant words chiefly treated with contemptuous mastery and thus made palatable for domestic consumption.[2]

Mimicry and mastery are on display in *The Man of Mode*. Sir Fopling Flutter is, of course, the archetype of enthusiastic close imitation—mimicry—of French and Frenchness, for which the play invites us to laugh at him, while suggesting in its Epilogue that its audience needs to recognize that it contains among its number many male followers and female admirers of his. We might well want, like some of the play's more recent critics, to resist the play's satire and put in a positive word for the fop.[3] What the play tends to suggest, meanwhile, is that the singular man of its title conceals others and their modes. The play offers, most obviously, the rakish Dorimant as the fashionable alternative to the foppish Flutter. The civil Young Bellair discreetly occupies the middle of the spectrum and, from that position, helps to bring the plot to its comic conclusion. The various modes these men display—gallantry, both libertine and decorous, and foppery—are all French in inspiration. However, an important difference between them is that gallantry, as both of its representatives perform it in the play, is a covert appropriation of a French mode to a new setting, whereas foppery is an overt representation. This difference is reflected in the way in which the various men speak. The modern gallants poke fun at Sir Fopling for his Frenchified way of talking, including his lisp, which Dorimant says 'he affects in imitation of the people of quality of France'. Yet even as they distance themselves from the slavish Frenchifying of the fop, Dorimant and Young Bellair use French words and phrases in their speech with discreet mastery, thereby indicating that they have judiciously selected and integrated elements of French elegance into the easy manner of the modern English gentleman. They typify a masterful English appropriation of French culture that the play presents as the height of London fashion.[4]

The London English did not, of course, go unchallenged in their desire to set the fashion in the three kingdoms of England, Ireland, and Scotland. There was, for example, a race in 1663 between translators in London and Dublin to produce for the stage the first English translation of Pierre Corneille's play *La Mort de Pompée*. Katherine Philips (1632–64), an Anglo-Welsh settler in Ireland who formed her own salon circle *à la française*, won the race. Her *Pompey* was performed in 1663 before the Duke of Ormond, a Francophile member of an Anglo-Norman Irish dynasty, thus furthering the claim of Dublin to a position of cultural autonomy in respect of London.[5]

Two of the writers who served on the Royal Society's committee for improving the English language in these years—Dryden and Evelyn—were meanwhile undertaking appropriations of French culture back in London. Evelyn sought to shape public policy towards the sartorial manifestations of French *à la mode*. This is the burden of his 1661 essay *Tyrannus, or the Mode*. He presents in this essay the well-to-do English as slaves to ever-changing French fashion in their clothing and accessories. These 'hang in the Ears, embrace the Necks and elegant Waists of our fair Ladies, in the likeness of *Pendants*, *Collers*, *Fans* and *Peticoats*, and the rest of those pretty impediments, without which Heaven and Earth could not subsist'. French fashions for English men are no less a tyranny, Evelyn claims, introducing a satirical vignette of a contemporary Londoner: 'It was a fine silken thing which I spied walking th'other day through *Westminster-Hall*, that had as much Ribbon on him as would have plundered six shops, and set up twenty Country Pedlers; all his body was dres't like a May-pole, or a *Tom-a Bedlam's* Cap.' The sartorial riggings sported by this effeminate fop, Evelyn says, sounded as loud as they looked. The author here adds a cutting comment to his vignette: 'So was our Gallant overcharg'd', he says—making *Gallant* here synonymous with the Frenchified fop—'that whether he were clad with this garment, or (as a Porter) only carried it, was not to be resolv'd.' The men-about-town who follow the mode slavishly risk losing their elevated place in the social hierarchy of Restoration England, in Evelyn's construction, for they appear to be carrying the latest clothes around on behalf of their French tailors, rather than wearing them, as gentlemen should. Evelyn even presents them as being at risk, by the same token, of losing their masculinity: were we to behold 'one of our silken *Came-lions* and aery Gallants making his addresses to his Mistress', he warns, we would soon be wondering 'which is the more woman of the two'.[6]

Evelyn was visibly worried that the addiction for imported alamodes and other such fashionable French materials and goods in England not only reflected the country's impaired sense of self, but would also damage its balance of trade. He was equally clear about the commercial benefits that were accruing to the French: 'Believe it, *La Mode de France*, is one of the best Returnes which they make, and feeds as many bellies, as it clothes Backs'. The remedy proposed in *Tyrannus* was for the newly restored Charles II to pass sumptuary laws, curbing expenditure on fashion goods, and then to encourage a new mode for homegrown designs and materials by using the clothes he wore to set a royal example to his court and the rest of the country. The picture Evelyn paints in that essay is of a Charles who—by discouraging foreign imports and making English fabrics newly fashionable—will, to his greater glory, 'give the Standard now to the *Mode* we next expect, and that not only to his own *Nation*, but to all the World besides'. Evelyn descends into sartorial particulars, championing the cause of the male vest. This was a kind of long under-cassock in 'the Eastern fashion' that, as Evelyn gave to understand in his diary entry for 18 October 1666, Charles took to wearing after reading *Tyrannus* and which he made fashionable in England. An improved market for homegrown designs and fabrics, a healthier balance of trade, and the prospect of men all over the world wearing English vests: there could surely be no better way to warm English hearts or to heal the damage caused to the nation's sense of self by its deferential addiction to French fashion.[7]

Evelyn was advocating for English fashion the domestic adaptation of the best practices found all over the world, including France and Italy, the countries he knew best and admired most. He offered in *Tyrannus* no direct criticism of the French or of their fashion per se. His quarrel was with English attitudes towards the French and, in particular, what might be called their servile, because excessively close and overt, imitation of French models in the realm of fashion. He said as much in his own name: 'For my own part, though I love the *French* well (and have many reasons for it) yet I would be glad to pay my respects in any thing rather than my *Clothes*, because I conceive it so great a diminution to our Native Country, and to the discretion of it.' There was, however, nothing to stop the English, in Evelyn's view, from making use of French designs, among others, in their home country. Such use had simply to be free from servility, in other words, actively adapted to the aesthetic and practical demands of the new setting: 'I affect whatever is comely, and of use, and to that I would be constant.'[8]

Evelyn practised, in *Tyrannus*, what he was preaching. He appropriated various French imports—now overtly, now covertly—and wove them into the fabric of his writing. These imports included French words, starting with the *mode* of his title and ending in the final sentence of his text with *mine*, a migrant French noun (akin to English *mien*) that Evelyn borrows in order to suggest that the face of Charles II possesses a certain cosmopolitan something in addition to comeliness.[9]

Evelyn also brings in ideas and examples from various French writers, including the late sixteenth-century essayist Michel de Montaigne, to whom Evelyn alludes after suggesting that, if the king were to set a new sartorial trend of sobriety at court, he would remove at one stroke the need to pass repressive sumptuary laws. Evelyn produces, in support of his suggestion, an example from the opening of Montaigne's essay on sumptuary laws: '*Mountaine* [Montaigne] tells us, that at the

Death of King Francis, one years mourning for him in Cloth, made Silk to be so despised, that had any Man appear'd in it for a long time after, he was taken for a *Pedant* or a *Mountebank*.' Evelyn displays this example as an overt borrowing. Meanwhile, he is borrowing covertly from the same passage, where Montaigne makes the very suggestion—that kings could curb excessive spending on clothes by setting a more sober trend—that Evelyn offers as his own in the new setting of Charles II's Frenchified court.[10]

Evelyn's covert adaptation of Montaigne may indeed be said to extend to the entire form of his text, for he describes *Tyrannus* as one of 'certain *Essayes*' he has composed, thus applying to the text a word that Francis Bacon and other English writers had borrowed from Montaigne to describe an excursion in prose that was usually short in length and informal in style. English writers of Evelyn's age were capable of displaying the essay's French provenance: another Fellow of the early Royal Society, Robert Boyle (1627–91), wrote of having adopted 'that form of writing which (in imitation of the French) we call essays'.[11]

Evelyn knew, in other words, precisely what he was doing. His appropriations of French linguistic and literary modes in *Tyrannus* do not contradict the spirit of his advice to Charles II about his sartorial policy. They replicate that advice at all levels of the text.

Dryden, meanwhile, placed the same mode of appropriation at the heart of English language, literary culture, and identity. He did not, of course, merely practise this mode towards French. He was well aware that the English language was an unstable mixture of several languages—including ancient and modern ones—and he cultivated a poetic idiom of his own by translating from these languages and weaving elements of their vocabulary and syntax into his written English. Paul Hammond has shown that Dryden turns to Latin in order to '[mark] out the gap between possible cultures and the actual nation' and, within this Latinate gap, 'dreams his own cultural space'. It is particularly striking to the reader of Evelyn's *Tyrannus* how often, in Hammond's account, Dryden is shown to access his Latin via Montaigne.[12]

While Dryden clearly had recourse to French culture for the modern mediation it could provide between Latin and English, then, he also looked directly to French for what it offered English. And what, in essence, was that offer? It amounted to an uneasy combination of cultural prestige by association and direct competition—the latter of a kind that the traces of classical Rome could hardly provide—to the kingdom and courtly culture of Charles II. *Marriage À-la-Mode* shows Dryden responding to this uneasy combination with characteristic poise. The creative adaptation of material from the French writers Madeleine de Scudéry and Molière that he undertakes in that play, discussed in the previous chapter, is quietly done. He brings, meanwhile, a discussion of the relative merits of English and French culture to the noisy surface of the play's comic plot. He does this by having Melantha and Doralice dispute that very topic when they meet in the masquerade scene as cross-dressed young men. When Doralice dismisses Melantha as an over-Frenchified urban sophisticate, Melantha returns fire, mocking Doralice as a witless English country bore. They all but come to blows.[13]

If Melantha's contribution to the dispute helped to provoke the attack on Dryden in *Remarques on the Humours and Conversation of the Town*, as it surely did, then the author of *Remarques* was missing the point. Dryden directs his satire, not at the partisans of English country life per se, but at the state of a cultural debate in England that is merely concerned with making the case for and against the influence of the country's cross-Channel neighbour. The playwright uses an overt satire of that debate, conducted between his cross-dressing characters, to direct attention away from the larger covert imitation of French sources he undertakes in order to create a double-plotted, genre-crossing, dramatic hybrid. Love the French or loathe them, as you will, but let us all help ourselves in the meantime to what of theirs we can make our own: this is the subliminal message that England's poet laureate offers his compatriots by means of his literary practice in *Marriage À-la-Mode*.[14]

Dryden had already made this subliminal message central to his literary theory. He had published in 1668 *An Essay of Dramatick Poesie* whose chief aim he described as being 'to vindicate the honour of our English writers from the censure of those who unjustly prefer the French before them'.[15] Overtly, then, he seemed, in the *Essay*, to be making the standard move in the familiar English game of minimizing French cultural influence. Covertly, though, he was putting to his own use insights gleaned from the recent and continuing debate about the state of culture in France. That debate, which was eventually put on spectacular public display in the so-called Quarrel of the Ancients and Moderns (c. 1687–c. 1716), explored how France should see itself in relation to the cultures of Greek and Roman antiquity that it claimed as its prestigious precursors. Should the arts and sciences of present-day France recognize that their Greek and Roman precursors provided norms and models to be followed but never surpassed, as the Ancients maintained? Or did Greek and Roman antiquity, as the Moderns instead proposed, offer principles and examples to be integrated into a process of perpetual development and, where appropriate, set aside?

These questions divided the French cultural establishment. The Ancients, who tended to be either men of the church or members of the laity connected with the austere Jansenist religious community of Port-Royal, had both benefitted from and promoted classical learning of a kind largely available only to well-born university men. The Moderns, who by contrast found their place in a salon culture presided over by women in high society, promoted *galanterie* as a quasi-aristocratic air of distinction combining worldly experience with wit and available to members of both sexes in France's social elite. The contrasting social and gender positions of the Ancients and Moderns help to account for the aesthetic preferences and achievements of both parties in the field of literature. The Ancients argued that epic, tragedy, and comedy should, in keeping with Aristotle's *Poetics*, remain separate; and, in the figure of Jean Racine (1639–99), produced a French tragedian to rival the likes of Euripides and Seneca. The Moderns developed new kinds of writing. The most important of these was prose fiction: its chief practitioners (as well as consumers) of the period were mainly women, most notably Madeleine de Scudéry and the comtesse de Lafayette, whose historical novella *La Princesse de Clèves* (1678) ranks as a landmark achievement in the history of the modern novel. The Moderns favoured, in addition to the creation of new literary forms, a progressive stance towards traditional ones. They advocated, for example, the mixing of genres such as tragedy and comedy in the theatre, as pioneered by Racine's rival Pierre Corneille (1606–84), whose genre-bending work polarized debate in the middle decades of the seventeenth century. The two parties eventually met in the recently founded *académies*, especially the Académie française, to fight it out. The Quarrel was, however, no French exception: a controversy of European dimensions, it was enthusiastically taken up in late seventeenth-century England, among other settings.[16]

Dryden played a part in the English propagation of the Quarrel. In his *Essay of Dramatick Poesie*, he returns to questions, discussed by Corneille and his critics in France, about the relative importance of ancient precedent and modern experimentation in respect of genre, the unities of time, place, and action in the construction of plots, and other theatrical conventions of the day. Dryden then firmly relocates these questions within a debate about the relations between, and relative merits of, English theatre and its French counterpart. This debate, conducted in a dialogue between four interlocutors, tends to suggest that English drama developed untouched by French influence; that it produced its own Ancients (represented by Ben Jonson) and Moderns (championed by Shakespeare and Fletcher); and that, since the Restoration, it has taken full possession of the 'empire of wit'. Neander, who sets out this case in favour of his English compatriots, announces two arguments: 'First, that we have as many Playes of ours as regular as any of theirs, and which, besides, have more variety of Plot and Characters; and secondly, that in most of the irregular Playes of *Shakespeare* and *Fletcher* (for *Ben Jonson*'s are for the most part regular) there is a more masculine fancy and greater spirit in the writing, than there is in any of the *French*.' Neander—whose arguments carry the day—even suggests that Molière and his contemporaries are now freeing themselves from their adherence to ancient theatrical convention by 'imitating afar off the quick turns and graces of the *English* Stage'.[17]

In that qualifying 'afar off' we may see Neander as tacitly conceding that, in suggesting a direct English influence over French drama at this time, he would be overstating his case. Neander, indeed, protests too much. He has much less to say, meanwhile—nothing, in fact—about everything that Restoration English theatre, including Dryden's, was borrowing from

French sources. He is equally silent about the degree to which Restoration English literary criticism and theory—starting with the *Essay* itself—was adapting these same French sources to the needs of the cultural debate in England.

While it is possible that Dryden hoped that his adaptations from the French would pass undetected, this seems unlikely, given how familiar the debates in the Académie française about Corneille's work were to Dryden and his fellow English writers. What seems much more likely is that Dryden was showing his peers how they might covertly redeploy the fashionable treasures of France so appreciated across the Channel in such a manner as to depreciate overtly, in the cause of English patriotism, the very culture that had produced those treasures in the first place. He was, in sum, performing for them a literary masterclass in the self-promoting English imitation of continental modes.

The seventeenth-century English did not invent such subtleties. They could draw on the rich set of responses, developed in the course of two centuries or more of debate on the continent of Europe, to the question as to how successfully to imitate the best models. Renaissance humanists all agreed that imitation was indispensable to the writer or artist who wished to produce the finest work: none of them advocated the view, which was to become fashionable in nineteenth-century Romanticism, that the making of beauty depended on the intimate experience of a creative subjectivity that had entirely freed itself from the imitation of previous models. Renaissance humanists all agreed, too, that the choice of model or models for imitation was crucial. They disagreed mainly about two related questions—what that choice should be, and how to imitate it—and they developed conflicting solutions to these questions that anticipate the opposing positions taken in the Quarrel of the Ancients and Moderns. The so-called Ciceronian debate of the fifteenth and sixteenth centuries pitted those (proto-Ancients) who thought that the work of Cicero was the single and supreme model of prose—as Virgil's was of poetry—against those (proto-Moderns) who favoured eclectic imitation in the service of self-expression. Seen in this way, imitation involved seeking out and selecting the most productive sources before judiciously integrating them, now overtly, now covertly, into a new whole.[18]

Writers of the English Restoration had these examples to draw on as they explored how best, in the service of their self-expression, to imitate the French. They could also reflect on the curious parallel between their own situation and that of their French predecessors of the previous century. The latter had found themselves responding to the fashion in their own country for a neighbouring culture, in their case Italian, as they explored the questions that this fashion raised about their national identity. French sixteenth-century writers, like their English successors, responded in various ways. They, too, developed forms of ambivalence. They were, for example, capable of noisily criticizing excessive Italianization of French language and culture—as Henri Estienne did, for example, in his 1578 *Deux Dialogues* (Two Dialogues)—while promoting so-called 'homegrown' alternatives that included naturalized Italian imports among their number. These included all manner of Italian words: one was *capriccio*, which, as we will see, the French quickly refashioned in their vernacular as *caprice*. They also adapted to their own purposes Italian movements such as the Neoplatonism of Marsilio Ficino (1434–99), social codes such as the grace of the Italian Renaissance courts, literary forms such as the sonnet, the culinary traditions of Florence, and a vast array of other objects and practices. French intellectuals tended to view this work as their contribution to the transfer of cultural power, the so-called *translatio studii*, which they hoped—in a century marked by Franco–Italian wars—would be accompanied by the movement of imperial power, *translatio imperii*, westwards to Paris.[19]

Restoration writers like Dryden wished, in their turn, to claim the new 'empire of wit' for what Shakespeare had called their sceptered isle. But England at that time had a long road to travel if it was to emulate its cross-Channel neighbour in the hard facts of cultural and imperial power rather than in mere fantasies. France had emerged from the civil and religious wars of the late sixteenth century. It had a strong ruler in Louis XIV, for better or worse, and it had begun much earlier than England to establish an empire through foreign conquest. Its imperial power was growing. So was its cultural power, starting with its language, which developed as a European-wide vernacular during the seventeenth century. It is little wonder, then, that the English watched with fear and loathing, as well as fascination, as French fashion broke in waves upon the shores of what they must have seen, in this connection, as their pestered isle.[20]

À la Mode *and the Modern*

To be à la mode in Restoration England was to be modern. It was also to be Modern, that is, to side, in the cultural debates of the age, with those who thought that the best practitioners of the contemporary arts and sciences should look back for inspiration to Greek and Roman antiquity, but not be ruled by its example, and that they had just as much to learn by imitating recent developments across Europe. Simply saying *à la mode* with a straight face in a seventeenth-century English sentence signalled a willingness to imitate one French development, namely, the invention of an elegant, linguistically pluralist, vocabulary of modern culture and society. To be à la mode in Restoration England was, therefore, inherently controversial. Some loved it. Others loathed it. Others, still, both loved and loathed it. *À la mode* thus entrenched attitudes, which persist to this day, towards the place of French in modern English.

The French phrase *à la mode* was, and indeed remains, able in English—depending on the manner of its use—either to concentrate the promise of being modern or to empty the modern of its prestige. This is true, also, of the phrase as used in early modern French. It had long been followed by an adjective or a noun (itself prefaced by the preposition *de*) that specified a particular manner or fashion (as in *à la mode ancienne* or *à la mode d'Italie*). In the seventeenth century, *à la mode* was increasingly deployed on its own to refer to fashionability itself. It did so across many areas of French society and culture. It became prominent in cooking: La Varenne's 1651 cookery book *Le Cuisinier françois*, which was quickly translated into every major European language, and in 1653 into English as *The French Cook*, included a recipe for *bœuf à la mode*—larded beef braised with vegetables and served in a rich winey sauce— which is thought to have been one of La Varenne's creations.[21] La Varenne's promise was that the modern could taste good.

In its 1694 dictionary, the Académie française shows *à la mode* being applied, above all, to the men and women who make it into the in-club, and to the clothes and fabrics they wear and the words they use to mark their modishness. The link between sartorial and linguistic fashion is explored elsewhere. The academician François de Callières published in 1690 a dialogue, entitled *Des mots à la mode* (Words in fashion), that reviews uses and abuses of contemporary French. The text both marks the hierarchical boundaries of the language as spoken by the various tribes that made up French society and presents the speech of the most distinguished people at the top of the hierarchy—the court—as the model of elegant French. Such people, Callières says at one point, treat new trends in words and the latest outfits with the same prudence: they are never the first to take them up nor the last to cast them off. Edmé Boursault described his 1694 comedy *Les Mots à la mode* (Fashionable words) as a theatrical 'bagatelle' inspired by Callières's dialogue of the same name. The play satirizes social climbers—such as a butcher's daughter married to a recently titled jeweller—who see fashionable words and ever more extravagant outfits as a means of raising their status. It offers members of the audience the pleasant prospect of feeling part of the in-crowd by transmitting to them what they need to know about the fashionable world while also teaching them to laugh at the ridiculous excesses of that world. It thus reveals fashion as a system of perpetual innovation and obsolescence in which to be in the know is to be one step ahead of the social climbers. The Académie française dictionary, first published in the same year as Boursault's comedy, shows an awareness both of this system and of its losers: it speaks of fashions that are 'bad', 'ridiculous', and 'extravagant' and of their victim as a 'fashion slave' (*esclave de la mode*). The fashion system was in place.[22]

À la mode has continued since the seventeenth century to enable speakers and writers of French to encapsulate what seems to them good and bad about fashionable society and culture. If anything, though, it was perhaps the English—for once, in this story, the trend-setters—who saw first that marriage, or what they quickly called 'marriage à la mode', could serve as a microcosm of fashionable society as a whole.

The rakish poet John Wilmot (1647–80), Earl of Rochester, had already written on this theme, probably in 1669, a poem that circulated in manuscript before being printed in two separate editions in 1679. Artemisa recounts in a verse letter from town to her friend Chloe, who lives in the country, her recent encounter with a 'fine lady' who had come up from the country with her husband in tow to see her 'gallant'. The lady is a fop and she speaks a fop's Frenchified English. She also takes the fashionable view of marriage. Artemisa reports her as saying, with due indiscretion, 'When I was married, fools were *à la mode*; / The men of wit were then held *incommode*.' The lady not only married by this maxim but, as she explains, continues to live by it. The wretched Corinna learned to do the same, she continues, after being left high and dry—and riddled with sexually transmitted disease—by a rakish man of wit: she has now ensnared a young country gentleman. He maintains her, his mistress, better than he does the cousin he was forced, for dynastic reasons, to marry: he has thus proved himself to be the fitting heir to and the latest flowering 'of a great family, / Which with strong ale and beef the country rules, / And ever since the conquest have been fools'.[23]

Dryden went on to make fashionable marriage a central— and controversial—theme of *Marriage À-la-Mode*. Etherege followed suit in *The Man of Mode*. Dryden dedicated *Marriage À-la-Mode* to Rochester and, in doing so, declared that he owed anything he had achieved in the play to 'your Lordship's Conversation'. The probable dating of Rochester's poem suggests that Dryden and Etherege were transposing to the theatre, in the 1670s, a theme that was already fashionable in Restoration culture.[24]

Dryden's play, and Etherege's, established themselves as the Restoration period's most enduring expressions of that theme. After 1700, *Marriage À-la-Mode* had its comic plot separated from its heroic double, making for a shorter, more pointed, comedy of modern manners. The dramatist Colly Cibber (1671–1757) mixed the comic plot of that play, in 1707, with scenes from another of Dryden's plays, *Secret Love*, entitling his compilation *The Comical Lovers; or, Marriage À-la-Mode*. For a command performance, in June 1715, its title was altered to *Court Gallantry; or, Marriage À-la-Mode*: gallantry, in other words, remained as prominently at the heart of the modern comedy of Frenchified English manners then as it had been in the 1670s. Cibber's remake was performed at intervals throughout the first half of the eighteenth century. In 1757 it was in turn remade by Henry Dell as a two-act comedy, *The Frenchified Lady Never in Paris*, which brought Melantha and her Francomaniacal antics to the fore. The scene in which Melantha has her maid Philotis furnish her with a list of French words to keep her à la mode survived intact in Cibber's and Dell's remakes of the play. This suggests that the ambivalence of the English towards the Frenchification of their language and manners—along with the sexual politics of marriage and modern life in England—remained appealing topics to English audiences well into the eighteenth century.[25]

While the title Dryden had chosen for his treatment of those themes became progressively detached from his play, that same title was appropriated by the English artist William Hogarth, who around 1743 produced six paintings as models from which a series of prints would be made under the title *Marriage À-la-Mode*. There is more of Rochester than of Dryden in Hogarth's narrative. Its opening scene, 'The Marriage Settlement' (fig. 2), shows a gout-ridden father pointing to a family tree in which William of Normandy has pride of place while the father's foolish viscount of a son gazes lovingly at his own foppish reflection in a mirror. The rash on his neck suggests that he is bringing into the marriage that most fashionable of STDs, syphilis, known in English of the period as 'the pox' but also as 'the French disease' or the 'à la mode disease'. Later scenes in Hogarth's sequence show that the viscount has infected a young girl with his disease and that his wife—who goes for lawyers on the make rather than child prostitutes—is just as sexually promiscuous and as addicted to other forms of French modishness

FIG. 2. Louis Gérard Scotin after William Hogarth, *Marriage À-la-Mode: plate 1, The Marriage Settlement*, 1745. Etching and engraving on paper. Courtesy National Gallery of Art, Washington.

as her husband. While Hogarth's series shows no direct connection with Dryden's treatment of the theme, it works that same theme into a melodrama of modern marital horror, recycling Dryden's title to brilliant satirical effect.[26]

Etherege's *Man of Mode* has endured, and, in the process, undergone its own creative reworkings. It continued to stir controversy among late eighteenth-century literary critics but was not then performed again in London until the Royal Shakespeare Company brought the play back to the stage in 1971. This was part of a broader revival of interest in the late twentieth century that saw much Restoration drama re-edited and performed, and its mode and idiom reworked by contemporary playwrights such as Edward Bond, who, in his 1981 play *Restoration*, trained the wit of that period upon its politics.[27] A similar pattern of performance and appropriation has continued to characterize the afterlives of *The Man of Mode*. The play had its initial setting temporally transposed, in a 2007 National Theatre production, to a twenty-first-century London in which Sir Fopling Flutter (played by Rory Kinnear) demonstrated, by his anglicized mimicry of French elegance, that such mimicry continues to provoke the self-implicating laughter of London audiences towards the character that, we saw at the end of the previous chapter, Dryden described as 'a people in a man'. Over a decade before this National Theatre production, *The Man of Mode* had inspired a successful contemporary spin-off, Stephen Jeffreys's play *The Libertine*. Jeffreys's play retells the colourful life of Rochester and weaves into its plot the long-standing idea that Etherege, in his characterization of the rakish Dorimant, was directly portraying Rochester on the London Restoration stage. *The Libertine* was first performed in December 1994 in association with a new production of *The Man of Mode*: the same theatrical company performed both plays. The effect of this theatrical pairing was to mark, as in a distorting mirror, the contrast between the polished gentility of Etherege's comedy and the rough realities of Rochester's life as a hard-living rake and political satirist. Jeffreys used the sensibility of his age to push the libertine gallantry that Etherege associates with Dorimant to a flamboyantly obscene and disease-ridden extreme, whose limits Johnny Depp probed in the 2004 film version of *The Libertine*, playing a hell-raising Rochester alongside Rosamund Pike in the role of Rochester's despairing wife.[28]

In all these ways and doubtless others, then, marriage à la mode has, for centuries now, moved with the times and across different cultures and media of artistic expression, revealing all the while the good, the bad, and the ugly faces of fashionable modern life. It thus reflects the wider history of French *à la mode* in English. English had no sooner received that phrase than it started to play exuberantly fast and loose with its modalities. As the *OED* charts, *à la mode* quickly spread to almost all parts of English sentences, being able to function as an adverb, adjective, noun, and preposition. Its history suggests that, by 1700, it would have been linguistically possible—if you wished to inform your interlocutors that the London in-crowd kept up with the times by wearing the most fashionable French silks in the French way—to say something along the following lines: 'The Alamodes remain à la mode by wearing the most alamode alamodes à la mode of the French . . .'. English (like French) came to dispense with the *mode* in the phrase *à la mode*, making *à la* a lexical unit in its own right, which can be specified by a noun or feminine French adjective in both languages (as in the phrase *à l'irlandaise*) or in English by any noun or proper name (as in the phrase '*à la* Beyoncé'). For those who remained committed to their modes, there remained plenty of further possibilities in English, a language in which the noun *à la modality* can even today still strike the ear as being alamodic, on occasion, even if no one seems to have used the noun *à-la-modeness* since Melantha's heyday.[29]

What travels with *à la mode* through the development of modern English, in all its modes, is a set of interconnected histories of consumables: silk handkerchiefs, cosmetics, and other accessories of modern life in the English-speaking world. *À la mode* is what you eat as much as what you wear. It is as British as beef stew and as American as ice cream. In the cultural meaning of the British dish and American dessert alike, French *à la mode* is no mere seasoning, but an essential ingredient.

The last word on the topic of *à la mode* in English must therefore go to the dysfunctional family whom we watch arguing their way across America, crammed into their ageing yellow Volkswagen van, in the 2006 road movie *Little Miss Sunshine*, directed by Jonathan Dayton and Valerie Faris. Failed life coach Richard (Greg Kinnear) and his wife Sheryl (Toni Collette) are taking their daughter Olive (Abigail Breslin) to a beauty pageant in California. Richard's unsuitable father Edwin (Alan Arkin) comes with them, as do Sheryl's teenage son Dwayne (Paul Dano), who has taken a vow of silence, and her brother Frank (Steve Carell), a depressed gay Proust scholar who has been living with the family since attempting suicide. The family stops for a four-dollar breakfast in a diner (fig. 3). Edwin orders a Lumberjack breakfast with coffee, Frank the fruit basket with camomile tea and honey, and so on. Olive is drawn to the waffles. But the menu says these come à la mode, and Olive (pronouncing it 'alamodee') asks what this means. The waitress explains: it comes with ice cream. Olive happily places her order, and the waitress departs. Her father intervenes. He wants to control his daughter's eating so she can become a stick-thin beauty queen. If he has his way, we infer, his daughter will only become truly à la mode in contemporary America if she foregoes the à la mode on the menu. The film in this way inserts the phrase into its satire of middle America with its material consumerism and its pernicious control of young female bodies. In its deployment of *à la mode*, the film poses Olive a question of identity: Who does she want to become? And what is the just measure for becoming that person?

We have already seen *à la mode* posing these questions, *mutatis mutandis*, of the Restoration English. These questions echo in the gloss on *à la mode* that Frank, the Proust scholar, offers Olive after the waitress has taken her order. But it is not

FIG. 3. A lesson in the meanings of *à la mode* for Olive, in Scene 6 of *Little Miss Sunshine*, starring Alan Arkin, Abigail Breslin, Steve Carell, Toni Collette, Paul Dano, and Greg Kinnear; directed by Jonathan Dayton and Valerie Faris; produced by Albert Berger, David T. Friendly, Peter Saraf, Marc Turtletaub, and Ron Yerxa (Los Angeles: Twentieth Century Fox, 2006), DVD.

clear that anyone is listening to Frank. Richard, who is threatened by Frank's linguistic erudition, refuses to let him finish what he is saying. *À la mode*, having promised to sweeten and illuminate the scene in the diner, is promptly dismissed:

> FRANK: Actually, Olive, *à la mode* in French translates literally as 'in the fashion'. À la mooode. *Mode* is derived from Latin *modus*, meaning due or proper measure . . .
> RICHARD: Frank, shut up.[30]

CHAPTER THREE

Creolizing Keywords

creolization, *n.*

Etymology: < CREOLIZE *v.* + –ATION *suffix*, perhaps partly
after French *créolisation.*

1. The action or process of taking on any of various
characteristics or other aspects of Creole people, their
culture, etc.; *esp.* the assimilation of aspects of another
culture or cultures; hybridization of cultures.

—*OXFORD ENGLISH DICTIONARY*

Either I'm nobody, or I'm a nation.

—DEREK WALCOTT

HOW, THEN, are we to understand the specific character of *à
la mode* and other French émigrés in English? What do these
words reveal of the cultural and
social processes in history that
have shaped them and have been,
in turn, shaped by them?

I argue, in what follows, that
émigrés are keywords of cultures and societies which have long
been, and still remain, caught up in a process of creolization.

My pursuit of this argument will cause me to draw together and adapt two hitherto unconnected concepts in cultural criticism: keywords and creolization.

Two Concepts

In his study *Keywords*, published first in 1976 and then in revised and expanded form in 1983, Raymond Williams—a Cambridge professor of English literature who came from the Welsh borders—set out to show his readers that the language they spoke was not a self-evident set of meanings, handed down to them from on high, but a process of making and remaking meaning in which they could choose to play a fully conscious and active part. He did so by composing for modern Britain what he called, in his book's subtitle, *A Vocabulary of Culture and Society*. He means by this vocabulary, as he says in his Introduction to *Keywords*, the set of words 'we share with others, often imperfectly, when we wish to discuss many of the central processes of our common life'. He explains that his attention was captured by these words while he was writing his book *Culture and Society 1780–1950* (1958), and that he came to see *culture* as 'the original difficult word' of this kind: 'The very fact that it was important in two areas that are often thought of as separate—*art* and *society*—posed new questions and suggested new kinds of connection.'[1]

Moving alphabetically from *aesthetic* to *work*, Williams examines over a hundred such difficult words in *Keywords*, excavating their particular and relational meanings in history. When a word raises problems of meaning, these need to be located in the context of specific historical relationships, but this approach is not meant to imply that language 'simply reflects the processes of society and history': 'on the contrary,' he observes, 'it is a central aim of this book to show that some important social and historical processes occur *within* language, in ways which indicate how integral the problems of meanings and of relationships really are'. He identifies lexical developments that may both reveal and effect change in cultural and social relationships. Such developments include the alteration of existing items of vocabulary and the invention of new ones. He insists on the sociocultural relevance of his enquiry for modern British readers—to whom the book was addressed—and gestures towards the contribution he hopes to make: not a resolution of the problems he has explored, but, perhaps, at times, 'just that extra edge of consciousness'. If they learn to recognize that the keywords of modern British culture bear within them opacity as well as clarity, carry a potential for coercion and resistance alike, then his readers will be starting to come to terms with that culture. His book is therefore anything but 'a neutral review of meanings': it offers, instead, 'a vocabulary to use, to find our own ways in, to change as we find it necessary to change it, as we go on making our own language and history'.[2]

Williams points out various limitations of his enterprise. He observes that many of the words he worked on 'either developed key meanings in languages other than English, or went through a complicated and interactive development in a number of major languages', and he notes that he had only occasionally been able—as he did in his entries for terms such as *alienation, culture,* and *ideology*—to integrate into his vocabulary 'crucially important' comparative analysis of this kind.[3]

Some of the work done in the wake of Williams has addressed this limitation of his vocabulary. A multilingual approach has characterized various important studies of words that—just like the émigrés I explore in this book—underwent complex developments in the early modern period. Individual words have attracted book-length comparative studies, such as *curiosity* in French and German by Neil Kenny, and *ingenuity* in early modern Latin and vernacular European languages by Alexander Marr, Raphaële Garrod, José Ramón Marcaida, and Richard Oosterhoff. Other studies have grouped words into clusters. The contributors to Ita Mac Carthy's 2013 collection *Renaissance Keywords*, taking inspiration from Williams's example, explore seven words—*allegory, disegno, discretion, grace, modern, scandal,* and *sense*—that crackled with a particular semantic energy in the languages of sixteenth-century Europe. While some of those words remain current and problematic in modern English, including *modern* itself, not all have made that journey. Roland Greene presents the terms at the heart of his 2015 study in 'critical semantics'—*invention, language, resistance, blood,* and *world*—as five words 'that maintain a disciplinary purchase but are also used in everyday life'. His polyglot investigation of these words in their sixteenth- and seventeenth-century uses helps to recover—as Greene hoped they would—'some of the wonder with which early modern people regarded particular words that crossed eras [. . .] and languages'. His historical focus on what he calls 'the age of Shakespeare and Cervantes' necessarily means, however, that the subsequent migrations of these words go uncharted.[4]

Other work has substantially broadened the cosmopolitanism of the enquiry undertaken by Williams while also maintaining its focus on contemporary language. The French historian of philosophy Barbara Cassin's *Dictionary of Untranslatables* is a case in point. Untranslatable terms in philosophy are those that invite and yet frustrate attempts to translate them across languages. The French and comparative literary scholar Emily Apter, who co-edited the English translation of Cassin's work, describes them as 'words that assign new meanings to old terms, neologisms, names for ideas that are continually re-translated or mistranslated, translations that are obviously incommensurate'. Apter uses the concept of untranslatability to mount a challenge to the assumption of all-too-easy translatability that, she argues, governs the academic discipline of world literature in its current, reduced form. She goes on (in the 2013 book that she wrote while working on Cassin's dictionary) to illustrate her thesis in essays devoted to what she calls, with reference to Williams, 'keywords': *cyclopædia, peace, fado* and *saudade, sex* and *gender*, and *monde*.[5]

It is hardly surprising that comparative work done since *Keywords* should have focussed on a more cosmopolitan vocabulary than the words Williams identified as being those 'we share with others, often imperfectly, when we wish to discuss many of the central processes of our common life'. 'We' meant for Williams, writing in 1970s Cambridge, British speakers of modern English. By contrast, it might mean none of the above for Apter and her colleagues, working in the more nationally and linguistically diverse environment of the twenty-first-century US academy. Meanwhile, not all untranslatables are widely applicable to common life, some of them being technical terms in philosophy. An increase in cosmopolitanism, relative to Williams's project, is accompanied by a loss of commonality.

I am interested here, as Williams was, in words shared by English speakers as they discuss the central processes of their common life today. But I should like to point out how many such words are of foreign derivation. We saw, in the previous two chapters, that English has received countless borrowings from French alone over the centuries. *Naïveté, ennui,* and *caprice* are examples of words of early modern French provenance that we users of English have long shared with each other and continue to share today—often imperfectly—as we talk about central processes of our common life, such as being true to our nature, feeling bored, and changing our minds.

I propose, therefore, to add to Williams's English vocabulary of modern culture and society a new category: that of the émigré. My proposal might meet with the objection that Williams has already integrated the category into his vocabulary by including a keyword like *ideology* (which he presents, in his entry on the term, as a 'direct translation' of the French word *idéologie*). My answer is that he did, yes, but only in respect of the kind of foreign-derived loanword (*ideology* being one such) that has been wholly adapted to English usage. There is no room in Williams's vocabulary for the residually foreign émigré. My contention is that room should be made.[6]

To this it might further be objected that—while we can indeed choose to call, in English, upon émigrés like *à la mode* when discussing central processes of our common life—we have for each of these processes more standard and more straightforwardly English words (like *fashion, boredom, innocence,* and *whim*) that deserve our primary attention. I would reply to this objection that it starts by granting the proposition: the residually French borrowings I have mentioned each meet Williams's definition of a keyword as a problematic term commonly available in the area of culture and society. I would want also to observe that English speakers and writers often choose to deviate from the standard and straightforward forms of expression, when discussing the central processes of their common life, and that it might be interesting to ask why and how.

Exploring the English uses of foreign-derived words would help us to do so. Such an exploration would, of course, be bound—as the case of *à la mode* has shown—to include in its remit interplay in particular uses between the apparently more standard and more straightforwardly English words available (such as *fashion*) and the émigré. It would acknowledge that recourse to French foreign borrowings is not a given for all English speakers, and depends on their access to, and the nature of their attitude towards, this foreign language. It could also usefully cause us all to consider further what 'standard and more straightforwardly English' might mean, precisely, in any given time and setting. And it would, at least, remind us—in relation to that last consideration—that the public garden of the English language has seen a thousand foreign flowers bloom.

Were we to have to do without French and other foreignisms in English, we would quickly find that 'we have hardly any words that do so fully expresse' their meanings, as Evelyn put it in 1665. At the same time, as the case of *à la mode* has shown, the importation of émigrés has tended to excite fear and loathing as well as fascination among speakers of English. What, then, might the study of the role played in English by these particular keywords reveal of the broader relations between neighbouring languages, cultures, and societies?

Answering that question means offering the theoretical conjecture I announced at the opening of this chapter: that this role is best understood as a specific instance of a wider process of creolization. It therefore brings me to the second of my two concepts in cultural criticism.

Caribbean cultural and social studies witnessed the development of creolization as a conceptual model for understanding processes of transcultural mixing in historical settings marked by highly asymmetrical power relations. Francophone

Caribbean cultural theorists shaped this development. Chief among these was the Martinican intellectual Édouard Glissant. Glissant defined *créolisation* as the process whereby several cultures, or elements of those cultures, form unexpected hybrids. He argued that the historical crucible of the creolizing process has been the Caribbean archipelago, from 1492 onwards, and that the European discovery and conquest of the Americas was the defining episode. If the early modern Caribbean was creolization's crucible, Glissant suggested, its catalyst in that region was the slave trade. Traces of language, belief, and behaviour from Africa survived the horror of the Middle Passage as cultural roots whose human carriers then came into contact with others. The result was new hybrids that took root in the soil of the Caribbean islands, so to speak, including speech varieties that developed between Africans and Europeans. Creolization emerged as a contradictory force in Glissant's account: the creative possibilities of its good side were made possible by and could not be disentangled from the actual circumstances—marked by inequality and domination—of its bad side. Inexorable as well as contradictory, it continued apace—for Glissant—in the era of globalization, as ever greater interconnectedness signalled the entrenchment of inequality yet also offered ever-increasing possibilities of creating new and beautiful cultural hybrids the world over.[7]

Creolization, when construed in this way, is distinct from *creole* as a description of a set of Caribbean and other languages. But the two may be related. The prevalent view among linguists for a long time was that creoles formed an exceptional class of languages. Each of these languages passed through an initial pidgin stage, in which people brought into sudden contact (such as slaves and their owners on Caribbean plantations) mingled their African and European mother languages so as to devise a rudimentary common tongue native to none, and this became a creole only once it was acquired by locally born children as their first language. This view, which came from the 1980s onwards to be particularly associated with the work of Derek Bickerton, was challenged by, among others, Michel DeGraff, a specialist in Haitian creole, who in 2003 mounted a case against what he termed 'Creole exceptionalism'. DeGraff's view, which he expanded upon during a robust academic controversy with Bickerton, was essentially that nothing intrinsic in the development and structure of Haitian and other plantation creoles sets them apart from other cases of language change via language contact. If there was a central difference between language change more generally and creolization, DeGraff argued, it was a sociohistorical one. Investigating further the sociohistorical context of the development of creole languages was to be part of the 'postcolonial creolistics' that DeGraff announced.[8]

This is not the place to adjudicate between the positions advocated by Bickerton and DeGraff. I merely observe that one productive consequence of the latter's position, with which I find myself in sympathy, is that it reconnects linguistic with sociohistorical and cultural studies of Caribbean creolization *à la* Glissant. DeGraff uses the term *creolization*, accordingly, to refer to 'the sequence of sociohistorical events that led to the formation of [the] languages known as Creoles'.[9]

Glissant, of course, went further. The Trinidad-born and British-based intellectual Stuart Hall considered, in a lecture first published in 2003, the wider, indeed global, conceptual applicability that Glissant had lent to creolization. Hall decided in that lecture to advance by means of a 'conjectural theorization' in two stages: first, by asking whether Francophone Caribbean notions of Creole and creolization could be 'expanded from their meanings and conditions of existence in the French Antilles' to the entire Caribbean; and second, to experiment with further expansion of the frame of reference 'by locating the question of "creolization" in the wider processes of globalization'.[10]

The first stage of Hall's argument sees him recalling the complex and contested word histories of *creolization* and *creole*. Hall reminds us that, while the English term initially had a connection with Spanish *criollo*, it eventually acquired a particular French colonial resonance. (Perhaps a French borrowing in English, then, *creole* is also, like *creolization*, an émigré.) Hall observes that Creoles were originally white Europeans, said to have acquired 'native characteristics' through long association with the colonial setting, and that the word was then also applied to black African slaves born in the island or territory. Only more recently, Hall points out, did the term *Creole* come to designate a person of *mixed* African and European blood in certain settings. Hall further shows that while this sense predominates in the Francophone Caribbean islands and neighbouring Anglophone islands, *Creole* means other things elsewhere in the English-speaking Caribbean (in Guyana, for example, it distinguishes Guyanese of African rather than Asian extraction), and that in the Gulf States of the USA it refers to the descendants and traditions of the early French and Spanish settlers.[11]

Hall then considers contemporary theoretical usage of the terms *creole*, *créolité*, and *creolization*. He argues, with reference to the Jamaican social historian Edward Kamau Brathwaite and the Canadian literary critic Mary Louise Pratt as well as Glissant, that this usage has tended to emphasize a process of transcultural 'entanglement' that takes place in what Pratt calls 'contact zones', in other words, 'social spaces where disparate cultures [. . .] grapple with each other often in highly asymmetrical relations of domination and subordination'. Hall sees this asymmetry of power as critical: 'Creolization *always* entails inequality, hierarchization, issues of domination and subalternity, mastery and servitude, control and resistance.' This distinguishes creolization from wholly affirmative syncretic concepts that have dominated the study of postcolonial cultures. By contrast, Hall emphasizes the contradictory nature of creolization, naming its defining features as being a fundamental asymmetry of power, on the one hand, and, on the other, a mutually constituting entanglement that makes a whole set of 'creative cultural practices' possible.[12]

Hall suggests that, just as the conditions of creolization exist everywhere in the Caribbean, so, then, do its associated creative cultural practices. He offers various examples of such practices from across the region: these include, from the Francophone islands, the *créolité* advocated in the wake of Glissant by Jean Bernabé, Patrick Chamoiseau, and Raphaël Confiant in their 1989 *Éloge de la créolité* (*In Praise of Creoleness*); from the Hispanophone Caribbean, Antonio Benítez-Rojo's postmodern critical study *La isla que se repite* (*The Repeating Island*), also first published in 1989; and from the Anglophone Caribbean, the work of the St Lucian poet Derek Walcott. Hall suggests of Walcott's 1990 epic poem *Omeros*, which brings together Homeric motifs and the verse form of Dante's *Divine Comedy* in a distinctively Caribbean setting, that it 'is, without question, a great poem of the creolizing imaginary'.[13]

Hall did not publish the second stage of his conjectural theorization, in which he proposed to consider creolization in relation to the wider processes of globalization, but he concluded the first stage by offering some preliminary remarks on this score. Creolization is 'the only basis in the present of creative practices and creative expression', Hall asserts by way of a recapitulation, in the Caribbean as a whole. How about the rest of the world? Hall ends his essay with a cliffhanger: 'Whether creolization also provides the theoretical model for wider processes of cultural mixing in the contemporary post global world remains to be considered.'[14]

Various scholars have pursued Hall's question. Some of these have done so by asking it of contemporary European culture and society. I should like to attempt a further and, I think, unprecedented exercise in 'conjectural theorization' by suggesting, in the wake of Glissant and Hall, that creolization provides a useful theoretical model for understanding processes of mixing in medieval and early modern European language and culture and, specifically, in the contact zone where English became entangled with French. That means bringing creolization back home, as it were, to the cluster of European countries that first devised it as a means of colonial domination.[15]

To do so is to recall that those countries not only exerted colonial domination abroad, but also experienced it at home, and that—in the case of England and France—they did so at each other's hands. It is to observe that a colonizing European people such as the early modern English may have had more in common than met the eye with their colonial subjects in the Caribbean, insofar as both knew what it was to be subjugated by an invading force and to find themselves mixing with it. It is emphatically *not* to imply, on the basis of that observation, that the two instances of subjugation are identical or equivalent to one another. It would be quite wrong—and I in no way mean—to claim that the English ever experienced colonial conquest and domination of the same kind or in the same manner as African victims of the slave trade did. By contrast with the Caribbean paradigm, creolization in the English setting was a long and complex process, amounting to centuries of entanglement between England and its continental neighbour. It did not involve the forced displacement and trading of slaves on a massive scale.

But the English did suffer conquest and domination, at the hands of William the Conqueror and his fellow Normans in 1066, and they have never forgotten it. The Norman conquest of England and its aftermath brought Anglo-Saxon and Norman language and culture together and forced them to coexist. It did so, too, in a palpably unequal setting, in which the Normans had supplanted the Anglo-Saxon landowning class and installed Norman (later French) as the dominant language and culture of government, law, trade, the church, the royal courts, and the creative arts.[16] The result was an entangling of languages and cultures that saw Latin (classical and medieval), Scandinavian, Celtic, and others drawn into the mix. That mix, the results of which varied according to circumstances of time and place, is irreducible to the binary of Saxon and Norman, of course, just as no Caribbean creole can be reduced to the mingling of African and European elements alone. Insofar as we can observe a fundamental asymmetry of power and a mutually constituting entanglement to have combined there, however, post-1066 England may be said to constitute a prime European example of a culture engaged in and defined by a process of creolization.

That process has lasted for centuries, of course, and has been marked by a myriad of subsequent political and military as well as cultural entanglements. The entity now recognizable as France was itself taking shape during this period. Conflicts on the mainland of modern France played their part in a slow and uneven process of nation-making. So did the mingling of peoples. The Normans—whose dukes proudly traced their descent back to the Vikings—initially set themselves apart from the Franks to the south and east of them. One key development, around 1200, saw the duchy of Normandy integrated into the patchwork kingdom of Philip Augustus. It was at this very moment in history, after he had captured Rouen (the capital of Normandy) from the English in 1204–5, that Philip Augustus started to style himself 'king of Francia' instead of, as hitherto, 'king of the Franks'. The cultural construction of French nationhood was, by then, already under way, as typified by the *Chanson de Roland* (composed c. 1100), a poem whose commemoration of the Battle of Roncevaux in the age of Charlemagne offered France a powerful (and lasting) 'fantasy of origins'.[17] The earliest extant manuscript of the poem, held at the Bodleian Library in Oxford, is written in the language of the twelfth-century Anglo-Norman elite.

The English kingdom, along with its dominant language and culture, came into being in the midst of the same mutually constituting entanglement. English invasions during the Hundred Years' War (c. 1337–c. 1453) were in part the expression of a continuing resistance to the prestige and dominance of Norman and French models in England. The remaining English territories in France had all been lost by the time Henry VIII's Protestant daughter Elizabeth came to the throne of England as its last Tudor monarch. But Anglo-French relations had, by then, become a cornerstone of English history and literature: playwrights such as William Shakespeare (1564–1616), for example, wrote history plays about the ebb and flow of English dominion in France and the challenges this posed to the English collective sense of self. The English remained, all this time, haunted by the prospect that the French might repeat the Norman conquest of 1066. The royal family that was to accede to the English throne after the Tudors, the Stuarts, had—as we saw in the previous two chapters—connections with the French royal family and (in some cases) pro-Catholic sympathies. Some in England viewed them as preparing a French invasion or indeed as *being* that invasion. Others, especially some English Catholics, hoped for a repetition in England of 1066 and all that.[18]

For one central instance of the way in which the Norman conquest has structured, since 1066, much political, religious, and cultural debate in England, we need look no further than the centuries-old motif of the Norman Yoke. The English historian Christopher Hill identified the outlines of the motif as follows:

> Before 1066 the Anglo-Saxon inhabitants of this country lived as free and equal citizens, governing themselves through representative institutions. The Norman Conquest deprived them of this liberty, and established the tyranny of an alien King and landlords. But the people did not forget the rights they had lost. They fought continuously to recover them, with varying success. Concessions (Magna Carta, for instance) were from time to time extorted from their rulers, and always the tradition of lost Anglo-Saxon freedom was a stimulus to ever more insistent demands upon the successors of the Norman usurpers.

Hill pointed out the historical insufficiencies of this theory even as he argued for its significance as a political rallying-cry that has served many purposes over the centuries. He showed that it has been used as a means, in some cases, of legitimizing but, more often, of contesting the power and privileges of the ruling class. In essence, the contestation is, as Hill puts it, that 'the people could conduct its own affairs better without its Norman rulers, whose wealth and privileges are an obstacle to equality'. The claim that it is time for England to cease being a Norman colony and to take back control is as old and as entrenched in English culture as is the story of the Saxon freedom fighter Robin Hood outwitting Guy of Gisborne and his Norman ilk.[19]

The Norman Yoke enjoyed a particular currency in seventeenth-century England, as the country lurched from parliamentary revolution against its monarchy to republicanism and back again to the restoration of its monarchy. The political radical John Hare, writing in the 1640s, called for all aristocratic titles, laws, and customs of Norman provenance to be rescinded and replaced. His proposals included exit from the language of the Continent. He asked, of English, 'That our Language be cleared of the Normane and French invasion upon it, and depravation of it, by purging it of all words and termes of that descent'.[20] Notice how easily Hare here conflates the Normans and the French—who were, after all, once separate, even enemy, peoples—in a single invading force. The identification of Normanization with Frenchification was, as I suggested earlier, well established in the popular English view of history by the time Hare was writing. Hare's anti-Normanism was reflected in a Puritan petition to parliament, published in the same year (1647) as Hare's tract, taking exception to the fact that English law books were all—as they had in fact been for centuries—written in Anglo-Norman. The signatories to the petition considered this fact to be 'a Badg[e] of our Slavery to a Norman Conqueror', as they put it, and therefore moved that 'all the Laws and Customs of this Realm be immediately written in our Mothers Tongue'. An Act to that effect was passed by the English parliament in November 1650.[21]

The Norman Yoke has remained a commonplace of English discourse ever since. Christopher Hill, writing in the 1950s, observed that 'anti-Normanism still had its vigorous spokesmen'. He could not then have predicted, of course, what new lease of life the Norman Yoke stood to receive in English parliamentary and popular discourse from the United Kingdom's evolving and fraught relationship with the institutions of the European Union. The 2016 Brexit referendum saw the majority of English and Welsh voters, by contrast with those in Scotland and Northern Ireland, support the victorious Leave campaign. In July 2018, the United Kingdom foreign secretary, Boris Johnson MP, resigned his office on the grounds that the government in which he served was, as he put in his letter of resignation, steering the country towards what he called 'a semi-Brexit'. Johnson drew his conclusion with a flourish as venerable as English parliamentary discourse itself: 'In that respect we are truly headed for the status of colony.' It seems that at least some of the English have yet to shrug off the Norman Yoke or to decolonize their imaginary.[22]

Three specificities of the creolizing process as it relates to England, then, are the longevity of the process, the reciprocity of invasion and counter-invasion of which it partook, and the continuing disputes about the nature of its legacy. All of these may be seen as significant departures from the Caribbean paradigm and as consequences of the fact that the creolizing process, in England, did not take place amid the forced displacement and 'seasoning' of slaves on a massive scale and within a relatively short period of time.

A further and related critical specificity of the creolizing process, as it relates to medieval and early modern England, is that England the colonized quickly turned colonizer. Collective identities were reforged as a once conquered people turned to conquering. Britishness emerged, after 1603, as a controversial geopolitical identity for what the critic John Kerrigan has called an 'archipelago' of kingdoms and cultures. It served eventually, above all, to present a common front to the rest of the world, starting with France, whose participation in the making of a former Norman colony was thereby denied. The historian Linda Colley suggested, in a controversial 1992 article, that historians of British identity had hitherto neglected to take full account of the insight, widespread among those working on continental Europe and the Third World, that national identity is both historically contingent and conceptually relational: that, in other words, 'we usually decide who we are by reference to who and what we are not'. Colley goes on in her article to apply that insight to the notion of Britishness that took hold in the period 1689–1815. She argues that the British in that period collectively took three decisions as to who and what they were (not). They defined themselves as Protestant where continental Europe was Roman Catholic; 'they defined themselves against France throughout a succession of major wars with that power'; and 'they defined themselves against the global empire won by way of these wars'.[23]

The complexities of Britishness remained considerable, then as now. Colley is right to speak of Great Britain as 'an invented nation' that was 'not founded on the suppression of older loyalties so much as superimposed on them'. That superimposition took different forms in each of the kingdoms that made up Great Britain. Colley's argument helps to explain why Ireland, whose population was more Catholic than Protestant, so often found itself treated as a 'colony', a 'laboratory of the British empire', rather than as an integral part of a supposedly united kingdom. England's place in that kingdom was central. Colley takes issue with those who exaggerate the specific role of English nationalism in the making of Great Britain and its empire. Yet that role should also not be overlooked. England was and remains, after all, the largest and most politically dominant of the three kingdoms, and home to Britain's capital city. By a kind of metonymy, which is as durable as it is objectionable, England is often seen—from both inside and outside the realm—not as one constituent part of the British isles but, rather, as the whole. English nationalists have long actively promoted this expansion of Englishness and appealed to anti-French sentiment in the midst of their nation- and empire-building. The anti-Normanism that Hare advocated in the 1640s, for example, was a programme for the 'defence and inlargement of the English Dominion', as Hare puts it in the peroration to his work, which he hopes will 'make Anglicisme become the only soule and habit of all both *Ireland* and great *Britaine*'. The idealized female figure of Britannia—a construction in print and song of the 1740s and 1750s, when the patriotic anthem 'Rule, Britannia!' first appeared, along with 'God Save the King!'—in that period sometimes personified England, and sometimes Britain, as those two collective identities overlapped. In both cases, however, Britannia was presented as a persecuted victim of the French in France and their Popish, pro-French, residually Norman stooges among the English ruling classes. Eighteenth-century Britons might well have traded in slaves; but they resolved, in the words of the anthem (still sung in Britain today), that they never, never, never would be slaves.[24]

Englishness is of course just as historically contingent and conceptually relational as Britishness and other national identities. Perhaps the most useful way forward, in light of the history sketched above, is to view Englishness as an identity that was forged—as the critic Simon Gikandi says—'in the ambivalent space that separated, but also conjoined, metropole and colony'.[25] Englishness and Britishness would, in that case, invite critical analysis as interrelated, in some respects overlapping, inventions of the same space. We would then be in a position to explore fully whether the cultural entanglements that took place in that space could usefully be defined as a process of creolization. To do so would be to pose Stuart Hall's question with specific reference to the peoples of Britain and Ireland in all the richness of their cultural practices and all the complexity of their history as colonized and colonizing. The extent of their colonizing would require an expansion of the geopolitical frame of reference to include the British empire, in its entirety, and so the mutual entanglement of languages and cultures across four continents. Such a project would act as a useful counter to nationalist histories of culture and society and to the separatist tendencies these histories are often used to reflect in debates about collective identity. It is a reminder that such identities are made, not given, and that they are made by being mixed (however painfully). It would approach the mixing of languages and cultures as neither affirmation nor negation, but as contradiction, because entailing highly asymmetrical relations of power yet enabling creative practices of language and culture.

Creolization encapsulates this contradiction while allowing it to be transposed from its first historical setting, the Caribbean, and to vary under specific conditions. Hall shows how delicately creolization may be handled as a non-reductive conceptual model in transit when, as we have seen, he uses it—varying its terms to reflect the specificities involved—to explore the language and culture of the English-speaking colonial and postcolonial Caribbean. What Hall does not do is connect one process of creolization—that which developed in the English-speaking Caribbean—with another, namely, the mutual entanglement of Anglo-Saxon, Norman, and other elements that produced English in the first place. Yet it is in the space conjoining, but also separating, those two historical processes, we might say, that creolization *à l'anglaise* takes place.

Transits and Transitions

To explore creolization *à l'anglaise* fully would be well beyond the scope of this book. Yet our topic provides a sketch of how such an exploration might work and what it might yield. Language has always been seen as one key marker of the wealth and privileges enjoyed by the Normans and their descendants in the nobility and gentry of the three kingdoms. The characteristic English reponse towards the importation of French language and culture—ambivalence—mixes, as we saw in the previous two chapters, fascination with fear of domination. Restoration writers like Evelyn and Dryden promised to exorcise that fear by redeploying the fashionable treasures of France while speaking the language of English patriotism. The fashion for French language and culture in England was, in this sense, inextricably entangled with the questions of inequality, hierarchization, control, and resistance that are central to the creolizing process.

As the English established their language in Britain and its colonies, that language came with its émigrés, and these encountered new circumstances in parts of the English-speaking world. In some of these places France already loomed large on the horizon, either because the place in question was close to France (as in the case of Ireland), or because the English and French had transported their age-old entanglement to a new theatre. Far-flung contact zones of this kind were to be found in many parts of the world including North America, the Caribbean, Africa, and Asia. Many have remained long after the colonial powers have retreated: to this day, for example, Anglophone and Francophone populations live in close proximity in eastern Canada (Quebec and neighbouring provinces), the Caribbean (the islands of the Lesser Antilles), and central and west Africa. In 'contact zones' such as these, a French word would be more immediately recognizable to the local population, which had already been exposed to French as well as to English. It could and did accumulate uses and meanings by being displaced to a new setting: think, for example, of what became of *à la mode* in North America.

The trio of émigrés to which we will be turning in the second half of this book—*naïveté, ennui,* and *caprice*—have their own creolizing stories to tell of transit and transition and of cultural entanglement and creativity. What they have in common with each other, and with *à la mode*, is that they have undergone creolization *à l'anglaise*. They all came to prominence in English, as was observed in the last chapter, when Restoration court culture imitated in its linguistic fashions the French models that Charles II looked up to. *Naïveté* and *ennui* both figure in the list of words that John Evelyn in 1665 said would fill notable gaps in English. *Naïveté* also appears in a second word list of the period, the one that Melantha acquires from her maid Philotis in Dryden's *Marriage À-la-Mode* (1673), and to which Melantha adds *caprice*. *Naïveté*, *ennui*, and *caprice*, while remaining in use since the late seventeenth century in both French and the English spoken by the English, have travelled far and wide. They have for centuries enabled people in many Anglophone countries to discuss central processes of their common life. They still do.

In what follows, I trace the Anglophone migrations of *naïveté*, *ennui*, and *caprice*, asking how particular English uses of these words have adapted and altered their French meanings and connotations, and what these words add to English today. I show something of what these words have contributed to the history of 'French literature abroad', as Simon Gaunt calls it, as well as to an English vocabulary of culture and society.[26] These two perspectives on the words—French and English in their orientations—are the non-identical twins of creolization when applied as a conceptual model to the present instance.

I explore instances of usage from a wide range of sources in literature, film, art, music, and everyday culture. I start from and return to lexicographical works such as dictionaries and word lists. I view these works not so much as guides to, but as participants in the making of, uses and meanings. We have seen how concerned intellectuals were in early modern France and England alike to establish their vernaculars as languages fit for purpose in the activities of government, law, the arts, sciences, trades, and commerce. Bilingual dictionaries mediated directly between modern European languages. A successful early example was Randle Cotgrave's French–English dictionary of 1611, to which Robert Sherwood added an English–French dictionary in 1632. Further editions, revised and enlarged by James Howell, appeared in 1650, 1660, and 1673. Guy Miège produced a rival to Cotgrave in 1677. This period also sees the rise of the monolingual dictionary in the main European languages. The labours and wranglings that surrounded the work of the Académie française on its dictionary had the happy effect of bringing in a golden age of French lexicography, in the late seventeenth century, as rivals and outcasts produced their alternatives. Like the dictionary of the Académie française, those of Pierre-César Richelet (1680) and Antoine Furetière (1690) are normative in their aims, and offer examples of actual usage taken, often, from the works of academicians. Where they differ is in respect of the norm they set for the proper use of the language, since Furetière favours the more inclusive notion of 'correct' usage, whereas Richelet and the Académie française promote 'elegant' usage. Taken together, they offer a complex picture of the language of polite seventeenth-century French culture and society, and have constituted a rich source of evidence on which later monolingual French dictionaries have drawn.[27]

English lexicography, in the absence of a state-sponsored Academy charged with setting norms for the language, took a different course. Bilingual and polyglot dictionaries were gradually complemented by 'hard word' dictionaries such as those of Thomas Blount (1656), Edward Phillips (1658), and Elisha Coles (1676). The last of these reflected the later seventeenth-century fashion for incorporating 'canting' (slang) words. The first half of the eighteenth century saw the emergence of expanded editions of some 'hard word' dictionaries, including that of Edward Phillips, and larger English monolingual dictionaries covering ordinary as well as hard words. Samuel Johnson's dictionary (1755), which followed significant works in the same vein by John Kersey (1702) and Nathan Bailey (1726 and 1737), is the landmark achievement of the period. In 1857, just over a century after the publication of Johnson's dictionary, members of the Philological Society of London decided to embark on a complete historical examination of the English language from Anglo-Saxon times to the present day: this was the origin of the *OED*, which was first published in the period 1884–1928, and which is now available in an online version that is being gradually revised. The *OED* records the language as it was and is now spoken across the Anglophone world.[28]

Other lexicographical works concentrate on the English that is characteristic of a particular part of that world. John Mendies, for example, in 1822 abridged Johnson's *Dictionary* to produce an English–Bengali dictionary that was—as its title puts it—'peculiarly calculated for the use of European and native students'. A second edition was published in Calcutta in 1851. *Hobson-Jobson*, a substantial Anglo-Indian dictionary, first appeared in 1886. Monolingual dictionaries have since been produced of Hiberno-English, American English, Australianisms, Canadianisms, Caribbean English, New Zealand English, and South African English. These are constructed on the same historical principles as the *OED* and add further regionally specific information to its account of the language. American English has been recorded in a wealth of other works, notably Noah Webster's dictionary (1828), whose successive editions have reflected wider controversies in lexicography. Where the second edition (1841) was prescriptive about the language and its correct use, *Webster's Third* (1961) adopted a more descriptive approach, cutting back on judgements of correctness and providing in their stead examples showing how people actually used the language. *Webster's Third* was promptly attacked for its permissiveness and a rival work, *The American Heritage Dictionary of the English Language*, appeared in 1969 to challenge its account of the language.[29]

French lexicographers are not alone, then, in thriving on controversy. English, French–English, and other polyglot dictionaries from the seventeenth century onwards are witness to the disagreements of their makers. Many of these in Restoration and post-Restoration England returned to wider debates about the state of the English language, the relative merits of English and French, and the extent and nature of borrowings in English from foreign languages (chiefly, among modern languages, French). The rival French–English dictionaries of Cotgrave (as revised by Howell) and Miège in Restoration England agreed on the international pre-eminence of French and its civilizing influence on the English even as they offered rival resources. Addressing his revised Cotgrave in 1673 to the 'Nobility and Gentry of Great Britain' and to 'Merchant-Adventurers' needing business French, as well as all those wishing to learn the language simply for their 'pleasure' and 'ornament', Howell emphasized that English existed in a linguistic contact zone with French and claimed that 'there be so many French words crept in and naturalized among us, that one had need to study French to speak good English'. Miège showed his agreement by quoting the final phrase of Howell's sentence in the preface to his *New Dictionary* (1677). Miège complained, nonetheless, that, despite his assurances to the contrary, Howell had failed to revise

Cotgrave sufficiently and the work continued to swarm 'with Rank Words and Obsolete Phrases'. Miège claimed that his own work, by contrast, offered a reliable guide to contemporary polite French usage for those desirous of reading the latest publications from France or of 'speaking the Court-French'.[30]

Samuel Johnson tried to stop the rot. In the preface to his *Dictionary* (1755), he referred to the Restoration mode for French, lamenting its deleterious effect on the current state of English: 'Our language, for almost a century, has, by the concurrence of many causes, been gradually departing from its original *Teutonick* character, and deviating towards a *Gallick* structure and phraseology, from which it ought to be our endeavour to recal[l] it, by making our ancient volumes the ground-work of stile.' He relied on pre-Restoration writers— such as Bacon, Raleigh, Sidney, Shakespeare, and Spenser—for the cultivation of an English style free from nefarious French influence. He confessed that he had flattered himself in hoping that his work might put a stop to the alteration visited upon English by commercial travellers, intellectuals, writers, and English speakers of foreign languages who, out of carelessness or 'refinement and affectation', are liable to import 'borrowed terms and exotick expressions'. Translators were the worst members of this last category: their 'idleness and ignorance, if it be suffered to proceed, will reduce us', Johnson thundered, 'to babble a dialect of *France*'. More in hope than expectation of success, he advocated Anglo-Saxon resistance to the invaders, redeploying the motif of the Norman Yoke on the battleground of language: 'Tongues, like governments, have a natural tendency to degeneration; we have long preserved our constitution, let us make some struggles for our language.'[31]

Johnson was of course recycling a commonplace notion of language as a battleground for a 'soft' power that paralleled the hard power of military conquest. Writers across Europe had long seen language as a field of conquest. Where Johnson and others saw the importation of foreign borrowings into their native language as a sign of its weakness, however, a French academician like François de Callières presented the same process as an indication of the strength of French: it was a vehicle for carrying home 'spoils of war' from France's military victories.[32]

Callières also points out the increasing importance of French beyond France. He presents this, too, as an indication of the country's international prestige. In a short poem, which appears towards the end of his 1690 *Des mots à la mode* (Words in fashion), the academician claims that the court of Louis XIV is now the centre of the world and serves as a model to many nations; that foreigners of distinction are daily flocking there from other illustrious courts; and that these foreigners migrate to the court of Louis XIV 'to copy its fashions and its language, / And to praise it even for its faults'.[33] Callières here uses the influx of foreigners into France as a means of reinforcing the prescriptive authority invested in him and his fellow academicians, by urging his compatriots to consider that what they said today, the world would say tomorrow.

How different was the state of the debate in early modern England about its language! English intellectuals who viewed language as power, and thought power desirable, could only envy French its international prestige at a time when English had none. They could hardly deny the fact that French words were turning and transforming English. They were left to disagree over what this fact said about English. Lexicographers showed themselves to be either receptive of or resistant to French-derived foreignisms in the minutiae of their work. Johnson's 'struggles for our language', for example, included him ignoring or depreciating gallicisms where he could. His dictionary includes no entries for *ennui* or *naïveté*. *Caprice* and *alamode* survive the cut, although once Johnson has defined *alamode* (as meaning 'according to the fashion'), he immediately dismisses it as 'a low word'. His dismissal is consistent with what he has to say in general about émigrés, by way of a carefully chosen quotation from Felton, in his entry on the word *gallicism*: 'In English I would have Gallicisms avoided, that we may keep to our own language, and not follow the French mode in our speech.' We have seen that John Evelyn took a contrasting view of gallicisms a century earlier, for he saw in them creative possibilities for the elegant completion of an English vocabulary of culture and society, whereas Johnson considered them to indicate that English was under the sway of French dominance.[34]

Perhaps they were both right. I do not mean by this to suggest that their perspectives may be reconciled, but rather that, when combined, they form the two halves of an unresolved contradiction. That contradiction is at the heart of creolization as a conceptual model. In that sense, then, we might say that Evelyn and Johnson—just like the authors of *Remarques* and *Remarks upon Remarques* in the 1670s controversy discussed in the previous chapter—formulated, between them, a characteristically ambivalent English response to creolization *à l'anglaise*.

The gallicisms explored in this book were, of course, here to stay. In 1851, almost a century after Johnson first published his dictionary, John Mendies added to the second edition of his English and Bengali *Abridgement* of Johnson's *Dictionary* a 'list of French and other foreign words and phrases in common use' in English. Mendies's list includes many of the émigrés that we have already observed establishing a place in Restoration English. The Frenchified language of gallantry, as promoted by Dryden's Melantha and Etherege's Sir Fopling Flutter, is well represented in the shape of *beau* and *belle, beau*

monde, billet doux, double entendre, éclaircissement, éclat, and
so on, all the way through the alphabet to the *valet de chambre*
that every English-speaking gallant worthy of that name employed. Mendies offered English and Bengali readers of his
dictionary a guide to the pronunciation and explanation of
these and the other words and phrases in his list. He included
an entry on *à la mode*: it was pronounced '*al-a-móde*', Mendies
informed his readers, and meant 'in the fashion'. *Ennui* also
found a place in the list: it was pronounced '*an-wée*' and meant
'tiresomeness'.[35]

Mendies was looking backwards, past Johnson, to the
French foreign words that had first turned English in the Restoration, and he was making these available to people learning
English as a language of empire, a long way away from England. He was contributing to a new chapter in the history of the
émigrés in this book as creolizing keywords.

PART II

Migrations

CHAPTER FOUR

Naïveté

naïveté, *n.*

Origin: A borrowing from French. Etymon: French *naïveté*.
Etymology: < French *naïveté* [...] < *naïve* NAIVE *adj.* +
-TÉ -TY *suffix.* Compare later NAIVETY *n.*

— OXFORD ENGLISH DICTIONARY

And the eyes of them both were opened, and they knew that
they were naked.

— GENESIS 3:7

NAÏVETÉ IN ENGLISH betrays,
like perhaps no other émigré, the
aspiration to partake in the cultural superiority that the English
attribute to the French. The French
noun and its corresponding adjective, *naïve*, figure prominently in
the list of words that the Franco-
phile Melantha obtains from her maid Philotis in Dryden's
Marriage À-la-Mode. Melantha looks at the list and pauses on
naïveté and *naïve*. She asks Philotis what these words mean.
Philotis specifies how they are to be used: 'Speaking of a thing
that was naturally said; It was so *naive*: or such an innocent

piece of simplicity; 'twas such a *naiveté*.' This sentence—containing the earliest instance of *naïveté* recorded in the *OED*—offers a first semantic sketch of an émigré that has established itself in English as a keyword of culture and society. It shows the relation of French *naïveté* and *naïve* to their classical Latin root, *nativus*, meaning 'native': a thing 'naturally said' is the product, after all, of a person's native wit. Philotis, in another life, would have made a fine professional philologist.[1]

Melantha eventually gets her chance to use *naïveté* and the other words on her list to maximum effect. The noble Palmyra—a prisoner of the usurper Polydamas at this point in the play's heroic plot—is led on stage. Melantha seizes her chance to show her quality. She checks her list of words—'*suitte, figure, chagrin, naiveté*'—to which she adds a transliterated idiomatic expression—'*let me die*'—before launching herself into a compliment: 'Madam the Princess! let me die, but this is a most horrid spectacle, to see a person who makes so grand a *figure* in the Court, without the *Suitte* of a Princess, and entertaining your Chagrin all alone.' Melantha then adds by way of an aside: '*Naiveté* should have been there, but the disobedient word would not come in.' The distressed Palmyra is astonished. An attendant court lady, Artemis, explains to her that Melantha is 'an impertinent Lady' and 'very ambitious of being known to your Highness'. Palmyra treats Melantha with haughty disdain. If *naïveté* confirms the Frenchified Melantha's fall from social grace in this scene, then it is not because 'the disobedient word would not come in', but because—as the play's editors, John Loftis and David Stuart Rhodes, put it in their commentary—it is oddly 'appropriate to Melantha's lack of sensitivity towards Palmyra's station and anxiety'. *Naïveté* thus proves disobedient, even twice so, on this, its first recorded appearance in English, in that it not only eludes Melantha but may be turned against her.[2]

This reversibility is explained by the pair of meanings that the word carries: 'innocence', 'artlessness'; and 'lack of experience', 'idiocy'. Whereas Philotis presents *naïveté* in an appreciative sense as meaning 'an innocent piece of simplicity', for example, Dryden's editors use the word in a deprecatory sense when applying it to Melantha's lack of experience. These meanings come into constant interplay in uses of the word. They betoken a profound difference of view about how *naïveté* is best conceptualized and how much it is to be valued. We will see— by charting a brief history of related instances, across cultures and centuries, from Dryden to Le Carré via Pascal and Schiller—how this difference has fed the antagonism of one French thinker towards another, captured the relationship of one German poet to another, and charted the course of triangular love between an Englishman, his wife, and her lover.

These are stories of innocence and experience, of simple natures and sentimental journeys, of rough diamonds and those that appreciate them. It is no coincidence that a diamond which is flawless in its natural state and is left either totally or partially unpolished is known as a *naïf* (a noun in English that otherwise, as we will see, means a naïve person). The rough diamond is a fitting emblem for naïveté because it betokens a luminescent innate quality that is thrown into sharp relief by the presence of its opposite. Needing no polish in order to shine, it is most keenly appreciated by the refined observer, whose refinement is anything but naïve: it takes sophistication—of a kind that the naïve, by definition, do not possess—to value a diamond in the rough.

It is to imply her possession of just this kind of sophistication that Melantha wishes to produce the words *naïveté* and *naïve* in front of the princess. She aims, that is, to exploit what might be called the subjective connotations of these words (what they imply about the speaking subject) in addition to their objective denotations (what they say about the objects they are being used to describe). It is a peculiar feature of *naïveté* and *naïve* that their use is often intended to connote in the speaker a quality (sophistication) that is the polar opposite of the quality in the thing it denotes (simplicity). In French, the same gap between the subjective connotation of *naïveté* and its objective denotation may be intended, but it is brought into view when the word travels into English. Its foreignness highlights the distance of the word from the natural state of affairs that it is being used to express. *Naïveté* is not merely a foreign word, moreover, but a French foreign word. Its use carries connotations of a cultural sophistication fashioned after the mode of *galanterie*. In English, then, the semantic force of *naïveté* lies in its deviation from standard native synonyms—such as *innocence* or *simplicity*—that might otherwise be used but that do not connote the sophistication of the person speaking. To speak of the naïve in English is inevitably to establish, as Melantha attempts to do, one's distance from, even elevation above, the naïve.

Stories of the Fall

Time and again, in their complex trajectories through history, *naïveté* and *naïve* have told stories of innocence and experience. These stories speak of children and the things they see and say, of adults who are oddly childlike in their style, of the world that children of all ages inhabit. They often tell of a fall from innocence and its aftermath from the perspective of experience. That perspective tends to reveal as much about the storyteller as about the contents of the story. An adult observer looks longingly towards a lost innocence, in one type of narrative, and, in another, looks down upon a lapse into idiocy.

The semantic tension between the appreciative and deprecatory meanings of *naïveté* is fundamental to the word in French. Early modern French dictionaries systematically alternate between these meanings in respect of *naïveté* and its adjective *naïf*: Furetière, for example, defines *naïf* as meaning both 'true, sincere, faithful' and 'artless, simple, heedless of consequences'. Recorded early French uses of *naïveté* and *naïf* suggest that the appreciative meaning of these words, related to Latin *nativus* and French *naturel*, predated the emergence of the deprecatory meaning. You might be tempted to say that there was an innocence to *naïveté* before its fall.[3]

These uses of *naïveté* and *naïf* do, indeed, often tell or imply the story of a fall. The single most important archetype here in European culture is the fall of Adam and Eve (as recounted in Genesis 3) after they succumbed to temptation, tasting of the apple of knowledge of good and evil, and thus knew they were naked. This was a fall from innocence into experience. It was also 'man's first disobedience' to God, as the English poet John Milton put it in the opening line of his Christian epic *Paradise Lost* (1667), for which Adam and Eve were expelled by God from Eden and therefore lost the chance to eat from the tree of life in the garden and become immortal. This first disobedience was by no means the last, according to many Christians, who see the doctrine of the fall as closely related to the doctrine of original sin. Central to the teachings of one of the early Christian church fathers, St Augustine, is the affirmation that all human beings are fundamentally inclined to evil since the fall of Adam and Eve from Eden, and that they are incapable of choosing good without being touched by divine grace, which God grants, exceptionally, to the chosen. While all should hope to be redeemed, and some will be, we lead—each of us—a fallen life. These teachings of the church structured the patterns of religious thought, everyday worship, and cultural expression in a Christian society like that of medieval and early modern France. It is no wonder, then, that the culture invented an abundance of stories according to which naïveté comes before a fall.

French writers and artists, in retelling such stories, probed the nature of naïveté by contrasting it with its opposite state. They asked whether naïveté, in the sense of an innocent simplicity, need inevitably become corrupt in this world and whether the naïve had any means of escaping the fall. Such questions carried implications for the storytellers themselves. Were they telling their story from inside or outside a state of naïveté? If it was from the outside, then how could they find an adequate means of representing naïveté, a means that was not itself corrupted by the fall from naïveté?

Michel de Montaigne explored the limits of such questions in his *Essais* (*Essays*) of 1580–95. He saw naïveté as a salutary affront to Christian civilization in Europe and an inspiration to him as a writer. He seems to have been fascinated by the possibility that there might have been no fall from Eden for some of his far-flung contemporaries. These were the Cannibals of the New World to whom Montaigne—a fierce critic of the manner in which the Europeans had conquered the Americas and subjugated their peoples—devoted one of his most provocative essays. In 'Des Cannibales' ('Of Cannibals'), he counters European moral superiority towards the so-called barbarities of the Brazilian Tupinambá, who wear no clothes, whose menfolk have several wives, and whose warriors ritualistically eat enemies they have defeated in battle. Montaigne judges their practice of cannibalism to be indeed cruel, but less so than the atrocities of the Europeans, who, blind to their own faults, condemn the Tupinambá. The argument is not relativistic, then, but contrarian in its reversal of perspectives: it meets European condemnation with a declamation in praise of communistic, polygamous, man-eating, naked folly. It proceeds, essentially, by overturning the negative uses to which Europeans put the language of barbarity in order to belittle the Tupinambá. The latter are barbarians, Montaigne retorts, only if *barbarity* is to be positively redefined: 'These nations, then, seem to me barbarous in this sense, that they have been fashioned very little by the human mind, and are still very close to their original naturalness [*naifveté originelle*].'⁴ Montaigne's implication here is that the Cannibals possess a naïveté foreign to the descendants of Adam and Eve.

Running through Montaigne's essay is the heterodox suggestion that, if the Tupinambá are naïve, this is because they are unfallen. The French literary historian Frank Lestringant has persuasively made the case for reading Montaigne's treatment of his Cannibals in the light of the polygenetic hypothesis of human development, derived from the Roman philosopher and poet Lucretius, whose work Montaigne read. Lucretius's idea was that humankind developed from the simultaneous and spontaneous appearance of humans in several parts of the globe. When applied to the situation that Montaigne describes, in which the Cannibals of the New World knew nothing of the many faults endemic to European societies, Lucretius's polygenetic hypothesis might suggest that the Tupinambá remained free from the effects of a fall that did not concern them and their ancestors as it did Adam, Eve, and their descendants. Since that hypothesis was anathema to the teachings of the Catholic church, and since Montaigne professed allegiance to these teachings, it should come as no surprise that he chose to let the suggestion run between the lines of his essay without ever stating it in so many words. That suggestion makes sense, meanwhile, of the great disparity

Montaigne sees between untainted Cannibal naïveté and ill-gotten European experience.[5]

Montaigne reasserts that disparity when he claims that the way in which the Brazilian Cannibals organize their collective life surpasses not just the experience of Europeans, but their conception of philosophy itself, not least the various attempts of European philosophers to picture the ideal society. He expresses his regret that Lycurgus, the ancient Spartan giver of laws, and Plato, the Athenian political philosopher and creator of ideal societies in his *Republic* and other works, did not live to witness Tupinambá society as it is organized. He imagines the two Greeks contemplating that society with wonder: 'They could not imagine a naturalness so pure and simple [*une nay-fveté si pure et simple*] as we see by experience; nor could they believe that our society could be so maintained with so little artifice and human solder.'[6] To describe the naïveté of the Cannibals, Montaigne here pairs the adjectives *pure* and *simple*, yoking them together by means of the initial intensifier *si* ('so'). He thus reveals, at the level of style, what he sees as the philosophical importance of Cannibal naïveté and the challenge it poses the fallen many. He, as one of the fallen, must search through his lexicon and pair word with word in the attempt to carry his reader with him, across the world, to a human society in which *naïveté* has known no fall.

Montaigne knew that his contemporary civil war-torn France was no such society. But he imagines his book as a virtual pure space, albeit a limited and conditional one, that he has created, in which to communicate his thoughts to the consenting lay reader. He does this in a note, addressed to the reader, which precedes the first chapter of Book I and serves as a preface to the work as a whole. Montaigne there describes his book as a limited but sincere exercise in unadorned self-portraiture, capturing his faults and all, and claims to have been constrained in the execution of this design only by a respect for public decency. The language of *naïveté* makes an appearance in these lines:

> I want to be seen here in my simple, natural, ordinary fashion, without straining or artifice; for it is myself that I portray. My defects will here be read to the life, and also my natural form [*ma forme naïfve*], as far as respect for the public has allowed. Had I been placed among those nations which are said to live still in the sweet freedom of nature's first laws, I assure you I should very gladly have portrayed myself here entire and wholly naked.[7]

Montaigne has in mind the nakedness and other sweet freedoms that the peoples of the New World, including the Tupinambá, enjoy in their naïveté. There is nothing more naïve, after all, than being naked and glad to be so. Yet Montaigne knows himself to be no Cannibal, but a son of Adam, and he must cover his nakedness for shame's sake. He indicates here that he intends nonetheless to write like a Cannibal, insofar as respect for public decency allows, conveying to readers everywhere, as best he can, the shapes of his *forme naïfve*.[8]

Montaigne had his naïveté confirmed by a writer who also opposed it. The ardent Christian and polymath Blaise Pascal (1623–62) chose to present his predecessor as a beguiling and dangerous naïf. Pascal saw himself as engaged in a battle for the soul of irreligious free-thinking France. He identified Montaigne as the archetype of the free-thinker he had in his sights, and Montaigne's naïveté, as a key expression of his free-thinking. Pascal's most sustained reading of Montaigne occurs in a text that purports to record an exchange about secular philosophy between Pascal and Louis-Isaac Le Maistre de Sacy (1613–84), then spiritual director of the Augustinian (Jansenist) movement based at Port-Royal, with which Pascal was closely associated. Pascal portrays Montaigne to Sacy as an innocent but self-centred Sceptic who throws all things—including even his own doubt—into doubt. Pascal, like so many commentators on naïveté before and since, finds it in others in a way that says more about Pascal than it does about the others. He savours the naïveté of Montaigne even as he prepares to turn it against him. Montaigne, Pascal asserts, 'rejects thoroughly that Stoic virtue which is portrayed with a severe expression'. His kind of virtue, by contrast, 'is natural [*naïve*], easygoing, amusing, playful, and, so to speak, full of tricks'.[9] This is a distinctly double-handed compliment. It shows Montaigne's naïve virtue to be as dangerous to its owner as it is to his Stoic opponents. It suggests that Montaigne needs urgently to correct his own natural inclination towards evil, if he is to stand any chance of finding the one true happiness, the grateful receipt of a God-given saving grace. He seems to have forgotten he is a son of Adam living in a fallen world. He has come, in short, to believe in his own naïveté. That, for Pascal, is a fall in itself.

Montaigne and Pascal write about *naïveté*, in their divergent ways, with the Christian story of the fall of humanity firmly in mind. Uses of the word in purely secular contexts are also common in seventeenth-century French. Dictionaries of the period report that the purveyors of *galanterie* are users of *naïveté* and *naïf* in a negative sense. Richelet, in 1680, for example, quotes a sentence by the celebrated *galant* writer Bussy-Rabutin in which some 'poor fellow' imparts a piece of news with a *naïveté* that is greeted, by a female interlocutor, with a knowing laugh. In the subsequent example it is a woman who utters '*naïvetés* that could make you die laughing'.[10] *Naïveté* here helps to define *galanterie* as a form of sophistication by capturing everything that *galanterie* is not in the distorting reflection of its polished surfaces. The art of *galanterie* consists, here, not so much in hiding the art as in unmasking what surrounds it as grotesquely artless because hopelessly naïve.

A Sentimental Journey

Naïveté travels to other languages as an ambassador of French civility. It does so in several more or less adapted variant forms. The noun *naïveté* has *naivety* as its typographical companion in English, the latter being more adapted to its new setting, having had its French suffix *-té* replaced by its English equivalent *-ty* and having lost the diacritical sign over the *i*. A middle way exists in the form *naiveté*: this preserves the French suffix but dispenses with the diacritical sign over over the *i*. That sign, called a *tréma* in French, indicates that the *i* is to be sounded separately from the preceding vowel. It also disappears from the *i* in one of two further pairs of words related to *naïveté*, for the adjective *naïve* is also (and perhaps more commonly) spelt *naive* in English, just as *naïf* tends to appear as *naif*. *Naïve* is the feminine singular form of the French adjective whose corresponding masculine singular form is *naïf*. The feminine singular form of the French adjective is more commonly employed as an adjective in English. *Naïf*, the masculine form, tends to feature as a noun meaning (as has already been noted) a rough diamond, as well as a naïve person. Even when their spelling is more adapted to their English setting, in the instances just mentioned, these words retain a French flavour in speech: *Fowler's Concise Dictionary of Modern English Usage* observes that, despite shedding its *tréma* on the page, '*naive* is generally pronounced in a quasi-French way nah-*eev* or niy-*eev*'. That quasi-Frenchness is critically important to the semantic development of *naïveté* in English, as I have already suggested, for it marks out—with greater emphasis than its native synonyms do in English and more than it tends to do in

French—the distance between the native simplicity of the naïve object and the refined civility of the speaking subject.[11]

Crucial to that development in English is the theoretical work of the German poet and philosopher Friedrich Schiller. Schiller, in 1795, wrote an essay, *Über naive und sentimentalische Dichtung* (*On the Naïve and Sentimental in Literature*), which marked a new chapter in the history of naïveté or, as Schiller preferred to call it, the naïve. He welcomed the distance that the word marked between the simplicity of which it speaks and the speaker. But he sought to resolve the semantic tension within the naïve between two forms of simplicity—innocence and idiocy—in favour of innocence. He asserted that it was a defining characteristic of the naïve that 'nature should stand in contrast to art and put it to shame'. He placed the naïve, thus redefined, in a new conceptual pairing with the notion of the sentimental.[12]

That pairing changed the course of *naïveté* through cultural history as other writers and artists took it up and explored its implications in art and life. The sentimental, for Schiller and others writing in his wake, stands, initially, in marked contrast to the naïve, although the two states depend upon each other, not least because no one is better placed to perceive the naïve than the sentimental observer. The distance of the sentimental observer from the naïve is essential to that perception. The questions that this distance poses—as to how you evaluate it, how you respond to it, and whether you espouse the naïve or seek to overcome it—have animated the sentimental journeys of *naïveté* from Schiller to Le Carré. They have, in the process, inspired the telling of new stories of redemption and fall.

Schiller deliberately imported *naive* into German as a French foreignism in order to exploit for his own purposes its previous meanings and connotations. These included the provenance of the word. This attracts a barbed comment from the German poet as he surveys a century or more of the French monopoly on fashionable culture: 'That nation which has gone farthest towards unnaturalness and the consciousness of it would have to be the first to be touched the most strongly by the phenomenon of the *naive* and the first to put a name to it.' That nation was the French, Schiller then confirms, before placing the experience of the naïve into a much longer and wider history than the French could provide by asserting that 'the experience of the naive and the interest in it [...] dates already from the beginning of moral and aesthetic corruption'.[13]

Schiller had his own fall story to tell. Human culture, he claims, has degenerated to such a degree since the time of the ancient Greeks that it has abandoned nature. This has been a gradual revolution, which started in antiquity. It is an incomplete one, for, in children, nature still remains unmutilated by the civilizing process, and the same is true of those adults who stand apart from the mainstream of human culture. Schiller is most interested in the poets that may be numbered among these adults. What he has to say about them is that they constitute one of the only two kinds of true poet that exist, that is, the naïve kind, which he opposes to the sentimental. *Sentimentalisch*, the term Schiller chose to use of the latter kind of poet, was a variant of *sentimental*, which German had borrowed from French and English in the eighteenth century, and which had positive connotations rather than the negative ones that surround it in modern English: it meant 'exhibiting refined and elevated feelings'. Schiller adopted the sentimental in this sense and redefined it, as fundamentally as he did the naïve, by pairing the two in a distinction that embraced the entire field of poetry. What all poets have in common, he says, is that they are 'by definition the *preservers* of nature'. But they preserve nature in contrasting ways, naïve poets simply by *being* nature, whereas sentimental poets '*look for* lost nature'. Hence Schiller's key statement: 'All poets who really are poets, according to the nature of the period in which they flourish or according to what accidental circumstances have an influence on their general education and on their passing mental state, will belong either to the *naive* or the *sentimental* type.'[14]

This statement belongs within a story of fall and redemption that differs markedly from that which Christian theologians derived from the Book of Genesis. Schiller's is a story about poetry. He asserts that poetry exists for nothing else 'than *to give humanity its most complete expression possible*'. His naïve poets live in an unfallen state of natural simplicity: their poetic task is therefore 'the most complete possible *imitation of the real*'. His sentimental poets, by contrast, live in a fallen state of culture: their poetic task is therefore 'the *representation of the ideal*'. Both kinds of poet, by fulfilling the task appropriate to the state in which they live, give humanity, each in their own way, its most complete expression possible. The only redemption for humanity that Schiller envisages is redemption through poetry.[15]

Redemption could be achieved by several poetic means. Schiller devotes much of his essay to an account of the various moods that sentimental poets adopt when responding to the lost world of nature from within the actual world of culture they inhabit. If they view that actual world as deficient, they write sentimental poetry in a satirical vein; if they mourn the loss of the natural world, they write it in an elegiac vein. Schiller—who thinks in pairs—subdivides the satirical and elegiac moods each into two further types: castigating satire 'achieves poetic freedom by passing over into the sublime', whereas jocose satire 'attains poetic content by treating its subject with beauty'; elegiac elegy expresses sadness that the natural world is lost or remains unattained as an ideal, whereas idyllic elegy expresses joy that the natural world or its ideal representation is at hand. The various terms borrowed here from poetics—such as *satire, elegy,* and *idyll*—are not to be understood in their traditional sense as referring to literary genres: Schiller stresses that they name the various moods of the sentimental and that a text belonging to any literary genre can be written in one or more of these moods. In this way Schiller's theory of poetry recalled, but also changed profoundly, the genre-based taxonomies of much previous work in poetics.[16]

It altered, in similar fashion, the terms of the long-standing Quarrel of the Ancients and the Moderns in respect of poetry. Schiller suggested that his account of the naïve and the sentimental provided a new conceptual principle capable of transcending a quarrel that, as we saw in chapter 2 above, had been concerned with the question of how much cultural value should be attached to ancient precedent. The mere question of precedent, as Schiller saw it, provided an insufficient account of what poetry was and should be. His story of a human fall from a naïve unity with nature into a sentimental striving for nature meant, of course, that for historical reasons more of the ancients were likely to be, in his definition, naïve poets (Homer and Æschylus chief among them) and more of the moderns would be sentimental poets (Milton, Kleist, and Klopstock being named as masters). But the gradual and incomplete nature of that fall allowed for there to be naïve works by moderns (such as Shakespeare, Molière, and Goethe), even if these were 'no longer of a completely pure type', given the increasing decadence of the age; and it equally meant that there were sentimental poets (such as Euripides and Ovid) among the ancients.[17]

Any comparison of ancient and modern poetry ought not, he warns, to be based on a definition of poetry derived one-sidedly from either kind. It should, instead, be undertaken with a view to 'a common but higher category'. Schiller allows this category to emerge in the course of his discussion. One possible approach to the comparison between naïve and sentimental poets, he says, would be to consider 'the relationship of both to their type and to their maximum potential'. This approach would find in favour of the naïve poets; for they, in their unity with nature, can achieve a perfect imitation of nature in their employment of a finite art; whereas sentimental poets, in their striving for nature through the cultivation of an ideal, can only ever reach an approximation of that ideal in their practice of an infinite art. When individuals are compared, Schiller says, the sentimental poet must always lose out to one 'in whom nature is functioning in all her perfection'. He ultimately prefers, however, a comparison between naïve and sentimental poets that starts from his earlier definition of poetry's single and lofty task, namely, that of giving humanity its most complete expression possible. This approach finds in favour of the sentimental poets as a whole. They, he says, share the goal of modern humanity, which has lost the unity with nature enjoyed by natural man, and which must use as best it can its available resources—ideas—to progress towards a new unity with nature achieved by means of an ideal. While an individual comparison between the two favours the naïve poet, then, 'there is no question as to which of the two deserves greater merit with regard to that ultimate goal' of humanity. The sentimental writer is the more deserving, on that score, as long as that writer is capable of rising to poetry.[18]

The French-speaking Genevan thinker and writer Jean-Jacques Rousseau (1712–78) looms large in Schiller's discussion here as one example of a failed poet of the sentimental kind. Schiller identifies Rousseau the thinker as a major modern seeker of the lost unity with nature once enjoyed by natural man (and Rousseau's influence on this part of Schiller's argument is significant). Yet Schiller goes on to criticize Rousseau the writer on the grounds that he seldom rises to the ideal of the true poet and prefers, instead, to lead humanity 'back to the mindless monotony of its first state'.[19]

Schiller observes, meanwhile, that many a naïve poet alive in the modern world will wish, by contrast with the likes of Rousseau, to help modern humanity progress towards a new unity with nature achieved by means of an ideal. In these cases, he suggests, the naïve poet will merge with the sentimental. He ends his discussion of the naïve and sentimental in poetry in this vein. Their combination becomes ever closer as the naïve and sentimental rise to the heights of poetry, he stresses, arguing that 'the poetic mood is an independent whole in which all differences and all deficiencies vanish' and that 'it is only in the concept of the poetic that both kinds of feeling can come together'.[20]

Schiller reveals nowhere in the course of his essay that he is reflecting, throughout, on his friendship and rivalry with his fellow poet Johann Wolfgang von Goethe (1749–1832). Yet reflect he does. Schiller was Pascal to Goethe's Montaigne, as it were, though without the religion. Schiller saw Goethe—who was older, more robust in health, and better connected than he—as the naïve poet of the pair and himself, the impoverished and sickly author of subversive political drama, as the sentimental. He claims in a letter to Wilhelm von Humboldt of 26 October 1795 that his essay addressed a specific question: 'Given my distance from the spirit of Greek literature, to what extent can I still be a poet and indeed a better poet than the extent of that distance seems to allow?' From this question, two further and increasingly personal ones followed for Schiller, which his editor and translator Helen Watanabe-O'Kelly has expressed thus: 'I am not a naïve writer. How is it then that I can still be good?'; and, 'Does this mean that I am necessarily a worse writer than Goethe who *is* naïve?' It is clear that Goethe saw Schiller's project in *On the Naïve and Sentimental in Literature* in these very terms: in 1830, long after Schiller's early death in 1805, Goethe described his friend's essay as his attempt 'to defend himself against me'.[21]

In the essay, Schiller shows the two friends initially standing apart from one another, yet poised to merge in the higher ideal of poetic humanity. In the middle of the essay its author introduces the unnamed Goethe as a 'naive poetic spirit' abroad in the modern, sentimental, world. Schiller has by then already suggested, in a footnote, that Goethe's 1774 epistolary novel *The Sorrows of Young Werther* is a masterpiece because it *unites* the naïve type of poetry with the sentimental. Goethe, at times seen as distinct from Schiller in poetic character, here joins his friend at the place where the naïve and the sentimental meet and merge. For his part, Schiller is and can only be writing his essay from that selfsame place, the sole vantage ground from which the interactions between the naïve and sentimental in poetry could ever be perceptible. Their sharing of this higher ground grants an equality of value to the two poet friends.[22]

Schiller chooses at the end of his essay to turn away from the poets and to sketch instead the relations between the naïve and sentimental in ordinary life. These relations amount, he says darkly, to a conflict that is without doubt 'as old as the beginning of culture and will scarcely be settled before the end of culture'. That conflict removes what is poetic from both the naïve and the sentimental character. It reduces the naïve to a form of realism and the sentimental to a form of idealism. By realism he means a combination of theoretical sobriety, commitment to the evidence of the senses, and resignation 'to that which is and which must be'; by idealism he means a combination of theoretical speculation, moral rigour, and a taste for 'the absolute in the actions of the will'. Schiller ends by warning that, as a result of their natural limitations, the realists can neither rise as high nor sink as low as the idealists. The idealists are of an 'infinitely perfectible' disposition, and since this is governed by the 'whims of the imagination' alone, it can lead 'to a never-ending fall into a bottomless pit'. This brings us back to the opposition, fundamental to Schiller's discussion of poetry, between a naïveté that is circumscribed by nature's limits and a sentimentality that knows no such limits. The difference is that, in ordinary life, all the poetry has been drained out of both the naïve and the sentimental.[23]

Three for the Road

William Blake (1757–1827) did not choose to call upon that notable pair of French émigrés, *naïveté* and *naïve*, when he wrote his *Songs of Innocence and of Experience* (1794). John Le Carré did, when his turn came, and he chose to do so through the conceptual prism of the essay Schiller published the year after Blake's *Songs* first appeared. This choice should come as no surprise to followers of Le Carré's work: the German literary tradition is the one that the novelist professes to admire most and to have 'devoured' whole.[24] He makes an entire novelistic comedy of modern English manners out of the naïve by sending it on a wild goose chase, in the company of the sentimental, to France and Switzerland and back again to England.

The novel in question is Le Carré's sixth, *The Naive and Sentimental Lover* (1971), an early scene in which has Shamus and Helen on a night out in Bath with their new friend Aldo Cassidy. Cassidy, a financially successful but unhappily married manufacturer of pram accessories, has just encountered Shamus and Helen when visiting a country pile he was considering buying as a weekend retreat from his London occupations.

First imagining them to be Haverdown's penniless ancestral owners, he was immediately struck by the couple's combination of beauty and charisma, and confided to Shamus that, if he were to buy the house from them, he would like 'to do some of the things that you might have done if . . . well if you'd had the chance'. This, he gauchely conceded, might make him 'rather a fool' in Shamus's book. Shamus immediately announces ecstatically to Helen in his Irish brogue that Cassidy is in love with them both, that Cassidy '*is* Flaherty', and that Shamus loves Cassidy. Helen insists on coming clean with Cassidy. She and Shamus are squatters. They 'go from one empty house to another'. Shamus is 'not even Irish', Helen confesses, 'he just has funny voices and a theory that God is living in County Cork disguised as a forty-three-year-old taxi-driver' by the name of Flaherty. Shamus is, in fact, a novelist whose time as an undergraduate at Oxford coincided with Cassidy's. He is 'altering the course of world literature', says Helen, 'and I love him'. 'As for Cassidy,' she announces to both men, putting her arms around Cassidy's shoulders, 'he's the sweetest man alive, whatever he believes in'. Helen's confession serves only to make the couple more alluring to Cassidy. The three get drunk together on whisky and head for the road. So begins Le Carré's story of triangular love and a fall without redemption.[25]

It becomes clear in the course of that night on the razzle in Bath that this is to be a comic novel woven from the threads of Schiller's opposition between the naïve and the sentimental. Le Carré draws that opposition into a searching novelistic exploration of the search for love in ordinary life. He uses the opposition principally to characterize the shifting roles that Shamus and Cassidy take up in the love triangle that involves Helen as the third party. Cassidy is Schiller to Shamus's Goethe, though without the poetry, we might say. But by including a woman as an observer of the opposition as well as a participant in its emotional logic, Le Carré transforms the approach taken by Schiller, who, in writing as the sentimental counterpart to his naïve friend, is personally implicated in his treatment of an opposition he presents as theoretical. Le Carré's transformation of Schiller's approach is discreetly done insofar as his narrator tends to place the relationship between the two men in the foreground, focalizing events through Cassidy and presenting Shamus as the stronger character, and thus appears to relegate Helen to the margins. Yet the transformation is decisive: it makes Helen at once chorus and protagonist, and she performs this dual role to her own advantage, telling truths that neither man can utter and using her commentary to intervene in the action.

It is she who introduces Schiller's opposition between the naïve and sentimental into the space of the novel. She reveals to Cassidy, in one of Bath's Italian restaurants, that Shamus has developed a theory which he plans to work into his latest book. According to her, the theory 'was based on someone called Schiller who was a terrifically famous German dramatist actually but of course the English being so insular had never heard of him, and anyway Schiller had split the world in two'. She continues: 'It's called being *naïve* [. . .]. Or being *sentimental*. They're sort of different kinds of *thing*, and they interact.' Cassidy wonders which he is. Helen—repeating Shamus's lessons—pronounces Shamus to be naïve 'because he lives life and doesn't imitate it', and because 'feeling is knowledge', as she tentatively adds. Cassidy is immediately clear that he is the 'other thing'. Helen agrees: 'Yes. You're *sentimental*. That means you long to be *like* Shamus. You've left the natural state behind and you've become . . . well part of civilization, sort of . . . corrupt.' Whereas Shamus, 'being *naive*, part of nature in fact, longs to be like *you*. It's the attraction of opposites. He's natural, you're corrupt. That's why he loves you.' Cassidy is thrilled. But he wants to know which side Helen is on. She is slow to break the silence:

> 'I don't think it works for women,' Helen replied at last. 'I think they're just themselves.'
>
> 'Women are eternal,' Cassidy agreed as finally they got up to leave.[26]

This opening sequence foretells much of what is to unfold. Helen has the measure of the two men. She is immediately aware that she is one party in a love triangle that deserves the name, for the two men are drawn to one another as well as to her, and she is to be both a witness to and a victim of their love. She can already see how Shamus wishes to shape that love. It will exclude her on the basis of Shamus's conviction that there is no room for a third kind of love in addition to the naïve and sentimental. She is left with little choice but to 'be just herself' alongside the two Oxford men, and to use this position to her advantage.

Helen understands the two men better than they understand themselves. Shaped no doubt by his reading of Nietzsche, but above all by his prejudices, Shamus has adapted Schiller's opposition between the naïve and sentimental to coincide with his own perspective on life. Helen faithfully reports Shamus's proclaimed adherence to the naïve, with which he closely associates himself, and to what he identifies as the naïve element in a series of binary oppositions: he prefers the working to the middle classes, the Old Testament to the New, free spirits to plodders, truth to sham, and taking from life as opposed to giving. When she declares Shamus to be 'a terrific innocent', she appears merely to be offering her homespun variant of the Schillerian epithet Shamus claims as his own, but is in fact expressing a more morally complex account of being naïve than Shamus ever offers. She comments to Cassidy, 'Of course anyone is a terrific innocent who is looking for love all the time, don't you agree?' She conveys here the warning that Shamus's innocence cuts two ways. His need to be loved is the source of his compulsive power to harm as well as to seduce those around him. She has recently told Cassidy, in front of Shamus, that Shamus beats her. She realizes that Shamus, the self-styled naïve, finds in Cassidy the sentimental lover he seeks. Cassidy stands to gain by this some of the love he craves, certainly, but she foresees that it will cost him dear: he will be cast as the corrupt one of the pair, saddled with the Bosscow and two veg (Shamus's phrase for Cassidy's wife and children); as the plodder and the giver. While Cassidy is unable to anticipate the costs that his sentimental love for Shamus will incur, she can already count them, as she can the bruises on her skin. Helen's warning to Cassidy serves, also, as an invitation to him: to become the '*gentle* lover' that she, a beaten wife, openly wishes for.[27]

Helen has worked Cassidy out, too, and her choice of the word *gentle* to characterize his role as her lover is intended to appeal to the better part of his upbringing as an English gentleman. Cassidy, the narrator tells us at the very beginning of the novel, 'might have served as an architectural prototype for the middle-class Englishman privately educated between the wars'. He remained in possession of 'those doggedly boyish features, at once mature and retarded, which still convey a dying hope that his pleasures may be paid for by his parents'. He had mannerisms that some might consider effeminate but 'most likely reflected a pleasing sensitivity towards a world occasionally too shrill for him'. A boarding-school-educated Oxford man, 'English to the core', Cassidy is not the worst such specimen. This is perhaps thanks to the fact that he clings for dear life to the chivalrous instincts and fine feelings that define the English gentleman. Helen immediately sees this in him and tries to make him her lover in this vein. 'I think you're a wonderful gallant man', she tells him during that first evening, after the three of them have played a game of billiards invented by Shamus which she has won. Cassidy reckons, privately, that he was in fact the winner, but that this doesn't matter since it was only fun, and that 'a female victory' in a 'man's game' was in any case 'chivalrous'. Helen must have read all this in his boyish features and decided to work with it. In throwaway remarks, whose depths Cassidy can barely fathom, she offers him and looks to receive from him the sense of self-worth that love brings to those who can give and take alike.[28]

The novel tells its story with a simplicity of plot that is counterbalanced by a restless multiplicity of style. This is a style that shifts between letter-form and fable, both exploited by eighteenth-century writers of prose fiction, and between various techniques associated with later novelistic developments, such as the omniscient narrator of realist novelists such as Honoré de Balzac (1799–1850) and Thomas Mann (1875–1955), the uses of focalization and free indirect discourse by Gustave Flaubert (1821–80) and later nineteenth-century writers, and the narrative flashbacks, dream sequences, and extended parodies of earlier literary idioms that are associated with James Joyce (1882–1941) and other practitioners of the modernist novel. The third part of the novel, which describes the time that Shamus and Cassidy steal from their wives together in Paris, is the most stylistically experimental. It deploys modernist techniques to disrupt the outer chronology of events and to represent, instead, the stream of Cassidy's innermost perceptions. It does so for reasons stated at the outset: 'Love affairs, Cassidy had always known, are timeless, and therefore elusive of sequence.'[29]

Cassidy's love affair with Helen, eventually consummated in a hotel room in London, is told more soberly in the language of giving and taking. Helen, made painfully aware of the fact that Shamus 'goes screwing all over Europe', decides to start 'a revolution of one'. She confirms that neither she nor Cassidy has ever had a lover apart from Shamus. She asks why. She observes that they are 'talking about ruin as well as love' and offers the thought that she would give up Shamus for her freedom. When Cassidy hesitates, she asks, 'Is it *really* so difficult to take? [. . .] After all the lessons we've had?' Cassidy, emboldened, decides he will give this his all: 'And suddenly he was kissing her, taking her [. . .]. Her touch took nothing; she steered and danced, lay passive, rode above him; but still she only gave [. . .], creating in him, of her obedience, a growing obligation to love her in return.' The writing here has earned its sobriety. Cassidy offers himself to Helen by taking her body; Helen reaches for her freedom by giving her body to Cassidy. This is perhaps the moment in the novel when its lovers come closest to—yet without ever reaching—the ideal of reciprocal exchange.[30]

The love triangle is no sooner completed in this way than it inexorably falls to pieces. Shamus, the 'taker and challenger of life', simply cannot bear to share Helen with Cassidy or Cassidy with Helen. Helen is in the end incapable of taking her freedom from Shamus on her own. She has chosen the wrong alternative to him in Cassidy. A child martyr to a grown-up world bereft of love, as he describes himself in a letter to one of his own sons, Cassidy the adult proves unable to value himself enough to escape that world and its loneliness. Helen the truth-teller shouts to Cassidy in their last meeting: 'For a while you really *did* care [. . .]. About yourself [. . .]. For God's *sake* do it again [. . .]. Find someone else. Don't go back into that awful dark.' But that is precisely what Cassidy does. He buys Haverdown and retires there. He and his wife patch things up 'for the children's sake'. He settles into a steady, passionless affair with a friend of his wife; he becomes a lay preacher, though 'his services were seldom called upon'. In time, Shamus sends him a copy of a novel he has written entitled *Three for the Road*, which Cassidy never reads. Cassidy comes in time, instead, to forget Shamus entirely. 'For', as the narrator explains, 'in this world, whatever there was left of it to inhabit, Aldo Cassidy dared not remember love.' In this, the novel's closing sentence, the narrator ushers Cassidy back into the darkness that he has carried within him since childhood.[31]

The *ménage à trois* depicted in *The Naive and Sentimental Lover* could hardly be more English. Not so the persona of the novel's author, born David Cornwell, who has repeatedly evaded questions about his adoption of John Le Carré as his *nom de plume* and, when pressed, dismisses it as a 'ridiculous name' even as he explains that he ignored the advice 'to choose a good Anglo-Saxon couple of syllables'.[32] However evasive he is on the subject, it surely befits him to have combined a traditional monosyllabic British first name with a floridly European surname, the latter an idiosyncratic émigré in its own right. That combination captures the work of a novelist who has consistently portrayed British institutions—and the suffering they have, in their gradual post-1945 decline, inflicted on individuals caught up in them—and who has chosen to do this from the outside, in particular, the critical distance of continental Europe.

If there is any significance to be gleaned from the French meanings of *carré* ('square') in respect of the author, it is perhaps that he has appeared to set his work squarely within the literary tradition of the spy novel, placing the British Secret Service in its Cold War and later predicaments, together with its networks of spies and the idiom of the trade, at the centre of stories of people caught between the opposing forces of personal and institutional loyalty. Of course, the apparent squareness of fit is an illusion, since the literary tradition around his work is as much Le Carré's creation as the intelligence jargon he purports to have imported into his novels. He has considerably enlarged the English spy novel, taking its form, content, and style in new directions, while maintaining a broad consistency of literary purpose and a core cast of characters. These include his single most important individual creation, George Smiley, the bespectacled British spymaster and unlikely holder of ideals in a vicious world. Smiley perhaps also speaks for his creator at the end of Le Carré's novel *A Legacy of Spies* (2017), when, as he takes leave of his former 'foot soldier' Peter Guillam, he looks back in retirement at a lifetime of espionage. He wonders what it was all for. '*Capitalism*? God forbid. Christendom? God forbid again.' There was a time, of course, when it was all for England:

> But *whose* England? *Which* England? England all alone, a citizen of nowhere? I'm a European, Peter. If I had a mission [. . .], it was to Europe. If I was heartless, I was heartless for Europe. If I had an unattainable ideal, it was of leading Europe out of her darkness towards a new age of reason. I have it still.[33]

Le Carré, we infer, has the same unattainable ideal. While putting the finishing touches to this book, I discover that the novelist has placed that unattainable pro-European ideal—and the political anger with Brexit and Trump that so often currently accompanies it in Britain—at the heart of his latest novel, *Agent Running in the Field* (2019).

The Naive and Sentimental Lover is perhaps Le Carré's novelistically most daring experiment to date towards that ideal. The fictional love triangle at its heart is known to correspond to an actual three-way relationship that saw David Cornwell entangled with the novelist James Kennaway and his wife Susan Kennaway in the mid 1960s. Both Kennaways have written about the affair, Susan in a memoir entitled *The Kennaway*

Papers (1981), James in a novel, *Some Gorgeous Accident* (1967), published a year before his death in a road accident. Kennaway writes himself into his own novel as James Link, a rough diamond of an Irish-American war photographer who loses Susie Steinberg, a glossy magazine journalist, to his friend Richard Fiddes, a socially polished and unhappily married doctor. The affair is further complicated by the fact that Fiddes, assisted by Steinberg, performs an illegal abortion on a London prostitute, for which he is brought to trial. Kennaway chooses to focalize the events of the novel through his alter ego Link, the biter bit, who heads for the sunset only to 'vanish in the fog'.[34] Le Carré has his fictional doppelgänger and focal consciousness, Aldo Cassidy, retreat into the darkness of forgetting. Perhaps the most eerie of the similarities between *Some Gorgeous Accident* and *The Naive and Sentimental Lover* lies in their shared experimentalism of style, for Kennaway deploys in his novel many of the modernist narrative techniques Le Carré adopted four years later in his own, as if the two friends both wished to rise to the literary ambitions they shared.

The literary ambition of *The Naive and Sentimental Lover* stirred controversy among its critics. The novel has more often than not been dismissed as 'wretched' and as 'a disastrous failure'. Its defenders have argued that the novel is in fact an exceptional achievement on its author's part and that its harsh reception says more about the pigeon-holing tendencies of the literary establishment than about the novel itself.[35]

The defence of exceptionalism, in my view, concedes too much. It implicitly denies Le Carré's other novels the literary experimentation that it recognizes in *The Naive and Sentimental Lover*. Yet these other novels experiment with style in enlarging the limits of the spy story: consider for example *A Perfect Spy* (1986), into whose heart Le Carré smuggles a psychological exploration of his protagonist Magnus Pym's damaging relationship with his disappeared mother and con artist father, concealing that exploration under the headline story of Pym's subsequent career in espionage as a British double agent. True, *The Naive and Sentimental Lover* deviates still further from familiar territory, and even emphasizes that deviation by comically embedding within the novel its own virtual double as a spy story. Shamus and Cassidy meet a Frenchwoman, Élise, during their time in Paris. Shamus introduces Cassidy to her as Burgess and himself as Maclean. Every Le Carré reader knows that these were the pair of British spies and friends who for years secretly passed information to the Soviet Union before their joint defection in the early 1950s. Shamus's conceit leaves the reader imagining an alternative, spy version of the novel, in which he and Cassidy love Helen and one another as double agents rather than as the struggling writer and the successful maker of pram fittings they are.[36]

The exceptionalist defence of *The Naive and Sentimental Lover* also tends to overlook the consistency of literary purpose the novel shares with Le Carré's others. That purpose is to diagnose, from a position of internal exile, the causes of the British failure to help lead Europe out of her darkness. In this instance, the cause of failure highlighted is the class system, which—in the novelist's portrayal—hollows out the individual's capacity for love in order to produce the stiff upper lip of those who are 'English to the core'. Any reader of the novel who feels that it ignores the institutions of governmental power—the Secret Service and the rest—might reflect that Le Carré time and again shows how the class system determines the implacable functioning of these institutions within wider British society.

It is, aptly enough, to a continental European idea, invented by the French and developed by a German, that Le Carré turns in order to portray the failures of the British class system. Le Carré is by no means the only artist to have adapted Schiller's opposition between the naïve and the sentimental.[37] The naïve and sentimental, in Le Carré's novel, are not to be confused with Shamus's reduction of them to a binary opposition that justifies him in his self-appointed role as an *enfant terrible* of naïveté and casts Cassidy as his sentimental sidekick. No one is less naïvely realist than Shamus, nor more in thrall to the hierarchies of the class system, in his reverse snobberies and his entirely conventional expectation that Helen will be the faithful wife while he goes screwing all over Europe. No one is less sentimentally idealist, less capable of striving for 'the absolute in the actions of the will', than Cassidy the damaged child of nature. The truth is that both men, like Helen, are a motley of competing textures and tendencies. Helen, who says, calculatingly, that she feels 'very *naive*' when she first goes to bed with Cassidy, fails to see that hers is and must be an individual woman's struggle for freedom. She traps herself within an opposition of Shamus's making. The interaction of naïve and sentimental in this novel transforms neither. We might observe, for this reason, that each member of the novel's *ménage à trois* is to be considered the naïve and sentimental lover of its title. In Le Carré's comedy of deflation, of course, none of them has what it takes—what Schiller might call the poetry of soul—to leave England, head for Europe, and pursue the ideal of love at the place where the naïve and the sentimental merge.

Le Carré undertakes, in *The Naive and Sentimental Lover*, a comic experiment in satirical reversal. We have already seen that he casts a quizzical light back on the exclusive masculinity of Schiller's treatment—the Goethe-Schiller show—by placing an ill-treated but lucid woman at the heart of his novel in the position of chorus and protagonist. He shows, again in satirical mode, the damage that unscrupulous Oxford men like Shamus can do when they get hold of an émigré like *naïveté* in a conceptual pairing like Schiller's. Shamus uses the sentimental to

blast the English middle classes as shams without ever ac-
knowledging that he is of their number and hoist with his own
petard. He is, as the spelling of his name suggests, a sham. For,
even as he attempts to separate himself from middle-class as-
pirations and constipations by denoting himself as naïve, he
cannot escape—indeed he trades upon—the superior connotations of that word.

These are connotations to which English users of the word
have long laid claim. Le Carré thus bears witness to a broader
truth about *naïveté* that we first observed in the company of
Dryden's Melantha. It is that *naïveté* is always ready to turn
English twice, once when it supports its user's aspiration to
partake in the cultural superiority the English attribute to the
French, and once again when it reveals the hierarchies of power
and class on which that aspiration is predicated.

CHAPTER FIVE

Ennui

ennui, *n.*

Etymology: < French *ennui*, Old French *enui* < Latin *in odio*
[. . .]. So far as frequency of use is concerned, the word might
be regarded as fully naturalized; but the pronunciation has
not been anglicized, there being in fact no English analogy
which could serve as guide.

—*OXFORD ENGLISH DICTIONARY*

The sufficient is not enough.

—A. L. HENDRIKS

ENNUI LOOMS IN the space between languages. It figures, alongside *naïveté*, in the list of words
that John Evelyn in 1665 said
conveyed meanings that English
could not otherwise fully express.
Evelyn said nothing specific about
those words and their meanings.
Naïveté quickly became current in English usage. *Ennui*, by
contrast, had fewer immediate takers. It seems not to have established itself fully as an émigré in English until the last decades of the eighteenth century. In one of the first instances of

usage recorded by the *OED*, which presaged much of the word's early fortunes in English, Lord Chesterfield in a letter of 1758 uttered the pithy observation that a man of his acquaintance who had worked in trade and industry found, after his social rise, 'that living like a gentleman was dying of *ennui*'. A string of English words—from *apathy* to *vacancy* via *boredom*—had acquired a prestigious foreign travelling companion.[1]

To personify ennui, as I have just done, is an imaginative act many centuries old. The Vulgate, the fourth-century Latin translation of the Bible of St Jerome adopted by the Catholic church, introduced a personification into a prayer telling the believer not to fear, among other things, 'the noonday devil'.[2] A Christian contemporary of Jerome, Evagrius of Pontus, associated the noonday devil with a dread listlessness and lack of interest in life he called *acedia*. French writers drew on the *acedia* of Evagrius and the personification of Jerome when developing their representations of ennui. The most famous expression of this development is, as we will see, Baudelaire's poetic dramatization of Ennui as a 'dainty monster' in the middle of the nineteenth century. Baudelaire, in personifying ennui, was well aware that he was doing nothing new. English writers before him had portrayed French ennui in the same terms: the *OED* records references to 'the dæmon Ennui' and the 'fiend Ennui' at the turn of the nineteenth century.[3]

Ennui turned English by naming in the language of the fashionable the demon of noontide that stalked members of the nobility and gentry: people who didn't have to work for a living. The prestigious French foreign derivation of the word reinforced the class connotations of the condition to which the word was attached. It was, however, soon extended to the men and women of the middle classes in Britain and Ireland and more distant parts of the British empire. We have already seen

how, in his English and Bengali dictionary of 1851, John Mendies included the word in his list of the 'French and other foreign
words and phrases in common use' throughout the empire. The
British would relinquish colonial possession of the Indian sub-
continent only a century or so later, by which time *ennui* had
been established in Indian English and its miseries had been
fully democratized. Arundhati Roy's novel, *The Ministry of Utmost Happiness* (2017), brings into view the outcasts of a contemporary India it portrays as a rapidly urbanizing regional
power that has learned a thing or two from its previous colonizers. It tells, among others, the story of a Kashmiri militant,
Musa, who goes underground after Indian soldiers open fire
during a funeral procession in Srinagar and kill his wife and
two-year-old daughter. The narrator describes how Musa, as a
fugitive, quickly masters arts of survival. Among these, 'he
learned the art of ennui, of enduring as well as inflicting boredom. He hardly ever spoke.' *Ennui*, as Roy's narrator uses it, is
a word that ventures into the territory of silence in which Musa,
like so many fugitives and militants all over the world, is forced
to live. Roy's narrator repeats, in the sentences just quoted, the
well-established relation of *ennui* to the native English *boredom*. An Anglophone's decision to pair the two in close proximity usually reflects, as it does in Roy's sentence, more than a
habit of lexical variation: it suggests that each carries a subtly
different shade of meaning. *Ennui* not only conveys a wider
and deeper truth than *boredom* can by itself, we might say, but
raises that truth to the level of art. This is what Musa does with
the boredom he endures and inflicts in the killing fields of
Kashmir.[4]

   It describes, equally, as we will see, what Anglophone artists
before him—such as the Anglo-Irish novelist Maria Edgeworth,
the German-born and London-based painter Walter Sickert,
the English essayist Virginia Woolf, and the Jamaican-born

poet A. L. Hendriks—have looked for and found in *ennui* in combination with *boredom* and other native English synonyms. *Ennui*, appearing so often as it does in these combinations, has thus been the instrument of a creolizing art. The word has migrated towards a transcultural 'contact zone' between English and French. Its entanglements in that contact zone have made possible a whole set of creative migrations, not only between languages, but also between different art forms.

Variation and Monotony

Seventeenth-century French dictionaries offer a coherent cluster of definitions for *ennui*. These reflect features of the word that remain true to this day. They display a wide spectrum of possible meanings, ranging (in English terms) from world-weariness and bitterness of soul via pain and worry to inconvenience and irritation, that last meaning reminding us of the etymological proximity of *ennui* to the contemporaneous English *annoy*. The semantic spectrum of *ennui* was already visible in Robert Estienne's 1549 bilingual Latin–French dictionary. Seventeenth-century dictionaries observe that its singular and plural forms tend in their usage to point towards different ends of that spectrum. *Ennuis* tend to be lesser agitations of the kind that 'wine and good company can charm away', as Furetière cheerfully puts it in his 1690 dictionary, whereas singular *ennui* is altogether more difficult to dissipate. In an exception to this observed tendency, French speakers today commonly use the singular noun in a semantically diluted sense more often associated with the plural, explaining that in this or that minor inconvenience lies the *ennui* of a situation. This semantically diluted use of singular *ennui* has by no means, however, supplanted its stronger meaning. If anything, this meaning has darkened over time, as we will see.[5]

Ennui, in that stronger and darker meaning, refers to a deep and dread weariness that is difficult to explain or even express. Furetière talks of 'pain [*chagrin*] and upset [*fâcherie*]'. Both he and the Académie française specify time as the principal dimension in which humans experience *ennui* of that kind. The Académie française dictionary defines the noun as a 'weariness of soul [*lassitude d'esprit*] caused by something that is unpleasant in itself or in its duration' and asserts that the reflexive verb *s'ennuyer* signifies 'that time wears on and feels long'.[6]

The temporal dimension of *ennui* has remained central to the word, and has elicited perhaps its most important philosophical conceptualization, that offered by the twentieth-century French moral philosopher Vladimir Jankélévitch in his 1963 essay *L'Aventure, l'Ennui, le Sérieux* (Adventure, ennui, and seriousness). Jankélévitch presents the trio of concepts in his title as three dissimilar ways in which humans inhabit time. Jankélévitch argues that ennui is caused by an underlying misconception of time. Where the dimension of time is properly conceived of as the irregular alternation of instants and intervals, of future becoming and present being, then *ennui* arises from the illusion that time is nothing but an uninterrupted interval of being in the present. The rot sets in—and ennui creeps on—when the instant is left to lose its shape and to subside into the interval. Ennui is in this sense 'the misfortune of being too fortunate'. The philosopher's remedy is essentially to reconnect the instants and intervals of time, which ennui put asunder, so as to 'impassion time in such a way that consciousness can rediscover in it both intensity and plenitude'.[7] He formulates that remedy in an impassioned style that seems to partake of the remedy itself. Jankélévitch's is a philosophy that consists in its manner of argument as much as in its matter, in the meditative poetry of his prose, its quasi-musical alternation of theme and variation.

Jankélévitch's essay contains a roll-call of the major French writers and thinkers who have left their mark on the history of ennui and of authors who have written in other languages: Shakespeare, Schopenhauer, Kierkegaard, Leopardi, Tolstoy, and Dostoïevsky. But Jankélévitch deploys these references as so many resources for a philosophy of time in the making rather than treating them as primary objects of his analysis. He gestures towards the contested word history of *ennui* only when seeking to intervene in it. We might say that he helped to establish *ennui* in the vocabulary of modern French philosophy while, in the process, tending to occlude the historical processes—the concerted conceptualizations and accompanying controversies—that made it a keyword of the culture in the first place.

It was by such means that *ennui* rose to prominence in seventeenth-century France. Those controversies had to do with those who might properly be said to feel ennui, what lay behind the dread weariness of soul it might mean, and what might be done to alleviate or overcome it. At stake in the seventeenth-century controversies was the centrality or otherwise to French society of the Catholic religion as an institution for the management of social behaviour and a system of belief. This conflict provided the context in which Pascal—as we saw in the last chapter—took issue with Montaigne concerning the secular attitude of naïveté on display in his *Essais*. Pascal was not acting alone. Other writers of devout intent, such as the essayist Pierre Nicole (1625–95) and Bishop Bossuet (1627–1704), deployed their considerable powers of eloquence in the same cause. Their gallant opponents—writers such as the novelist Madeleine de Scudéry, the comic playwright Molière, and the poet Jean de La Fontaine—wrote in secular appreciation of life in the here-and-now. In many respects, the controversy between the godly and the gallants was a further ramification of the Quarrel of the Ancients and Moderns, and many of the people involved on both sides were the same. Both sides sought, ultimately, to determine the direction taken by French society and culture, starting at the very top, with the king and his close circle.

A key treatment of ennui in gallant mode is Madeleine de Scudéry's 1684 conversation 'De l'ennui sans sujet' (On causeless ennui). Scudéry deploys the notion to compliment the king on his unrivalled *galanterie* and thereby urges him, implicitly, to remain as *galant* as ever. The young and witty Aminte suffers from inexplicable ennui. She confesses to her female friends and their male admirers that she finds all of the usual entertainments for well-born women weary, stale, flat, and unprofitable. She points out that one might do better to alternate between 'diversion' [*divertissement*] and 'occupation'—thereby introducing into one's experience of time, as Jankélévitch might say, a pattern of interval and instant—but that an alternation of this kind is open only to men: 'How are people of my sex, who have no occupation, to avoid often becoming bored?'[8] She leaves the conversation, thoroughly *ennuyée*, only to re-enter in order to hear a report of the 'ingenious and gallant diversion' [*ingenieux et galant divertissement*] that the king has just given for his courtiers at Marly. This was the château that Louis XIV had recently had built as a retreat from Versailles. Clindor surfaces to tell the tale. He describes how the château, an architectural marvel, was revealed to the court magnificently lit up and packed with rare and beautiful goods from all over the world that were to be won at the gaming tables. The king played first, to encourage the others, and only later did it become known that he was picking up the tab for all losses incurred at the tables. Aminte listens, mesmerized. She ends the conversation promising she will eventually shrug off her causeless ennui on condition that she be allowed to indulge it for the next few years, except when attending the king's parties, where she appreciates that it would be quite 'impossible to suffer ennui' [*on ne se pouvoit jamais ennuyer*].⁹

The offer that Scudéry conveys in her conversation on ennui is that she become a gallant writer in the service of a gallant monarch. This offer is never made explicit. To make it so would, after all, hardly be gallant. Scudéry nonetheless finds an indirect means of suggesting that, by writing about it in a witty and diverting way, she can dispel ennui. Her offer applies, not just to the likes of Aminte and Therame, but to the king himself. He, too, may be a prey to ennui. Perhaps, on days when there is no party planned at court, the king might pick up a copy of her *Conversations* and find there a gallant diversion fit to dispel ennui. Madeleine de Scudéry was granted a royal pension in the year before she first published the work. In this context, as Elizabeth C. Goldsmith says, 'the book of conversations in which "De l'ennui sans sujet" appears functions [. . .] as a text offered to the king in exchange for a gift he had accorded its author'.¹⁰

Pascal had already presented a godly account of ennui by the time Scudéry published her conversation on the topic. He did so with conceptual depth and literary stealth in his *Pensées*, a collection of some eight hundred fragments first published in 1670, eight years after his death. He provided the depth by analysing, from an austere Augustinian perspective, the ordinary experiences that well-to-do lay French people like Aminte and indeed her king had. Since Pascal was aiming his defence at such people, not at professional theologians, he wrote for them in an idiom and a style they could understand. Therein lay his literary stealth. He drew on references from aspects of culture and society with which they would identify. He adopted the words they associated with secular codes of manners. He saw and treated *ennui* as just such a word.

Like Scudéry, Pascal pairs the word with *divertissement*, but in his case it is to show that *divertissement* succeeds only in distracting the godless from the step towards salvation that ennui offers them. Entitled simply 'Ennui', fragment 515 of the *Pensées* portrays in list form the horrible sense of emptiness that humans feel when they are left to their own company in a room, bereft of occupation or diversion. That is the moment when ennui leaks out from the innermost depths of the human heart and stirs feelings of sadness, bitterness, and despair. No one is exempt from this desolate experience, Pascal says in fragment 169, not even the most privileged members of society: catch him when the party is over and you will see that 'a king without diversion [*divertissement*] is a man full of miseries'.[11] The most common response of the godless is to redouble their efforts to find entertainment that will distract them from their desolation. While, by this means, diversion provides us with our only consolation from the misery of our godless lives, Pascal says in fragment 33, it is in fact the greatest source of our misery insofar as it prevents us from considering our true predicament: 'Without it we would be bored, and this boredom [*ennui*] would drive us to seek a more solid means of escape. But diversion [*divertissement*] amuses us and guides us imperceptibly to death.'[12] Death offers no prospect of the salvation that might have been granted to those whose ennui had brought them—as Evagrius had hoped *acedia* would bring its sufferers—to seek out God.

Pascal does not say quite how an experience of ennui could, by itself, bring a godless person to seek out God. It is clear, however, that he saw Christ as an inspirational exemplar in this respect. Christ in the final hours of life—which he spent alone in the Garden of Gethsemane while his disciples slept—is portrayed by Pascal as suffering 'abandonment in the horror of the night': as 'Jesus in a state of ennui'.[13] As the literary historian

Nicholas Hammond says, Pascal presents Jesus as having responded by entrusting himself entirely to his Father, thereby suggesting by 'spiritual implication' that fallen people suffering the ill effects of ennui should do the same.[14] The question nonetheless remains as to how Pascal imagined such people might be brought to see Christ as their exemplar in the first place. The answer, of course, is that he hoped to play his part in bringing about just such a conversion in the readers of the *Pensées*.

French writers at the turn of the nineteeth century reactivated seventeenth-century controversies about ennui in a context changed by the French Revolution of 1789 and its aftermath. Synonymous with the *mal du siècle* of Romantic writers at the beginning of the century, ennui mutated thereafter with succeeding shifts in literary sensibility all the way to the *fin de siècle*, being picked up and exploited as a leitmotif along the way by all the major novelists—including Stendhal, Balzac, Flaubert, and Zola—and by poets as diverse as Lamartine, Baudelaire, Verlaine, Laforgue, and Mallarmé. Even as nineteenth-century writers and thinkers disagreed about ennui—its nature, causes, and remedies—they experienced it as an intimate threat to their activity as artists and struggled with that threat in the fabric of their work.[15]

Two leading French writers took up that struggle, from opposing positions, in the changed circumstances of the years following the Revolution of 1789 and the subsequent rise of Napoleon. These were François-René de Chateaubriand (1762–1848) and Germaine de Staël (1766–1817). Roger Pearson has made their contrasting approaches central to his monumental study of the role of the poet as lawgiver in nineteenth-century France. Pearson shows how poets on the Right and Left—'the modern division of political opinion that sprang from the Revolution itself'—disagreed, in its aftermath, about what the

Revolution meant and what the future of French society and culture, particularly poetry, should be.[16] He uses a contrast between Chateaubriand and Staël to capture these disagreements. I would like to offer a modest addition to Pearson's account by bringing into focus a single word, *ennui*, which I suggest proved to be key for Chateaubriand and Staël alike.

Chateaubriand renewed, from the Right, the godly approach to the bitter experience of ennui. He worked to achieve the restoration of a constitutional monarchy and the Catholic church to the centre of French political life. He argued in his works of the late 1790s and early 1800s that political revolutions—including that of 1789—derive from a fundamental sense of dissatisfaction and that it was the role of poetry, in the broad sense of that word, to show that dissatisfaction to be, as Pearson puts it, a 'sacred and God-given condition of lack that [. . .] only Christianity can properly treat'. Chateaubriand portrays that dissatisfaction in *René* (1802), his short Christian prose odyssey, whose eponymous protagonist came to be seen as the exemplar of French Romantic *mal du siècle*. René's sense 'of being caught between a mutilated past and a yet-to-be constructed future', Pearson says, 'mirrors the predicament of his countrymen' in the aftermath of the Revolution of 1789.[17] Chateaubriand in *René* talks of a 'disgust for life which I had felt since my childhood' and 'a profound sense of ennui'.[18]

The poet, in Chateabriand's view, could help the post-Revolutionary French to overcome their ennui by teaching them to devote themselves to the restoration of social and political life and to search for a pathway to the divine within nature. Staël opposed Chateaubriand's godly conservativism from the progressive Left and proposed, to a secular Europe, a new poetry that would dispel ennui. She did so in *Corinne ou l'Italie* (1807), a novel weaving political allegory, poetic theory, and

travelogue into the story of an unhappy love affair. The eponymous protagonist is a beautiful and independent woman poet
living in Rome. Like Chateabriand's René, Staël's Corinne is
an exemplary figure, but Corinne embodies—in stark contrast
to René—European Romantic ideals of political emancipation
and poetic enthusiasm for women as much as men. As Staël's
title suggests, Corinne *is* Italy, and Staël celebrates in the novel
the peninsula's long cultivation of these ideals in the face of
tyranny (without once mentioning its latest embodiment, Napoleon, who had been crowned King of Italy in 1805). Staël,
whom Napoleon had exiled from Paris in 1802, reimagined
Europe as home. Corinne is Italy at the heart of Europe, being
the cosmopolitan and polyglot daughter of an Italian widower
whose second wife is English, and having lived in England as
well as Italy. In Rome, she falls in love with a young Scottish
aristocrat by the name of Oswald, Lord Nevill. Staël presents
Oswald as inhabited by a British variant of ennui *à la* Chateaubriand, a black hole of emotional exhaustion, resulting from
the unresolved tension between his innate poetic sensitivity
and the austere social conformism he has inherited from his
father. His is a negative Northern melancholy of restless lack,
which—as Pearson shows—Corinne meets with its positive
Southern counterpart, a melancholy caused by intense feeling
in the here-and-now when this exceeds the limits of her expressive powers.[19]

Corinne, it turns out, tasted British ennui *à la* Chateaubri-
and long before she met Oswald. In Book 14 of *Corinne* she tells
Oswald of how, from the age of fifteen, she spent six years living
with her father, English stepmother, and half-sister in a small
town in Northumberland. The word that Corinne repeats again
and again in her account of these years is *ennui*. Corinne's stepmother Lady Edgermond possessed the same austere social
conformism as Oswald's father and evidently experienced

Corinne's Italian abundance of wit and spirit as an affront to English ladylike virtue. The winters Corinne spent in the town were, she says, 'a collection of ennuis, both diverse and monotonous'.[20] She endured countless hours of insipid tabletalk between women bored by their own company. The long-awaited arrival of the men changed nothing: they continued to talk amongst themselves. Society in such a town made a deliberate habit of ennui, in fact, for 'people [. . .] do not like to enjoy themselves on one occasion, only to realize that they are bored every day'.[21] Corinne, in the end, simply could not bear the all-pervading ennui of a woman's life in a provincial English town. A creole poetic hybrid ready to burst into flower in the right conditions, who had by then absorbed the meditative seriousness of English poetry without losing the imaginative liveliness of her Italian compatriots, she decided to return to Italy—sacrificing her family, rank, and name—in order 'to lead an independent life entirely devoted to the arts'.[22] She chose the melancholy of the warm South over the ennui of the chilly North.

It works, beautifully, until she falls for Oswald. She hopes that she will win him and warm him up by the force of her love and the gifts of her poetic soul. She misjudges him. What happens instead is that Oswald chooses to accept his dead father's legacy to him rather than Corinne's gifts. In accordance with the father's wishes, he concludes eventually that Corinne is wrong for him and marries her half-sister Lucile, an English purebred drained of life and colour by the upbringing she has suffered at the hands of her mother. Corinne learns of the marriage on an impulsive journey back to England in search of Oswald. She returns to Italy, puts away the lyre she can no longer use, and dies of a broken heart. The narrator ends the novel refusing either to blame Oswald or to absolve him. By implication, it invites the novel's readers to form their own judgement, and not just on Oswald. Which of the two responses to ennui on display in the novel do we endorse? Do we prefer Oswald's conformism and godliness *à la* Chateaubriand to Corinne's enthusiasm and gallantry *à la* Staël? If we were to prefer Oswald's way, of course, we would be helping to realize a situation in which, to adapt Pearson's elegant formulation, *Corinne* met the fate of Corinne.[23] Which of us would have the coldness of heart to collude in that? Not I. No novel should have to endure the ennui to which that woman was subjected in a small English town at the edge of the *monde*.

Creative Hybrids

Writing creatively about ennui never happens at a safe distance, it seems, for the experience always threatens to creep over the writing and drain it of activity. How is the writer to respond to the threat of ennui? While one response is to lapse into an exhausted silence, of course, another is to search for expressive forms for coming to terms with that threat. That search took a new direction in the nineteenth century as *ennui* underwent a process of creolization. This process goes unnoticed by the comparative literary scholar Reinhard Kuhn in his panoramic 1976 study of ennui in Western literature. Kuhn claims at one point that 'the vocabulary to express ennui at the disposal of writers of Anglo-Saxon, Romance, or German background is a very limited one'.[24] What he overlooks, in making that claim, is the fact that some writers found subtle ways of mixing the vocabularies of these languages. Yet this hybridizing process marked a key development in the history of creative literary response to ennui. It afforded new possibilities of expression and forged creolizing connections between the literary culture of nineteenth-century France and that of its neighbours.

The creolizing of *ennui* may be seen in the work of two nineteenth-century writers, one the author of a novel in English bearing the word in its title, the other a French poet who made it central to the organization of his most important collection. The first is the Anglo-Irish novelist Maria Edgeworth. Her novel *Ennui* (1809) was quickly translated into French and no less a writer than Germaine de Staël said, in 1813, that it had 'charmed' her.[25] Yet the novel is conspicuous by its absence from Kuhn's detailed survey of ennui in Western literature, for it is not only an early landmark in the Englishing of that French émigré, but also an important part of a corpus of work that took the English novel in new directions. The second writer, to whom Kuhn gives due recognition, is the French poet Charles Baudelaire (1821–67). In the opening poem of his major work of lyric poetry, *Les Fleurs du Mal* (*The Flowers of Evil*) of 1857, Baudelaire establishes Ennui as a demonic figure presiding indolently over the entire collection.

Edgeworth and Baudelaire share the same creolizing approach to the language of ennui. Both deploy a word or phrase from their native language in a pairing with a word or phrase they have borrowed from the foreign language of a neighbouring culture that is widely viewed as prestigious. Both lead with the foreign-derived word, as if they felt that its prestigious and oblique relation to their native language helped it to mark the elusive position of the word's strange referent, on the margins of language itself. They then combine the foreign word with native synonyms in microcosmic lexical contact zones—phrasal pairings—whose precise meaning is irreducible to either of its constituent elements. They create, in this way, a language of ennui composed of creole hybrids.

For Edgeworth's narrator, writing about his early years as the young Earl of Glenthorn, the foreign-derived word is *ennui*. The synonymous English noun or phrase with which he pairs *ennui* varies: in the first paragraph alone of his memoir we encounter *apathy, brown study, incapacity, indolence, restlessness*, and *vacancy*, some of these embedded in phrases. Glenthorn justifies the need for such variation when, in the same paragraph, he introduces his readers to the condition from which he once suffered:

> Whilst yet a boy, I began to feel the dreadful symptoms of that mental malady which baffles the skill of medicine, and for which wealth can purchase only temporary alleviation. For this complaint there is no precise English name; but, alas! the foreign term is now naturalized in England. Among the higher classes, whether in the wealthy or the fashionable world, who is unacquainted with *ennui*?[26]

Glenthorn is obliged to vary his English terms because he feels that none is adequate to the task without the aid of the 'now naturalized' *ennui*. That he regrets this state of affairs is revealing of the cultural inferiority complex that he, like so many English gentlemen before and since him, feels towards France.

For the lyric subject of Baudelaire's poems, who describes a bohemian artist's modern urban life, the foreign-derived word is the English *spleen*. Baudelaire had every reason to view English as a language of political and cultural prestige. Born six years after Britain and its continental European allies had defeated the Napoleonic French, he lived in an age of British imperial expansion, when the international spread of English— which was already established as the common tongue of the United States of America—was mirroring that expansion. He was an ardent admirer of English and American literature and the translator of Edgar Allan Poe and Henry Wadsworth Longfellow. No wonder, then, that he looked to English for the resources he needed to creolize *ennui*.

There was more to the creolizing of *ennui* in the work of
Baudelaire and Edgeworth, however, than the mere mixing of
languages. There was also the making of literature. *Ennui*, as
the two writers found it, circulated among a wide range of discourses of knowledge, including theology, medicine, politics,
economics, and the *moraliste* literary tradition of social and
moral analysis. Edgeworth and Baudelaire mixed representations of ennui from these various discourses in the crucible of
the literature they wrote. They produced, by these acts of creative alchemy, new tales of ennui that served as allegories of
their practices as literary artists.

Baudelaire, by pairing *ennui* with *spleen*, was able to draw
on the rich traditions of religious and medical writing in which
these notions loomed large. He writes as though he had thoroughly absorbed the haunting depictions 'of the ennui that
comes to the godless' found in seventeenth-century religious
writing, such as the work of Pascal, while remaining impervi-
ous to the spiritual implication that Pascal and others of his
persuasion hoped readers would draw from that depiction. The
poet of ennui in *Les Fleurs du mal* is a despairing sinner sun-
dered from God.

Baudelaire seems equally conversant with medical accounts
of the spleen of the kind that the English physician George
Cheyne gave in his treatise *The English Malady* (1733). Cheyne
used his title to group together various chronic disorders that
he described as '*nervous* Distempers, *Spleen*, *Vapours*, and
Lowness of Spirits'. He did more than merely relabel the age-
old idea that the spleen was the seat of melancholy in the body.
As his modern editor notes, Cheyne saw the English malady as
a syndrome resulting not from purely physiological factors, but
from the social and cultural configurations of the English way
of life: these included, for his well-to-do patients, ever richer
diets and the demands of polite sociability. The result was a

modern melancholy that Cheyne claimed to have suffered personally, describing it as 'a *melancholy Fright* and *Pannick*, where my Reason was of no Use to me'. *Spleen* first appeared, in the decades following publication of Cheyne's work, as an anglicism in French.[27]

Baudelaire turned the word and its previous conceptualizations to his own purposes. He ignored the diagnoses of the medical doctors as much as he did the remedies of the soul doctors. He connected *spleen* and *ennui*, instead, in webs of metaphor describing the mental turmoil of an indigent poet living in a Parisian attic.

He does so most intensely in a sequence of poems all entitled 'Spleen'. This sequence comes towards the end of the first and longest part of the work, 'Spleen et Idéal' ('Spleen and the Ideal'), whose title names the opposite poles of the poet's inner state and the expression of each of these in his verse. Exalted representations of poetic flight in the realm of the ideal characterize the early poems. In the third of them, the poet reminds himself that his 'elevation' is also a flight from 'the ennui, past troubles and ordeals / That load our dim existence with their weight'.[28] This is an intimation of the spleen that comes to dominate the mood and mode of the later poems in the first part. While the poet, at first, succeeded in taking flight, now he fails, remaining rooted to the ground and imprisoned under an oppressive sky whose kingdom will have no end. The poet starts 'Spleen (II)' claiming he has 'More memories than if I'd lived a thousand years!' He likens his mind to a 'giant vault / Holding more corpses than a common grave' before bemoaning the long limping days when 'Ennui, the fruit of dulling lassitude, / Takes on the size of immortality'.[29] In 'Spleen (IV)' he describes the atrocious anxiety that comes upon him on days when the sky weighs down like a heavy lid on a mind 'moaning in ennui'.[30] *Spleen*, as Baudelaire uses it, is a one-word condensation of the downward spiral. The poems written in this mode possess energy, but it is a negative energy, a nightmare of death by paralysis rather than a vision of extinction. The poems are created by alchemy, but through a reverse of the usual process, whereby the poet—as he says in 'Alchemy of Suffering' ('Alchimie de la douleur')—transforms gold into dross and turns heaven into hell.[31] This is, of course, a *poetic* alchemy. It happens in the verse. It is, indeed, what makes the verse happen. Baudelaire thus converts ennui into a modern poetry that reflects on its own processes.

Ennui is, as has been said, tied to one of the two opposing poles of that poetry. The irregular movement of poetry between those two poles is writ large in *Les Fleurs du mal*. Kuhn says that Baudelaire ends the collection 'with the triumphant exaltation of one who has conquered ennui'.[32] I am not sure that the poet tells so affirming or so neat a tale. Ennui in *Les Fleurs du mal* is now conquered, now conquering, always there. It is a secret of human existence that the poet and his reader share. Baudelaire establishes it as such in the opening poem of the collection, 'To the Reader' ('Au lecteur'), which serves as the preface to the 1868 edition of the work. 'To the Reader' ends with a personification of Ennui as a 'dainty monster' lurking among the menagerie of vices that the poet has just shown inhabiting him and his reader alike. Ennui is at once the ugliest of these vices in intent and the most casual in attitude, an esoteric figure ready to swallow the whole world in a single exhausted yawn, but—for now—dreaming of the scaffold as he smokes his water-pipe. The poem's famous closing lines establish reader and poet in a relationship of bottomless complicity on the basis of the secret knowledge of ennui they share: 'Reader, you know this dainty monster too, /—Hypocrite reader,—my double,—my twin!'[33] Only with this complicity established does the collection begin its tale of a modern poetic life in turmoil by telling, in the ironically entitled opening poem 'Benediction' ('Bénédiction'), of the poet's birth into 'this bored world'.[34]

Edgeworth's narrator describes, in *Ennui*, his escape from that very world. His tale is that of a super-rich fashionable young English gentleman cured of his ennui by his travels in contemporary Ireland and by the bewitching age-old plot Ireland turned out to have in store for him, involving changeling children, extravagant reversals of fortune, and the revelation to him of the pleasures and benefits of professional work and companionable marriage. Edgeworth chooses to have Glenthorn tell this tale of fashionable life in an autobiographical narrative. She spins from his narrative two interrelated allegories. One is political: that of a true union between England and Ireland based on the renewal of the aristocracy; the other is literary: that of the creolizing creative processes at work in her fiction. This literary allegory sees the novel in English, in her deft hands, rid itself of ennui thanks to its transformative encounter with an Irish culture seasoned with French insight. By the end of his narration, our hero is able to confide in his reader that 'the demon of ennui was cast out for ever'.[35]

Edgeworth mixes English, French, and Irish modes in her novel's account of its headline condition. The young Glenthorn joins a list of upper-class English characters in her novels afflicted by the modern melancholy and other nervous distempers that George Cheyne, as we have seen, described in *The English Malady*. Edgeworth, as various scholars have pointed out, drew on two medical sources closer to hand than Cheyne: Erasmus Darwin, a friend to the Edgeworth family, whose *Zoonamia* (1794–96) traced the causes of such distempers to a mixture of physiological and psychological causes; and Thomas Beddoes, Darwin's protégé and Edgeworth's brother-in-law, whose *Hygëia* (1802–3) argued that the pathologies of modern life were conditioned by the lifestyle choices of wealthy fashionables. In her novelistic depiction of such people, Edgeworth mixes English medical discussions of ennui with French *moraliste* dissections, which appear as epigraphs to some of the chapters. These tend to confirm, in an epigrammatic register, the oral insights of the Irish characters that Glenthorn meets. The young English earl is on the verge of suicide—with his 'old malady' risen 'to an insupportable height'—when his childhood Irish nurse Ellinor O'Donoghoe persuades him to visit his Irish estate. He settles there, having travelled the country, and befriends Ellinor's son Christy. Christy observes, late in the novel, that 'any man, you see, may be made a lord; but a gentleman, a man must make himself'. With all the insight of the French *moraliste*, yet in his characteristic Irish mode of speech, Christy is telling Glenthorn's story.[36]

What happens to young Glenthorn is precisely that, once relieved of his status as an English lord, he learns to make himself an Irish gentleman. Ellinor reveals to him shortly before her death that she is his natural mother and swapped him and Christy at birth, meaning that Christy is the English earl, and he an Irish changeling. Our hero responds by relinquishing his title and his lands to his foster-brother and starting afresh. The new Earl of Glenthorn and his family's enjoyment of their new wealth and privilege—for which nothing had prepared them—ends in the ruin of the castle and the death through alcoholism of the Earl's now dissipated son. The former earl, meanwhile, takes his Irish name (O'Donoghoe) and moves to Dublin to train in the law.

There he meets Cecilia Delamere. She is charming, independent-minded, and, as it turns out, independently wealthy because heiress in law to the Glenthorn estate. Our hero, having lost his title and rank, stands no chance with her until Lord Y——, an elderly and well-meaning Anglo-Irish peer, takes him under his wing. Lord Y—— presents Ireland to him as a meritocracy in which 'the highest offices of the state are open to talents and perseverance'. He intimates that, if his young friend were to make proper use of 'time and industry' in his legal studies, he would stand, not only to make of himself a gentleman with a befitting profession, but also to win the hand of Cecilia freely given.[37]

So it turns out. The ingeniously plotted modern romance that is *Ennui* ends with our hero returning to Glenthorn castle on the verge of a new era in its history. He will now restore the castle and manage the estate, no longer (as he was last time) an over-privileged lounge-lizard in flight from self-inflicted ennui, but a self-made man, possessed of the new understanding 'that a man may at once be rich and noble, and active and happy'.[38]

This moral tale crackles with the energy of allegorical invention. Its plot has been rightly described by one of the novel's most astute readers, the literary critic Mitzi Myers, as 'a brilliant strategy enacting an emblematic answer to the identity politics that trouble Irish history'.[39] Two major events of the period covered by the action of *Ennui* (1798–1804) troubled Irish history and affected Edgeworth personally as a member of a landowning Anglo-Irish Protestant family that supported Catholic emancipation and social and educational reform in Ireland. The first of these events was the Rebellion of 1798 against the dominance in Ireland of the Anglo-Irish Protestant minority whence Edgeworth came. The Rebellion—which was inspired in part by the French Revolution—saw, among other things, the advance of a combined force of French soldiers and Irish rebels towards the Edgeworth family seat. The second of these events, which followed the suppression of the 1798 Rebellion, was Ireland's constitutional Union with England, of 1800. Maria's father R. L. Edgeworth voted against the Union as it was presented to the Irish parliament in 1800, but he and his daughter then sought in their writings to 'conciliate both countries', as they put it in their co-authored *Essay on Irish Bulls* (1802).[40]

Maria employed indirect symbolic means in her fiction. She made the 1798 Rebellion central to the action of *Ennui*. Nowhere in the novel, by contrast, does she mention the Union of 1800. In its place, she imagines at the end of the novel an alternative future for Ireland and England by means of a symbolic marriage of the two countries, represented by a former English aristocrat turned professionally trained gentleman and an Irish wife every inch his equal in talents and perseverance. Their marriage promises at one stroke to rid European aristocracy of an ennui that had precipitated its demise in the French Revolution of 1789, to overcome age-old social divisions in Ireland, and to improve the political standing of the country and its social well-being in an improved Union.

How seriously Edgeworth meant her readers to take this political allegory is hard to ascertain. Life would certainly have to imitate art by executing some improbable twists and turns if it were to realize the novel's vision of Ireland's future. Then again, as Glenthorn observes with a nod to the French seventeenth-century poet Nicolas Boileau, 'the romance of real life certainly goes beyond all other romances'.[41]

In the brilliance of its allegorical invention, meanwhile, the romance of *Ennui* casts light back on its source to reveal the novelist at play and at work. We see her mixing Irish, French, and English modes, not just in the account of ennui that her tale offers, but in the very manner of its making. Edgeworth, as Mitzi Myers has observed, allegorizes the literary creation of her novel by 'making "novelists" out of a whole string of colourful female characters'. These women shape the movement of the plot around her lethargic protagonist and, in so doing, represent different elements of modern Irish culture and society. Ellinor is Mother Ireland. The embodiment of the country's Gaelic heritage and a prophetic figure in its oral storytelling tradition, she foretells the auspicious return to the land of a high king, the O'Donoghoe, who will do much good. Lady Geraldine, Glenthorn's next female guide to Ireland, is from an old Anglo-Norman Irish family and thus represents Ireland's direct relationship with France and the rest of continental Europe. To mark her cosmopolitanism, and to keep the English in their place, she playfully mixes French words and witticisms into her speech. Feminist in outlook and fiercely patriotic, she openly resists Ireland's voluntary servitude to England, setting her compatriots a challenge: 'Let us dare to be ourselves!'[42] Lady Geraldine passes Glenthorn on via Lord Y— to Cecilia Devereux, Glenthorn's third Irish female companion and the deviser of a modern Anglo-Irish plot for him, thanks to which the local boy—for remember that Glenthorn is an O'Donoghoe—dares to be himself and, in this way, makes good.

Ennui represents, at one level, the successful collaboration of these three tutelary figures. Behind them stands the novelist herself. Edgeworth was already the author of novels concerned with life in Ireland (*Castle Rackrent*, 1800), France (*Madame de Fleury*, 1805), and England (*Belinda*, 1801, a novel to which we will return). She went on, in her six-volume series of novels entitled *Tales of Fashionable Life* (1809–12), to show in various ways the intermingling of the peoples of these countries and of their societies and cultures, most usually in a bilateral form: *Émilie de Coulanges* (1812) explores English responses towards French culture as represented by the aristocratic émigrés who had fled Revolutionary France for London, for example, while *The Absentee* (1812) uses a comedy about the Anglo-Irish family of an absentee landlord to analyse the cultural attitudes that both connect and divide the English and the Irish. *Ennui*, which appeared in the first volume (1809) of her *Tales of Fashionable Life*, is an important development in Edgeworth's intermingling art. The result is an unexpected creative hybrid that recalls the satirical tales of Jonathan Swift and Voltaire and the novels of Ann Radcliffe and Edgeworth's contemporaries, Germaine de Staël and Sydney Owenson, while taking the novel in English in a new and distinctive direction. For *Ennui* combines the enchanted mode of Irish Gaelic storytelling with the disenchanted mode of the French *moraliste* fable in order to rework a romance plot of changelings and conversions that is as old as English fiction.

That reworking is the expression of a creolizing art. Edgeworth starts her story of ennui from a situation marked by a fundamental asymmetry of power—England in its colonial dominance of Ireland—and then, with assistance from France, performs a transformative entanglement of cultures that furnishes the novel with a whole set of new creative possibilities.

Three More for the Road

A comprehensive study of *ennui* as a creolizing hybrid is beyond the scope of this book. My more limited aim is to explore why and how, among its fellow French émigrés, *ennui* turned English. My answer, as I hope already to have suggested, is that the residual Frenchness of *ennui* has appealed to English writers and speakers as a way of indicating how hard it is to find any language capable of expressing its meaning. *Ennui* in this guise has accompanied native English synonyms, such as *boredom* and the other words that Glenthorn drew into its bleak semantic ambit, and served to complement and complete their meanings in sentence after English sentence. As a result, it has come to be a prism through which the writers of these sentences reveal the creative processes of their work as a whole, indicating new directions for the form they practise and connecting it with other forms of expression across the creative arts.

A trio of interrelated instances suggests that *ennui* has continued to function in this way in the English-speaking world. This trio shows *ennui* in migration, shaped in its successive appearances by different contact zones between Anglophone and Francophone culture, while crossing generic borders from painting to poetry via the essay. The first of these instances, a painting entitled *Ennui* (c. 1914) by the German-born Camden Town artist Walter Sickert (1860–1942), set off a small chain reaction across the creative arts, for the Bloomsbury essayist and novelist Virginia Woolf (1882–1941) chose to write about Sickert's painting in the course of her essay *Walter Sickert: A Conversation* (1934), while the Jamaican-born poet A. L. Hendriks included a poem inspired by the painting in his 1988 collection *To Speak Simply*.

Sickert's painting depicts ennui as the mood that has engulfed a markedly ordinary English domestic scene (fig. 4). Sickert realized several versions of the painting, including one in a large format now owned by the Tate, and a later and smaller reworking in the collection of the Ashmolean Musueum (Oxford). Hendriks, in a footnote to his poem, describes Sickert's *Ennui* in the following succinct terms: 'The picture shows a man and a woman in the corner section of a twentieth-century middle-class parlour. The two people are looking in opposite directions; they have turned their backs on one another.' The intimate mutual isolation of the man and woman suggests that they are many years unhappily married. Both appear to be in their sixties. The man leans back in a chair, pulls indolently on a cigar, and gazes vacantly into his self-absorption; the woman stands with her elbows down on a chest of drawers, one hand

FIG. 4. Walter Richard Sickert, *Ennui*, 1917–18. Oil on canvas. Image
© Ashmolean Museum, University of Oxford, WA1940.1.92.

supporting her head, and dejectedly faces the wall. The décor, all faded browns and sickly yellows, encloses the two figures as surely as the glass domed bell-jar standing on the chest of drawers entraps the stuffed birds it contains. The painting in the background of a bare-shouldered female figure, an idealized representation of some goddess, seems entirely removed from the drab scene over which she presides. A decanter on the mantelpiece contains some remnants of port or claret in which neither the husband nor his wife seeks temporary solace. A beer glass stands on the table in the foreground. It offers no promise of alcoholic cheer to anyone seeking just one, let alone three, more for the road. It contains what looks like water in a measure that, in the circumstances, you could only describe as half empty rather than half full. In that beer glass, half filled with nothing other than cold water, Sickert provides English *ennui* with its visual emblem.[43]

His painting enters into dialogue with its predecessors in the literary and visual arts. He had read depictions of ennui in nineteenth-century French realist novels—by Balzac, Flaubert, and Émile Zola (1840–1902)—and made of these an English painting. Some of the painting's early critics drew the same parallel: one, for example, saw in *Ennui* 'the quintessence of a Balzac translated into paint'.[44] Others associated it with the painterly movement that came to be known as the 'London impressionism', of which Sickert was a leading member, and which aimed—in emulation of its Parisian counterpart—to capture beauty in all parts of a complex city. Sickert had claimed to dislike 'impressionism' as a label, but concluded that it was 'useless to protest', and so came to 'use it like everybody else'.[45] The label certainly helps, given its French provenance and its use in this period in respect of the literary as well as the visual arts, to situate Sickert's work. Sickert had lived in Paris in the years 1898–1906 and was a friend and admirer of the impressionist painter Edgar Degas (1834–1917) and the post-impressionist painter Maurice Asselin (1882–1947). He wrote about them and other French artists of the age, such as Maurice Denis (1870–1943), with a contagious enthusiasm and in a distinctly Frenchified English.

Sickert's appreciations of his French counterparts illuminate his choices in *Ennui* of subject matter, style, and execution. He celebrated Denis's ability to 'tell his story like Balzac', in other words, 'with relentless impartiality' and by making it 'dense with suggestion and refinement'. These were abilities that Sickert displayed in his painting. His decision to entitle it *Ennui*—an émigré word we cannot assume either of the painting's subjects would necessarily know—created a productive distance between those subjects and the artwork that captures, in a single moment, their inner emptiness. Sickert wrote appreciatively about Degas's choice of a single word for the title of *L'Absinthe* (c. 1876, Musée d'Orsay, Paris), concluding that 'Degas measures the exact range of a word as carefully and as unerringly as he does that of a line or tone'.[46] He brought Degas's insight to bear on the execution of the painting in which he measures visually the exact semantic range of *ennui*. The choice of a title for any painting draws the painter, of course, into verbal language. Sickert argued in a 1910 essay that the visual 'language of art' was irreducible to words: 'The real subject of a picture or drawing is the plastic facts it succeeds in conveying', he insisted, such that 'if the subject of a picture could be stated in words there had been no need to paint it'. At the same time, he expressed sadness at what he perceived to be the 'hostility' of English literary culture towards painting, and as a painter asserted his belief that visual and literary artists had much to say to one another: 'We believe our thoughts, which are not verbal thoughts, would be as interesting to them, are in fact as necessary to them, as theirs are interesting and necessary to us.'[47]

Virginia Woolf took up that assertion and responded to *Ennui* in her short conversational essay, of 1934, on Sickert. She purports to have fashioned her piece out of the reported dinner-party conversation of seven or eight friends who have recently seen the painter's work shown at a London gallery. Her diners start from and return to the belief, also expressed by Sickert in his 1910 essay, that, as one of Woolf's speakers puts it, 'painting and writing have much to tell each other'. The companions experiment with different literary analogies for Sickert's character as a painter. They quote, by way of justification, one of his pronouncements about himself: 'I have always been a literary painter, thank goodness, like all the decent painters.' One declares him to be a biographer and asserts, 'Not in our time will anyone write a life as Sickert paints it.' Another argues that Sickert 'always seems more of a novelist than a biographer', and likens him to the realist novelists. The similarity resides in the kind of story that his paintings tell, in which each of the figures 'has been seized in a moment of crisis', meaning that 'it is difficult to look at them and not to invent a plot'.[48]

It is when reading Sickert in this way, as a realist novelist working in paint, that Woolf's diner alludes to the Ashmolean *Ennui*:

> You remember the picture of the old publican, with his glass on the table before him and a cigar gone cold at his lips, looking out of his shrewd little pig's eyes at the intolerable wastes of desolation in front of him? A fat woman lounges, her arm on a cheap yellow chest of drawers, behind him. It is all over with them, one feels. The accumulated weariness of innumerable days has discharged its burden on them. They are buried under an avalanche of rubbish. In the street beneath, the trams

are squeaking, children are shrieking. Even now somebody is tapping his glass impatiently on the bar counter. She will have to bestir herself; to pull her heavy, indolent body together and go and serve him. The grimness of that situation lies in the fact that there is no crisis; dull minutes are mounting, old matches are accumulating and dirty glasses and dead cigars; still on they must go, up they must get.[49]

Woolf in this passage takes up the invitation, which her diner sees in the painting, to exercise the novelist's licence and 'invent a plot'. It is the plot of ennui, brought to a halt by the 'accumulated weariness of innumerable days', the temporal disorder identified by Jankélévitch. Sickert's execution of that plot, another speaker adds, makes 'beauty and order prevail' in the 'other world', that of pictorial representation, of which the publican 'is mysteriously a part without knowing it'. Persuaded of this view, Woolf's companions come to see Sickert as having recreated in pictorial form not the idiom of the novel so much as the heightened language of poetry, and to count him among 'the poets who have kept close to the earth, to the house, to the sound of the natural human voice'. Sickert, we might say, is a poet of common life: that life whose central processes I have suggested are the stuff of keywords.[50]

He is, more specifically, the poet of English ennui. Woolf, meanwhile, discreetly establishes herself as its essayist. Even as her speakers find that 'painting and writing have much to tell each other', they keep reiterating that the two arts 'must part in the end', because 'there is a zone of silence in the middle of every art' and, in particular, 'a great stretch of silent territory in Sickert's pictures'.[51] That zone of silence is not one that language can ever hope adequately to fill when it has been heightened into poetry or formalized as criticism. Language can do more, perhaps, when it has been given the freedom to play in the space of the Woolfian essay, that hybrid art of conversation and meditation, that 'sunny margin where the arts flirt and joke and pay each other compliments'. Sickert, the self-avowed literary painter, is a fitting subject for an essay because, like the essay form as Woolf practises it, he is a 'hybrid'—mixed by birth and cosmopolitan of mind—and one of those who 'are always making raids into the lands of others'. One of Sickert's most prodigious raids took him into the territory of *ennui* and, in her essay, Woolf offers herself as his literary companion.[52]

A. L. Hendriks undertook a quite different raid into the territory of Sickert's painting in a short poem, entitled 'Ennui', which Hendriks included in his 1988 collection *To Speak Simply*. With a nod to the painter's London impressionism, perhaps, Hendriks describes the poem in an accompanying footnote as having been 'written upon reflecting on *impressions* received from [. . .] Sickert's painting with the same title'.[53] Hendriks (Michael Arthur Lemière [1922–92]) was a decade or less older than two of his fellow Anglophone Caribbean writers, the poet Derek Walcott (1930–2017) and the novelist V. S. Naipaul (1932–2018), who spent much of their working lives in Britain (Naipaul) and the US (Walcott) making literature of the African, Asiatic, and European elements that combined variously in the societies and cultures of the Caribbean islands of their birth and upbringing (St Lucia, in the case of Walcott; Trinidad, in the case of Naipaul). Hendriks by no means achieved the same recognition in his lifetime as these two Nobel laureates in literature. Yet Hendriks, a Jamaican-born writer and broadcaster who divided much of his adult life between Britain and the US, may be said to have much in common with Walcott and Naipaul in respect of his life's geographical trajectory and of his work's contribution to the 'creolizing imaginary', in Stuart Hall's phrase, of modern and contemporary Caribbean literature. Hendriks, who was of Jamaican and (on his mother's side) French parentage and for a period of his life lived in Paris, added more French elements into the mix and mingle of his work than either Walcott or Naipaul. In poems such as the long sequence, 'D'où Venons Nous? Que Sommes Nous? Où Allons Nous?', which appears in *To Speak Simply*, Hendriks works French phrases (starting with those of his poem's title) into elliptical lines of free-form English verse to produce a meditative vision that starts and ends with a plunge into light.[54]

The poet treats *ennui* in similarly mixed fashion in *To Speak Simply*. Like Anglophone artists before and since, Hendriks connects *ennui* with native synonyms such as *boredom* to create creole hybrids, which he places between language and the silent zone beyond language. The first poem in *To Speak Simply*, 'The Construction of Cities', asks what expectations early humans brought to their making of urban settlements. It finds these to have been 'an old lure' and 'a mirage of comforts / Blossoming out of wasteplaces and deserts / To cosset and assuage the heart's cold stone'. They were a mirage, the poet concludes, because 'What we found was boredom, middleclass discomforts / Beyond our imagining: a kind of bland despair'.[55]

Hendriks returns by another route, in 'Ennui', to the poetry of defeated expectation and of boredom, discomfort, and despair. The poem states its case in seven stanzas of clipped verse:

> The sufficient is not enough,
> Nor is total absolute.
> I cannot know what fills your stuff;
> Soul, mind, body; no one's that astute.
>
> What rings us though is loss,
> The attitude to failure;

That's what signs to us, that dross
Is more to us than gold in future;

We value it more
Because it's really ours
Won by vain attempt; or
Perhaps better, like those tided shores

Where we all live once, alone
Trying to float small craft carven
Of wood, and laden with impossible stone
We have resolutely graven.

The sufficient then, leaves us
Anxious, empty, forsaken;
While enough deceives us,
And like total cannot be taken.

Is all, in the end, another person
Thinking in a small room
About the absolute of doom.
Even valiantly, when light must darken?

That is like the illusory black after lightning,
Fooling the eyes when the bright flash is spent,
When what we really need is more excitement
Even if frightening.[56]

There are echoes here of Pascal, the religious dissector of ennui, and of Baudelaire, the poet of reverse alchemy, who makes dross of gold. There are, however, no strains of Woolf's essay. In contrast to the conversational sociability of Woolf's essayistic prose, there is a bleak economy to Hendriks's poetic diction, an elliptical quality which adds an underspecified complexity to the poet's avowed intention, as in the title of his selection, 'to speak simply'. Hendriks's elliptical poetic expression is perhaps more akin to the pictorial language of Sickert's *Ennui*: it creates silent territory of its own—in the spaces surrounding the stanzas on the page—and thereby invites us to read it for a plot in which the speaker of the poem comes into voice. Sickert's composition provides the characters in the drama, of course, but the poem does not assign its utterance to any of them in particular. It leaves us wondering, in other words, who is speaking. Perhaps more than one person voices the poem in turn: the poem certainly leaves open that possibility. At any given moment, however, we seem to be hearing one voice speaking. Its most likely owners would appear to be the man or the woman hemmed into that small room. But there is also the figure of the poet to consider and, indeed, that of the painter. Nor may we overlook the possibility that Ennui itself, that creole hybrid of a dainty monster, is murmuring in the darkness that follows a flash of light.

CHAPTER SIX

Caprice

caprice, *n.*

Etymology: < (after 1660) French *caprice*, Italian *capriccio*: see CAPRICCIO *n.*, and CAPRICH *n.*, which both preceded this.

—*OXFORD ENGLISH DICTIONARY*

I had [. . .] a hundred thousand pounds, or more; and twice as many caprices.

—MARIA EDGEWORTH

CAPRICE EMBODIES DEVIATION in—and deviation of—language: it represents, we might say, a queer turn of events. The French word entered English in Dryden's *Marriage À-la-Mode* (1673) to mark a sexual *frisson* for the play's resident female Frenchified fop. As we have already seen, Melantha is betrothed to Palamede while amorously entangled with Rhodophil, whereas Doralice, who is married to Rhodophil, is conducting a flirtation with Palamede. Act 4 sees the lovers meet during a masquerade. The women have disguised themselves as young men and each has revealed her identity to her lover alone. Enter *caprice*. The scene is a titillation of transgressive desire. The men, who are friends, betray homosexual as well as heterosexual extramarital fantasies and, in particular, express their desire to cheat, each on the other, in plain sight of his unsuspecting friend. Palamede, looking over at Rhodophil, whispers to Doralice: 'I will storm the Out-works of Matrimony even before his face.' By then, Rhodophil has already shared with Melantha 'the oddest thought' he is having about Palamede, which is what fun it will be 'to cheat him when he looks upon us'. Melantha replies: 'This is the strangest *caprice* in you.'[1]

Melantha is, as ever, deliberately Frenchifying in her choice of language. There were ways to couch Palamede's *caprice* in current English words. Cotgrave provided plenty of synonyms for the French noun in 1611. These are: 'A humor, caprichio, giddie thought, fantasticall conceit; a suddaine will, desire, or purpose to doe a thing, for which one hath no (apparent) reason.'[2] It is striking that Cotgrave includes the French word's Italian cousin, *capriccio*, among the lexical choices available to speakers wishing to translate *caprice* into English at the turn of the seventeenth century. This inclusion is confirmed by other sightings of that Italian migrant in early modern English, which spells the word with various degrees of adaptation, ranging from the unaltered *capriccio* to the entirely adapted *capriciousness* via partially adapted forms, *caprich* and *caprichio*, whose spelling also reflects the influence of Spanish *capricho*. Melantha was therefore deliberately bringing French *caprice* into a continental mix. In so doing, she anticipated the future course of English, since the word has since gone on to name a thousand capricious things in that language while keeping a residual Frenchness at the level of its pronunciation (with the stress falling on the second syllable whose close front unrounded vowel, or long *e*, means that *caprice* rhymes with English *fleece* or the city of Nice).[3] Melantha did not cause the

French émigré to oust its Italian cousin; far from it: the two words continue to be used in English today and receive separate entries in the major works of English lexicography. *Caprice* and *capriccio*, along with their shared adjective *capricious* and other associated words, functioned as a lexical contact zone in which early modern English users brought ideas and cultural forms from several of their dominant continental neighbours into a mutually constituting entanglement that continues to this day.

That entanglement of ideas and forms includes not just the giddy thoughts and apparently irrational motions of will of which Cotgrave speaks, but also the turn of mind that produces these in people and animals; and it detects similarly whimsical behaviour as a characteristic of natural forces. Joseph Glanvill speaks, for example, of the 'shifts, windings, and unexpected caprichios of distressed nature' in the preface to his 1665 essay in sceptical philosophy, *Scepsis Scientifica*, which Johnson quotes in his entry for the noun.[4] *Caprice* and *capriccio* also describe forms of creative practice that share the same winding and whimsical characteristics: the early modern English lexicographers Edward Phillips and Nathan Bailey note, for example, that these terms are used to name (in Phillips's words) 'pieces of Musick, Poetry, and Painting, in which the force of Imagination goes beyond the Rules of Art'.[5] The idea of a sudden and pleasurable deviation from the norm, which Melantha calls a *caprice* in her lover, returns here embedded within an entire culture of imaginative and irregular creativity in which the composer, the poet, and the painter collaborate and compete with one another.

Caprice and *capriccio* feature in English and other European languages both as twinned examples of that culture and as its key linguistic expression. To focus on one of the words to the exclusion of the other—to overlook *capriccio*, say, in a single-minded pursuit of *caprice* as a French word that turned English—would therefore be to overlook the multi-transcultural creolizing hybridity that lends these words their purchase and pungency in Anglophone settings.

We have already seen this creolizing hybridity at work in the history of other French words that turned English. In this respect as well as others, *caprice* offers a fitting final choice of émigré, an emblematic instance of that particular category of English keywords. *Caprice* carries with it the web of connotations—of fashionable poise, modern gallantry, access to literature and learning, and a cultural prestige born of political power—that surrounds with pain and possibility the Anglophone reception of all the émigrés explored in this book. Like them, again, *caprice* possesses specific differences of meaning in English within its semantic field. It is more commonly used than *capriccio*, for example, to describe an alluring or frivolous deviation of behaviour (where *capriccio* tends to portray that deviation in darker and more disturbing tones). The words have rather different material referents. *Capriccio* has lent its name, in Italian restaurants all over the English-speaking world, to a popular pizza topping (treat yourself if you can, dear reader, to a *pizza alla capricciosa* followed by apple pie à la mode in celebration of migrant words in English and their accompanying culinary pleasures). *Caprice*, by contrast, is sometimes used to refer to a broad-ribboned scarf.[6] You need only picture a figure of indeterminate gender called Caprice wearing that flowing scarf—its broad ribbon breaking into a wavy line—to emblematize *caprice* in visual form. For *caprice* is unique among its cognates and synonyms in existing as a proper name, and a gender-crossing one, moreover.

These various differences lend the word a set of creative possibilities that—in the course of a cartwheeling tour—we will see activated and reactivated by Anglophone writers (of more than one country) all the way from John Dryden in the 1670s to George Bowering in the 1980s via Maria Edgeworth in the 1800s. The word has not only acquired creative possibilities in the course of its migrations, indeed, but—as the case of *capriccio* in 1940s Germany confirms—has come to be synonymous with creativity itself as a surprising and innovative deviation from the norm. When viewed in this way, *caprice* may be said to act as a figure for émigrés as a whole; for, that is, those words that come into the language from outside and turn it in new and unexpected directions.

Sheep and Goats

Caprice, by the time Dryden's Melantha coaxed it into an English sentence of the early 1670s, was already rising to prominence as a modern French keyword. Writers of French treated it in ways that confirm much of what has already been said of a period in French history marked by the transfer westwards, to Paris, of cultural as well as imperial power. They were the inheritors of a language and culture of capriciousness shaped by Italian and Spanish artists and scientists. But they sought to make of it something at once quintessentially French, and modern. They differed amongst themselves, in relation to *caprice* as to so many other things, about the legitimacy of this process of cultural appropriation and about its chances of success: *caprice* became, then, another site of the conflict between the Ancients and Moderns, and between the godly and the gallant, in late seventeenth-century France.

All of this may be glimpsed in the entries that *caprice* receives in the great monolingual French dictionaries of the period. Furetière reveals that *caprice* started life in French as one of the Italian words that, as we saw earlier, entered the language in droves in the second half of the sixteenth century. He does this obliquely by commenting that 'the word *caprice* was new in the time of Henri Estienne and seemed strange to him'. Henri Estienne was the author of a well-known work of 1578, *Deux Dialogues* (Two Dialogues), which railed against the excessive Italianization of contemporary French courtly language and manners. Estienne singles out as an example of this the importation, into French, of *capriccio* as *caprice*, and offers alternatives, some of them homegrown and others taken from ancient Greek and therefore—for a humanist like Estienne—of more dignified derivation.[7]

The range of meanings and associations that Italian *capriccio* and its Spanish cognate possessed made the journey, with *caprice*, into French. Furetière and his rivals in the Académie française, like Estienne, define the word as meaning a sudden deviation of thought or behaviour from reasonable norms. In his 1684 French translation of the 1647 book of maxims that the Spanish Jesuit author Baltasar Gracián (1601–58) devoted to the art of worldly wisdom, Amelot de la Houssaye (1634–1706) made *caprice* key to Gracián's verbal portrait of the rash disposition of those who act without due circumspection, in which the author quips that the surest way to rid oneself of such obdurately wilful 'monsters' is to head to the opposite ends of the earth.[8]

Seventeenth-century European society was dominated by adult males who appointed themselves as the judges of which behavioural norms were reasonable and identified other groups as only too likely to deviate from those norms. These groups included children and others under the sway of an unruly will; artists and others prey to the power of the imagination; and— possibly the most deviant of all—women, the rationality of whose behaviour was seen as undermined by the unpredictable dictates now of the will, now of the imagination, and often of both. These groups surface time and again among the examples of capricious behaviour given in works of early modern European lexicography. Those examples are not always cast, however, in a negative light. The ambivalent language of caprice could serve, as it still can, the purposes of praise as well as blame. Furetière and the Académie française distinguish between positive and negative meanings of the word, as well as between its uses in respect of social behaviour and of cultural creativity.

These distinctions overlap in the definitional space the dictionaries afford *caprice*. Both dictionaries perceive the word to have negative meanings when it is applied to social behaviour that goes against all reasonable norms. In such cases, it is 'a disorder of the mind', says Furetière. These uses of the word continue to this day in French: frustrated parents and others commonly berate children for the *caprices* or temper tantrums that go against the sweet reason the adults implicitly claim to enjoy.[9] The Académie française and Furetière both portray *caprice* as potentially positive in its meaning when it is used to describe the flash of imaginative wit at the heart of cultural creativity: in this case, says the Académie française, 'it may be taken in good part'.[10] The implication here is that it may be, but need not, since some might see the artist working in fits and starts as no more than a child who has refused to grow up. One person's fancy might be another's folly. *Caprice* admits of such reversals of perspective, and early modern French dictionaries make this plain, capturing the ambivalence of the word by setting out first its negative sense and then its polar opposite.

The word carries its ambivalent meanings in the company of a veritable bestiary. That there was felt to be something animal about caprice is hardly surprising. Animals were widely held to lack entirely the faculty of human reason and so offered lexicographers a conspicuous spectacle of stubborn, capering, or frolicking conduct. Animal analogies could serve, again, to praise or blame that conduct as replicated by humans.

Furetière observed that the adjective *capricieux* applied to humans and animals alike, and offered the example of an unpredictable mule. That mule joined the host of other animals that recurred—and still do—in accounts of the origins of the *caprice* family of terms. The etymologist Julia Cresswell has argued that *capriccio* was formed from the combination of two Italian words, *capo* ('head') and *riccio* ('hedgehog'), to reflect the sensation of hair standing on end—the 'hedgehog-head'—produced by horror or some other sudden emotion. Over time, she suggests, *capriccio* came to mean 'a sudden start, a sudden change', perhaps influenced by the Latin word *caper* ('goat'). Creswell here ushers in the frolicking goat whose Italian name—*capro* (male) and *capra* (female)—was widely seen to be at the origin of *capriccio* and related words in early modern Europe.[11] In a medical treatise of 1575, which was translated into many languages, including English in two versions (1594 and 1698), the Spanish physician Juan Huarte de San Juan exploited the goatish etymology of the Italian adjective *capriccioso*: 'The Inventive Wits are termed in the *Tuscan* Tongue *Capritious*, for the resemblance they bear to a goat, who takes no pleasure in the open and easy Plains, but loves to Caper along the Hill-tops, and upon the Points of Precipices, not caring for the beaten Road, or the Company of the Herd.' Furetière used his mule to exemplify a negative capriciousness. Huarte de San Juan, by contrast, separated the sheep from the goats in order to identify as positively capricious the characteristics that set 'inventive wits' apart from the other types of human mind.[12]

Huarte de San Juan was contributing to a European-wide discussion across the arts and sciences about the scope and nature of human ingenuity. The publication of his treatise marks the key moment in the story when *caprice* enters stage left, accompanied by the goats, to stir things up. The word does this by specifying ingenuity as rule-breaking and innovative—

in a word, capricious—inventiveness. In the association of ingenuity with Spanish *capricho*, as Marr, Garrod, Marcaida, and Oosterhoff put it in their word history of ingenuity, 'we begin to see [...] the gradual convergence of certain characteristics—loftiness, whim, inventiveness—around certain social types: writers and artists. In other linguistic contexts, e.g., English, this shift would soon be articulated using the language of genius'.[13]

French provides another such linguistic context, and a significant mediating one for English culture, for all the reasons already given. Furetière, in his entry on *caprice*, defines the word, in its positive sense, as referring to a product of inventive wit: the word, he says, is used of 'pieces of poetry, music, and painting that succeed thanks to the power of wit [*la force du génie*] rather than through observance of the rules of art, and which have no settled name'. This definition of *caprice* places it firmly in the vocabulary of the Moderns in their Quarrel with the Ancients. *Caprice* was a modern French name for the Modern attitude which said that the rules of art were there to be bent ingeniously out of shape and that, while the sheep followed the straight lines of classical form, the goats would trace capering lines of their own invention. It lent a name to these creations as well as to the underlying spirit of irregular invention whence they sprang. Furetière mentions three examples of such creations: he observes that the poet Saint-Amant (1594–1661) entitled some of his works Caprices; he invokes the caprices of the engraver and printmaker Jacques Callot (1592–1635); and he says—though without naming any of their composers—that there are 'caprices in music'.[14]

Musicians were, indeed, among the first artists to make *caprice* define a spirit of invention. The historian of art David Rosand has shown this in an expansive history of *capriccio* and its cognates. Rosand quotes the German music theorist Michael

Prætorius's 1619 definition of the term as meaning a 'sudden whim' [*phantasia subitanea*]:

> One takes a subject, but abandons it for another whenever it comes into the mind to do so. One can add, take away, digress, turn, and direct the music as one wishes, but while one is not bound strictly by the rules, one ought not to go too much out of the mode.[15]

To be capricious, in Prætorius's terms, the piece needs to take the player and the listener on a hill-top journey, not into free form, but towards and away from a mode of music that is familiar. It will be 'based upon the very compositional conventions that it undermines', as Rosand says, if it is to produce its effect. It will rapidly pass through more than one mode—and vary its themes—in its capering search for form.[16]

Artists working in visual media soon turned, also, to the language of caprice when promoting an art of fancifully combining and varying themes to surprising effect. Jacques Callot, the exemplary figure named by Furetière, was an engraver and printmaker from Lorraine who learned and practised his craft in Italy. Callot first published in Florence, in 1617, a series of fifty small etchings entitled *Capricci di varie figure*. These were a combination of disparate themes, including cityscapes and battle scenes, the artist's variations on which enabled him to show off, as Rosand puts it, his 'inventiveness as a designer and his skill as a printmaker'. To etching, a medium that enabled rapidity of execution, Callot appeared to bring an equal rapidity of capricious invention.[17]

He elevated that invention to become a theme of his work by finding ways of suddenly drawing the spectator's attention to the artistic illusion that the etching creates. In one of the 1617 *capricci*, 'La Promenade' ('The Promenade'), Callot com-

FIG. 5. Jacques Callot, 'The Promenade', in *Capricci di varie figure* (Rome: Calisto Ferrante, [1617]), [29ʳ]. Etching on paper. Courtesy National Gallery of Art, Washington.

pletes a view of a landscape with a distant city by adding two viewers (fig. 5). These are an elegant gentleman and lady who may, we surmise, be fashionable residents of or émigré visitors to the city. They occupy the entire right-hand side of the etching and frame the work for the spectator insofar as we watch them, from behind, contemplating the scene.

A later example of Callot's capricious art is *L'Éventail* (*The Fan*) (1619). It commemorates a mock battle staged each year on the river Arno between Florence's guilds of weavers and of dyers (fig. 6). Once again, Callot not only represents that carnivalesque urban scene, but makes his representation part of the scene. He chooses the fan as his artistic medium, peopling its frame with a motley collection of figures who are witnessing the scene from afar, one of whom is holding up just such a

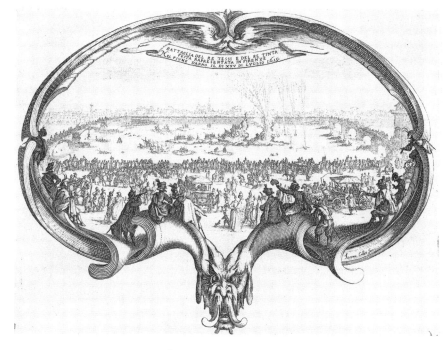

FIG. 6. Jacques Callot, *The Fan*, 1619. Etching and engraving on paper. Courtesy National Gallery of Art, Washington.

fan—perhaps, we can only imagine, a copy of the very fan that is before our eyes. This fan, meanwhile, is itself looking back at us: the scene portrayed is supported by the curvaceous horns of some hoary god, whose head forms the base of the fan, and who is fixing us with a beady stare. Perhaps, we surmise, this is a capricious god who has dreamt up the whole representation— invented it—on a whim. If so, then the god has succeeded in depicting a day of celebration in the life of a city, while also causing us to stand back from the depiction and observe both the manner of its making and our consumption of it as its be-dazzled spectators. As we watch, so are we watched watching, an interactive process that the etching makes visible. The capriciousness of Callot lies precisely, as the art critic and literary historian Louis Marin has said, in the flowing lines of connection the artist traces between the matter and manner of his work, by representing the pleasures and miseries of human life even as he draws attention to the opaque surface of that representation, to its artistry, to its power of invention. The graphic line, in Callot's work, no sooner meets *caprice* than it breaks into a wave, turns inward and outward, visibly goes beyond the rules of art.[18]

Callot set a pattern for later seventeenth- and eighteenth-century artists working in the capricious visual tradition, such as Salvator Rosa (1615–73), Giovanni Battista Tiepolo (1696–1770) and his son Domenico (1727–1807), and—perhaps most famously of all—Francisco Goya (1746–1828). All of these artists inflected *caprice* to their own ends, at times emphasizing its playful whimsicality, at others portraying its bristling horror. All drew attention to the nature of the artistic illusion. All sought, not merely to congratulate themselves on their artistry, but to test out its powers on a knowing public that had been taught to value the power of wit over observance of the rules.[19]

So did French writers. *Caprice* emerges, as we have seen, in the midst of the controversy surrounding sixteenth-century French lexical borrowing from Italian. It expands in scope, towards the end of the century, in Montaigne's *Essais*, whose composition is characterized by a free movement in and out of familiar literary modes—the letter, the dialogue, and so on—in the informal space of the essay.[20] It comes to prominence, as I have already suggested, at a time when the seventeenth-century Ancients and Moderns of French literary culture were drawing up the battlelines. Pierre Corneille, arch-Modern in the theatre, drew on the term to defend, publicly, one of his most notoriously genre-bending works, *L'Illusion comique* (*The Theatrical Illusion*) of 1636, which uses the device of a play-within-a-play to combine tragic and comic elements in a demonstration of modern theatre's power to disturb and surprise. Emphasizing its 'bizarre and extravagant invention', as well as its novelty, Corneille described it as a 'capricious play' [*pièce capricieuse*] and a pleasing one for that.[21]

One might look to *caprice*, also, to account for the irregular wit of eighteenth-century prose fiction, as pioneered in English by Laurence Sterne (1713–68), and in French by Sterne's admirer, Denis Diderot (1713–84). Like Sterne's novel *Tristram Shandy*, Diderot's novel *Jacques le fataliste et son maître* (*Jacques the Fatalist and his Master*) simultaneously awakens in its reader the desire for a single line of narrative, and frustrates that desire by wantonly multiplying its storylines and wilfully veering off course at every opportunity.

To trace here a capricious history of experimental French writing, though, would be to wander, goatlike, from the path we have chosen to follow in pursuit of *caprice* across cultures. Let us return, instead, to the sole exemplary figure in the French poetry of caprice that Furetière chooses to name in his entry for that term: Saint-Amant. This now largely forgotten Normandy poet merits inclusion in the dictionary, for he provides a close parallel in poetry to the caprices that Furetière identifies in Callot's engravings and in music. Like Callot, Saint-Amant uses the word as a title under which to gather a combination of disparate themes, including—in the poet's 1643 *Œuvres* and in his later works of the 1640s—a failed melon crop, a sleepless night in grotty lodgings, the pungent delights of Cantal cheese, a naval battle that did not happen, the return to fashion of a poetic form, the lameness of his horse, the relaxing powers of wine, the joy of cider, the risible spectacle of

Rome, the pain of venereal disease, and the perfidy of Albion. Saint-Amant foregrounds the ingenuity of invention involved in this capricious combination in such a way as to make it, at moments, the theme of the work. Here, too, there is a direct parallel with the work Callot does to lure the spectator's attention away from the ostensible matter of his engraving to its inventive manner. Yet Saint-Amant is working with language, not pictorial image, and with the poetic line rather than the graphic one. The poet must find other means of drawing the eye of the beholder to the caprice of invention that lies behind the title of his poems. He varies the length of his poetic line and its arrangement on the page to reveal the process of poetic invention. He mixes poetic forms into surprising combinations, as Corneille (whom he admired) did in the theatre, and he usually performs this mixture by rapidly passing—as do the composers—from one form to another within the same composition. He comments on what he is doing either in the paratextual space surrounding his poems or inside the poems themselves. He creates caprices within caprices as he moves across cultures.[22]

Saint-Amant's 1643 poetic account of the naval battle that did not happen, 'Le Passage de Gibraltar' (Passing through Gibraltar), is a case in point. It celebrates the expedition of French naval forces led by the poem's dedicatee Henri de Lorraine, count of Harcourt (1601–66), to wrest from the Spanish the small Provençal islands of Sainte-Marguerite and Saint-Honorat (off Cannes). The French expected to encounter the amassed might of the Spanish navy on their passage through the strait of Gibraltar, but met not even a fishing boat, thus creating for Saint-Amant ideal material for what he terms, in the poem's subtitle, a 'Heroicomic Caprice'. The poet duly mixes the heroic with the comic, inflating and deflating his subject along the way, listing in detail the French boats engaged in the non-action and anticipating the future repossession of the islands while passing freely through various poetic modes and moods to end with a drinking song in celebration of a day spent spilling wine rather than blood. The subtitle is only the first of the paratextual spaces in which he draws attention to the poem's Modern irregularity of invention. The second is a prefatory prose 'Argument'. Like French practitioners of caprice in the pictorial and musical arts, Saint-Amant had learned much from the Italians, and he fills the 'Argument' with praise of Alessandro Tassoni (1565–1635) for his mock-heroic poem *La secchia rapita* (The stolen bucket) of 1622. Saint-Amant says that, by whimsically mixing two opposed poetic spirits, the heroic and the comic, Tassoni wrought effects that are extraordinarily difficult to reproduce, and which Saint-Amant then claims to have successfully imported into French poetry. 'Le Passage de Gibraltar' is an example of that importation and an advertisement of the poet's capricious French style: it encapsulates his variations of line length and register, as well as of theme, and his passing from the decorous mode of *galanterie* to the libertine in a performance of inventive poetic wit.[23]

Once he has established caprice as a modern French vehicle for such wit, Saint-Amant travels freely in it across Europe, mocking the squalor of present-day Rome (where he saw military service) in *La Rome ridicule* (Risible Rome) and attacking the barbarity of Protestant England (where he sojourned) in *Albion*. There is a keener edge to the satirical treatment of contemporary culture in these later and longer poetic exercises. They nevertheless recall Saint-Amant's earlier experiments in the art of caprice and his metapoetic reflections on that art. These are most visible in the 1643 poem in which Saint-Amant laments the recent return to fashion of a fixed poetic form, the *rondeau*, which the poet's contemporary Vincent Voiture (1597–1648) had rescued from the annals of medieval and Renaissance French poetry and made the subject of high fashion among the literary practitioners of French *galanterie*. This is a poem about poetry, then, and more specifically a caprice about caprice. It starts with a lament for the various poetic forms that the *rondeau* has supplanted. First of these is the caprice, which—with its capacity for pictorial representation—'makes nature rut with art', and which the poet personifies as 'a godlike madman wealthy in invention, / Bizarre of word and lively of description'.[24] Part god, part goat, caprice, in Saint-Amant's freakish Pan-like personification, embodies the power of irregular invention. It is, in the words of Louis Marin, nothing less than 'poetry itself, divine madness, that sudden stroke of genius [. . .] where, by means of "impetuousness of wit" and "vehemence of spirit", the representation exceeds its own limits in the artifices of language'.[25]

Sibling Rivalries

The capricious thus capered its merry way across the languages of early modern Europe and the realms of different arts. It marked their borders by leaping over them. It captured the inventive spirit of each art in turn. The connections it sketched between poetry, music, and painting tended to take the form of parallels suggesting that, as it capriciously was in painting, so it was in poetry . . . ; and so it was in music . . . : the language of capriciousness conveyed these productive artistic parallels. So did a set of metaphors, chief among them the capering line of witty invention, and a set of personifications—animal, human, and divine—at the head of which skipped Huarte de San Juan's ever headstrong goats. French *caprice*, in the company of Italian *capriccio*, placed itself at the heart of these cross-cultural and intermedial developments.

What had yet to befall *caprice*, however, was the mingling of the inventive energies it possessed in poetry, music, and painting. The German composer Richard Strauss (1864–1949) achieved that mingling in his final operatic work. *Capriccio* (1942) is both a summation of his career and a witty development of the capricious conversation between the arts of early modern Europe. It offers a recapitulation of that conversation in its original Italo-French setting by taking an Italian title and subject and transporting these to Paris as the heartland of fashionable European culture. That I propose now to explore—in Strauss's *Capriccio*—the German afterlife of an Italian word, in order to show how a French word turned English, may appear to be a waywardly tangential course of action. But it bears out my initial observation that *caprice* and *capriccio* feature in English and other European languages as twinned examples of a culture of creativity and as key linguistic expressions of that culture.[26]

Strauss and his librettist Clemens Krauss (1893–1954) chose to call *Capriccio* not an 'opera' but—as the work's subtitle has it—*A Conversation Piece for Music in One Act by Clemens Krauss and Richard Strauss*. The work recalls those 'shorts', witty conversational pieces of theatre about theatre itself, that early modern companies staged as an accompaniment to the evening's main billing. Molière was a master of the genre: he followed his brilliant and controversial 1662 verse comedy *L'École des Femmes* (*The School for Wives*), for example, with a one-act prose *Critique* (1663) of the play in which the protagonists discussed his latest *succès de scandale*—none other, of course, than *L'École des Femmes*—in ways that enabled the playwright to defend the play against its critics and to commend it and its author to the wider public. The conventional comic plot resolutions of a wedding and a recognition scene are not available to the author of a one-act conversation piece, as a character in the *Critique* points out to the audience in the play's final flourish of self-aware wit, so the play ends with the serving of supper. So does *Capriccio*. What distinguishes *Capriccio* from Molière's *Critique* and other such theatrical exercises in witty self-awareness is that it is a conversation piece conducted in and for music. It takes its own condition of being—the relationship between words and music—and makes of this its theme. That theme is brilliantly transposed to all levels of the work and is mirrored in the subtitle, which names the librettist Krauss and the composer Strauss as the work's co-authors, thereby casting the relationship between words and music as one of creative collaboration between artists.

The theme provides *Capriccio* with a plot that adds the edge of amorous competition to that relationship of creative collaboration. The action takes place in a garden salon of a château near Paris in the late 1770s. This is a perfect setting for the portrayal of a French eighteenth-century higher society given over to *galanterie* and unperturbed by any future prospect of Revolution: the aristos command everything except their feelings, the artists seek social advancement through their art, and nothing is lost upon the servants. The Countess Madeleine, an embodiment of grace and beauty and a wealthy widow, is to celebrate her birthday. A composer, Flamand, has written a string sextet in her honour: its *andante* movement is being performed for her at the beginning of *Capriccio* and forms the work's overture. A poet, Olivier, has composed a love sonnet for her that he will shortly read to her. Both men love the Countess and are competing for her hand in marriage. They express their competition in terms of the age-old priority dispute between their sibling arts, the poet insisting that the words come first and the music follows after, the composer maintaining that the opposite is the truth. 'We're rival suitors', says one; 'Friendly opponents', says the other. 'Tune *and* words . . .', says one, '. . . are brother and sister', completes the other, their sharing of the sentence discreetly confirming the mutual dependence of their competing arts. The erstwhile slumbering theatre director, La Roche, now wakes up. He is organizing the birthday celebrations for the Countess, and plans to include music by Flamand and a drama by Olivier as well as an opus of his own. He sets to work. He reminds them that he alone can provide them not only with the décors they need, but with a home for all of the sibling arts, by combining them in a single art-form, opera.[27]

Strauss and Krauss were looking back in *Capriccio* to opera as it developed in early modern France and Italy. The Austrian writer Stefan Zweig (1881–1942) had drawn Strauss's attention to a short libretto by Giambattista Casti (1721–1803), *Prima la musica e poi le parole* (Music first and then the words), which Mozart's rival Antonio Salieri (1750–1825) had set to music, and which was first performed in Vienna in 1786. Casti's text and its reception were shaped by a distinctively French context. The 1774 première in Paris of *Iphigenia in Aulis*, an innovative opera by the Paris-based Bohemian-Austrian composer Christoph von Gluck (1714–87), gave rise to the last in a series of controversies about musical theatre in eighteenth-century France. The controversy divided supporters of Gluck and his various innovations from partisans of Niccolò Piccinni (1728–1800), the Neapolitan composer of French and Italian operas, who in late 1776 had moved to Paris. In the ensuing din, the controversy between the Gluckists and Piccinnists seemed at times to be pitting Moderns against Ancients and French opera against Italian, thereby as it were rekindling two major cultural battles of the previous century in a single conflagration. Yet, as the cultural historian Mark Darlow has shown, issues specific to the cultural life and institutions of contemporary Paris were at the heart of the controversy. These took theoretical form in the much debated question of the relative importance to opera of words and music, in response to which the Gluckists asserted the primacy of poetic drama, and the Piccinnists that of musical form.[28]

This was the question Strauss wanted to explore, and he eventually found a willing collaborator in the conductor Clemens Krauss, who produced a libretto loosely based on Casti's. Strauss and Krauss found in Casti's libretto and the surrounding Gluckist–Piccinnist controversy the makings of their opera about opera. The controversy surfaces in *Capriccio* as the talk of the town—nearby Paris—and of its cultural institutions. The theatre director, La Roche, attacks the French innovations of Gluck, ironically saluting him as 'the prophetic successor to the mighty Corneille', and prefers the Italian comic opera of a Piccinni. The Countess Madeleine, by contrast, speaks of a 'genius' who 'proves it is possible to write a musical tragedy': we are to infer that she has in mind none other than Gluck.[29] La Roche produces as an amusement for the Countess and her brother—and as an indirect reply to Madeleine—a pair of Neapolitan singers who sing a plaintive duet in the Italian style of *bel canto* that the theatre director says is being eclipsed by operatic innovation.

The controversy thus continues in the decorously gallant setting of a garden salon. It provides Strauss with the opportunity for manifold capriciousness at the level of musical form: as the talk ranges from Gluck to Piccinni and from French *tragédie lyrique* to Italian *bel canto*, the music travels with it, wittily parodying these and other musical forms and idioms as each, in turn, rises to the surface of the conversation. Strauss turns some of these musical jokes upon himself: he has the Count roundly declare that 'every opera is itself absurd', for example, to a tune recycled from the composer's own *Krämerspiegel* song cycle of 1918.[30]

The Count's sister, meanwhile, has started to see that opera might be a solution to her problems in love. No sooner has Olivier the poet begun, in Scene 4, to recite to Madeleine the love sonnet he has composed for her than Flamand the composer—not to be outdone—sits down at the keyboard and improvises a harmony to accompany the poem. The composer then reappears in Scene 6, triumphant, to perform his completed musical setting of the sonnet in front of its author and the woman they both love. Strauss, in this scene's dramatization of the encounter between words and music, succeeded in lifting *capriccio* way beyond the reach of any mere *jeu d'esprit*. He did so by taking as his text the 1555 sonnet 'Je ne sçaurois aimer autre que vous' (I could not love another, only you) by the French Renaissance master of the form, Pierre de Ronsard (1524–85), in a free German translation by the Hungarian conductor and writer Hans Swarowsky (1899–1975). In the sonnet, the poet offers his beloved the power of life and death over him by picturing her as the very blood flowing through his veins, and awaits a response that never comes. To the musical setting of the sonnet, Strauss brought all his expertise as a composer of German lieder. He adopted a basic five-bar musical pattern, so that the end of each vocal phrase corresponded with the end of each line in the poem, while freely introducing variations of rhythm and modulations of key to capture the shifting emotional purchase of the sonnet.[31]

Strauss's musical setting, which shapes the rest of the opera, is immediately reworked into a comic trio in the course of which the composer sings phrases of his setting, the poet complains that his verses have been mangled in the making of this 'seducing' song, and the Countess celebrates the intertwining therein of words to music and music to words. Finding himself suddenly alone with her, Flamand presses Madeleine to choose between the two men, and she promises that she will give them her reply the following morning at eleven o'clock.[32]

It is when faced with this dilemma, in discussion with her brother, that the Countess lights upon her solution. The arts must set aside their rivalry and unite in an opera. The poet and the composer, in collaboration with the theatre director, will thereby create for the sibling arts—of painting as well as poetry and music—'one home and one desire'. The solution was there from the beginning. One question remains: what will the opera be about? Here it is the Count—hitherto no lover of the form, as we have seen—who casually provides the artists with the inspiration to make an opera with a difference: 'Write about conflicts in our experience. Write of yourselves. Take the happenings of this afternoon—all that occurred here today—write it, and then compose it, and perform it as an opera.' The artists agree to this suggestion and disappear.[33]

Capriccio comes to a close amidst the remains of the day. The moon rises early and floods the terrace with light, accompanied by a solo horn, which plays a silvery and beauteous interlude (a further reprise of the *Krämerspiegel* song). The Countess reappears and learns that she will dine alone. Her major-domo tells her that the poet desires to pay her a visit tomorrow morning, at the appointed hour, so that she can 'tell him the ending of the opera'. Well aware that the men expect her to make a choice between their two hearts as much as their two arts, the Countess sings Olivier's sonnet in Flamand's setting, accompanying herself on the harp. She is torn. She interrupts the song to observe that it blends word and music so thoroughly as to create in her the 'mysterious experience' of 'finding one art restored by the other'. 'Deciding on either', she can see, means 'losing the other'. She looks to her mirror in vain for enlightenment. It shows her an aristocratic woman of considerable poise, wearing an evening dress no doubt fashioned after the latest French mode, but it takes her no nearer to a decision. It leaves her still in search of a *dénouement* that is not, as she says, 'trivial'. Her solution, it seems, has only displaced the problem. It is at this point that supper is served. The Countess takes her leave with a curtsy. The curtain falls. *Capriccio* has concluded in the only way it could. The opera has found no ending, yet we have just heard it in the making.[34]

A deep undercurrent of nostalgia flows through *Capriccio*. Its composer surveys a lifetime of writing music. He makes connections between the different parts of his career and the different musical forms his works have taken, and he alludes to many of the operas he has composed in the course of this, his final operatic work. He also looks back—with the close collaboration of his librettist—over the history of opera. *Capriccio* sketches opera's controversial development as a form, and re-works musical phrases by Rameau, Gluck, Rossini, Wagner, and other notable practitioners; tells of opera's patronage by the cultivated wealthy; and reveals the passion it inspires in its artists, the personal ambitions they nourish, and the storms in teacups they orchestrate. It recreates opera, in front of its audience, as a new home for the sibling arts. These are the arts that otherwise tend to caper along the hill-tops of culture until Krauss and Strauss coax them down to the garden salon of a château near Paris and into Frenchified eighteenth-century conversation.

Nostalgia for the past is more often than not, as has often been observed, the trace of a flight from the present. There is surely no more powerful illustration of this observation than the fact that Strauss and Krauss worked on the gallantries and graces of *Capriccio* in Nazi Germany during the first three years of World War II. The opera was first performed in Munich in October 1942. How different the result would have been, had Strauss and his librettist chosen to follow the advice that the Count offers the artists in *Capriccio*, and made an opera by writing about conflicts in their experience. . . .

These conflicts shaped the making of the piece in decisive, if invisible, ways. They notably caused Stefan Zweig, the writer who had first drawn Strauss's attention to Casti's libretto, to withdraw from the project. Zweig was the composer's friend and the two men had worked together on the opera *Die schweig-same Frau* (*The Silent Woman*). Its first performance, in Dresden in June 1935, took place amid political controversy. Zweig was Jewish. Since April 1933, shortly after Hitler seized total power in Germany, Jews had been barred from government employment in the country and, by September 1935, they would be forbidden from marrying non-Jews. Strauss had been made president of the Reich Music Chamber by Goebbels in November 1933 and had accepted this honorary position. He came under serious pressure to avoid being seen to work with Jews, which he resisted, securing, through Goebbels, Hitler's approval that the première of *Die schweigsame Frau* could go ahead and insisting that Zweig's name appear on the poster. Just before the première took place, it seems that Zweig told Strauss that he would not be willing to collaborate publicly with the composer on any future projects, both because he feared that to do so would do Strauss no good and because he wished, for the sake of his fellow Jews, to avoid being associated with an artist who had exposed himself politically by accepting commissions from the National Socialists.

In his written reply to Zweig, which survives, Strauss proudly declared his contempt for the anti-Semitic theory of Aryan superiority so dear to the Nazis: 'I know only two types of people: those with and those without talent.' He pleaded with Zweig to continue openly working with him and to let him manage the public relations. But he and Zweig never worked together again. The Gestapo intercepted Strauss's letter, meanwhile, and sent it to Hitler. The Nazi hierarchy punished Strauss for the sentiments it expressed by forcing him, in July 1935, to resign as president of the Reich Music Chamber for reasons of ill health. Strauss eventually found a librettist for *Capriccio* in Clemens Krauss. He continued to assert his independence as an artist from the political interference of the Nazis. He was subject to direct threats from Goebbels at a meeting in February 1942. Strauss received from other leading figures in the Nazi government—especially Hans Frank (1900–46), Reich minister of justice, and Baldur von Schirach (1907–74)—a measure of protection for his family, including his Jewish daughter-in-law Alice, and for himself. He sought and welcomed such protection. He stayed working in Germany—and composed, among other things, *Capriccio*—during a period in which many other artists fled the country or died, including Zweig, who along with his wife committed suicide in February 1942.[35]

This raises troubling questions about the artist's responsibilities, choices, and their consequences. Did the thought ever occurr to Strauss and Krauss—or, before his death, to Zweig—that the project promised to establish the equality of the arts and marry them in a symbolic new whole in a country that had recently passed a law banning marriage and criminalizing sexual relations between Jews and non-Jewish Germans? If it did, that thought remains forever beneath the unruffled surface of *Capriccio*, which appears as an exercise in pure operatic high art escapism from an intolerable present. Strauss described the work as his last operatic Testament.[36] One wonders how he could have written it.

Three Flights of Fancy

French inherited a language and culture of capriciousness shaped by Italian and Spanish artists and scientists, but then naturalized it, gradually making of *caprice* something exclusively French. By contrast, English—like German, as in the case of Strauss's *Capriccio*—has maintained a more culturally composite lexicon. This has enabled Anglophone writers to deploy *caprice* in ways that both confirm its Frenchification and call that Frenchification into question.

Eighteenth-century English dictionaries offer synonyms for *caprice* that stem from different languages: *fancy*, deriving from Greek *phantasía* via Latin; *capriccio* and *capricho*, borrowed from Italian and Spanish; *whim*, probably of Scandinavian origin; *freak*, thought to arise from English dialects; and—in a striking English addition to the continental European bestiary of capricious goats and hedgehogs—*maggot*, a word that Johnson thought might come from Welsh *magrod*, but which the *OED* thinks more likely to be an alteration of the Germanic *maddock*. In early modern English, a *maggot* can refer to a capricious action or person, and this sense survives in contemporary Irish English (at least as I hear it spoken in West Cork) where you say of people who play the fool that they are 'acting the maggot'.[37] Of these synonyms for *caprice*, Italian *capriccio* is the closest and most frequent associate in English, as has already been noted. The two often appear side by side in English sentences, as emigrant variants, and their corresponding adjectives are at the origins of the English adjective *capricious*. An early usage of *capricious* is the 1698 English translation of the Spanish physician Huarte de San Juan's witty exploitation of the goatish etymology of the Italian adjective *capriccioso* to describe the wayward caperings of the inventive wits. That sentence, quoted earlier, marks one of those moments when English visibly turned to the Romance languages of early modern Europe and their prestigious cultures of invention to nourish its own fledgling efforts.

Anglophone wits have long exploited the culturally composite lexicon of capriciousness at their disposal. They might pair the Germanic earthiness of *maggot* with the French fragrance of *caprice*; they might choose, instead, to remain within the sphere of Romance borrowings by associating *caprice* with *capriccio*; or they might cleave to a native vocabulary of the *freak* and the *whim*. Such choices enable the working of any manner of semantic effect in respect of capriciousness, its meanings, and its connotations. It has long made stylistic sense, in certain circumstances, for English writers to deviate wittily from a homegrown lexicon construed as standard and to turn to foreign-derived words in order to capture the idea of a whimsical invention that deviates from the witless norm. This is how *caprice* has been turning English ever since, it seems, Dryden's Melantha first reached for it in her surprised response to one of her lover's stranger propositions. She would never have dreamed of looking anywhere other than French for her foreign word, of course, Melantha being Melantha. It nevertheless makes broader historical sense that English culture should have turned to a French émigré, in this particular field of meaning, when one considers the long history of importing modes of French invention and impulse to England. A mixture of fear and fascination has long accompanied that history, as we have seen, and it is a characteristically ambivalent response of English culture to its émigrés to identify their pretensions even as it deploys their energies.

One form of this response, in respect of *caprice*, involves exploiting the word for what it adds to the English language while maintaining that French culture cannot be said to have invented *caprice*—despite any claim to the contrary made from across the Channel—since the Italians, for example, manifestly got there first. This is one of the ways in which English culture uses the composite lexicon at its disposal in an attempt to undermine the supremacy of its rival and erstwhile political master.

Shakespeare scored a subtle hit of this kind against the French and their *caprice* even *before* the word seems to have entered English (thus confirming what A. D. Nuttall identified as the playwright's eerie 'ability to anticipate our thoughts').[38] Shakespeare chose to set his comedy *All's Well That Ends Well* (c. 1604) in France and war-torn Tuscany. Helen secretly loves Bertram, who on the death of his father became a ward of the king of France. Helen has cured the king of a life-threatening fistula. In gratitude, the king grants Helen's wish to marry his ward, but the snobbish Bertram refuses to consummate the marriage and goes off to the Tuscan wars in the company of his braggart sidekick Parolles. Shakespeare reminds his audience periodically that these people are all French. When Parolles lets loose a flood of comic invective against the rigours of female virginity, for example, he likens virginity to 'one of our French wither'd pears'.[39] Parolles's name, alone, suggests he is entirely made of French words. Such reminders draw the audience's attention to the linguistic element of this play's dramatic illusion: we are to assume, even as we hear their conversations conducted in English, that they are in fact speaking French. This fact lends salt to the exchange in which Bertram announces his rash decision to abandon his unwanted wife and go off to the wars. 'Wars is no strife / To the dark house and the detested wife', Bertram declares, to which Parolles replies: 'Will this capriccio hold in thee, art sure?'[40] This is the earliest recorded instance to be found in the *OED* of *capriccio*; and yet we need to remember that the aptly named Parolles is speaking

French, if we are to grant our assent to the dramatic illusion. We are to draw the inference, then, that the French, too, sometimes need to reach for a foreign word—in this case, a linguistic representative of Bertram's declared destination, Italy—when, in their surprise, the normal words fail them. In a flight of theatrical fancy, then, Shakespeare both introduces his audience to *capriccio* as a synonym for French *caprice* and puts the French in their place.

Caprice has gone on to distinguish itself from its cognates and synonyms. More headstrong goat than horrified hedgehog or freakish maggot, it remains a foreignism in English, albeit less conspicuously so than *capriccio*. It is unique among its cognates and synonyms in having emerged as a proper name. The most famous living wearer of the name is probably Caprice Bourret (b. 1971), an American businesswoman, model, and actress, who in 2006 launched a lingerie range carrying her name ('By Caprice'), then expanded her business into home goods, which in 2018 she was planning—as her personal website puts it—'to launch in multiple global territories' while 'developing the core product range'.[41] Her example speaks for itself in the contemporary world of economic globalization. There are other Caprices who have a central part to play in our story, however, since they are to be numbered among those artists—the composers, poets, and painters—who have put the imaginative wit the name betokens to altogether more capricious purposes than the core ranges and rules of a global business could ever allow.

In what follows, I shall concentrate on two Caprices, one of them in name and both of them in nature. Their flights of fancy extend the Anglophone migrations of *caprice* along lines that I have sought to trace in respect of each of the émigrés at the heart of this book. Where Shakespeare's witticism in *All's Well* belongs to the prehistory of English *caprice*, these two are part of its afterlives, being reactivations in new contexts of a word long established in the lexicon of English as a French émigré. Taken together, they show *caprice* undergoing its own creolization *à l'anglaise*, a process of linguistic and cultural mixing that occurs in contact zones with French throughout the English-speaking world and which reveals, at one and the same time, asymmetries of power and creative possibilities. One asymmetry of power that these two instances highlight is the inequality in gender relations that, as we have already seen, has long enabled misogynists to dismiss the behaviour of women as a caprice in that word's negative sense of a deviation from reasonable norms. In both instances, *caprice* is waiting to be reclaimed by women from the misogynists and turned to positive purposes, and literature offers them the means of doing both.

The first of my flights of fancy marks a return to the cross-cultural creolizations of Maria Edgeworth. Her 1801 novel *Belinda* is set in a fashionable English society that has long viewed French culture as the acme of modishness and is being reshaped by the arrival of aristocratic émigrés from across the Channel in the years following the French Revolution of 1789. *Belinda* might well have been entitled *Caprice*, for it explores that word and its implications for women of the upper and middle classes in their pursuit of the sole occupation that English society judged respectable for them, marriage. What the novel suggests is that successful women, when choosing a partner for life, need to work together to bend the rules. They need, collectively, to exploit women's reputation for caprice.

Belinda has at its heart the relationship between the novel's eponymous heroine, who is on the marriage market, and the charismatic Lady Delacour, who decides to take Belinda under her wing. Lady Delacour—while in no sense naïve—is a walking and talking encounter between the other French words at the heart of this book. Like other à la mode English men and women of her period and class, including her fellow literary creation the Earl of Glenthorn, she suffers from that profound boredom which the French word alone can name in English. The narrator of *Belinda* reports Lady Delacour's self-portrayal in these terms: 'Lady Delcour confessed that, in the midst of the utmost luxury and dissipation, she had been a constant prey to ennui'. Her ennui stems in large part from a miserable marriage that she claims to have entered into through pure caprice. While no Caprice by name, Lady Delacour is Caprice by nature, and she presents herself as a marriageable young woman in these very terms to Belinda:

> I was a rich heiress—I had, I believe, a hundred thousand pounds, or more; and twice as many caprices. I was handsome and witty—or, to speak with that kind of circumlocution which is called humility, the world, the partial world, thought me a beauty, and a *bel esprit*.

Lady Delacour continues to show these character traits throughout the novel. She falls out with not only her husband, but even Belinda, subjecting her protégée to the worst excesses of her capacity for caprice.[42]

The thoughtful and deep-feeling Belinda, meanwhile, is free from caprice. Surrounded by women who decide on a whim that they know what is right for her—including the otherwise faultless Lady Anne Percival, who wants her to marry Mr Vincent, a white European Creole who turns out to be an inveterate gambler—the unflappable Belinda thinks for herself. She quietly but passionately chooses a suitable partner for life in the wealthy and charismatic aristocrat Clarence Hervey. It remains for her to win his hand, however, in a *dénouement* that the twists and turns of the novel's plot—combined with her irreproachable but ultimately limiting prudence of conduct—threaten to put beyond her reach.

Re-enter Caprice, in the figure of Lady Delacour, to secure a happy ending for her friend by imaginative, indeed, highly irregular means. In Edgeworth's first sketch of the novel, which survives, Lady Delacour was to die at the end of *Belinda*, a victim of her own capriciousness, 'the last whimsical ambition' with which she is 'seized'—in the words of the sketch—having been 'to conceal from all the world that she has a cancer'.[43] Edgeworth revised the ending of the novel in such a way as to have Belinda first save Lady Delacour from her capriciousness and then Lady Delacour use that capriciousness to secure Belinda's happiness. This ending transforms Lady Delacour into yet another of those colourful female characters in Edgeworth's fiction who, as we have seen, figure within the plot of the novel as proxies for the novelist herself. In so doing, Edgeworth also transformed the story her novel had to tell of caprice, which suddenly reveals itself to be a resource for women, in the realization of their ambitions, if they decide to make proper use of their talents and to write their own endings.

The second of my flights of fancy is George Bowering's 1987 novel *Caprice*. While less internationally renowned than two of his Canadian contemporaries, Margaret Atwood (b. 1939) and Michael Ondaatje (b. 1943), Bowering is much celebrated in his native Canada as both a novelist and a poet of the experimental avant-garde. Born and brought up in British Columbia, the westernmost province of Canada, Bowering has suggested that writers based in central and eastern Canada—such as Atwood—offer a view of the entire country and its literary culture that is not applicable to Canada's remote West. Bowering's project, to write that West into a new Canadian literature of the edges of empire, lies behind his *Caprice*.[44]

I have contended throughout this book that the appearance of a word in the title of a work may not only signal that word's cultural prominence, but also condense its complex of meanings. How significant a performance of its title the work is depends, of course, on the import of the work itself. I am sparing you—believe me—any number of indifferent English Edwardian novels variously called *Caprice*, ranging in tone from the light comedic to the melodramatic, each reducing the keyword in its title to a colourless reproduction of what the word can do and mean. Bowering's *Caprice*, by contrast, makes and remakes all sorts of capricious sense. A Canadian western with a difference, set in British Columbia in around 1890, *Caprice* reactivates the capricious tradition of border crossing and hill-top capering far away from the scene of its first emergence in early modern Europe.

In this respect, *Caprice* mirrors the procedures of the entire trilogy of novels about British Columbia of which it is the second publication, coming between *Burning Water* (1980) and *Shoot!* (1994). *Burning Water* takes as its subject the first encounters in the 1790s between the native population of what was to become British Columbia and its European explorers, focussing on the historical figure of George Vancouver, but reimagining Vancouver's story in a wilfully subversive comic parody of the colonial travel narrative. *Shoot!* focusses on the McLean Gang—a group of 'halfbreeds' (Canadians of mixed white and native parentage), the youngest of them barely a teenager, who were hanged in 1881 for the murder of a policeman. The novel tells their story from the boys' point of view, against the grain of conventional history, probing the dark side of Canadian creolization. Bowering views the whole of Canada as a 'contact zone', as the literary critic Sherrill Grace has put it, and in his trilogy of novels he explores the British Columbian part of that contact zone over two centuries of cultural entanglement.[45]

The second novel in the trilogy, *Caprice*, earns its name in the sense defined for composers by Michael Prætorius early in the seventeenth century: it errs from the mode on which it is based, but never too far, to create something different. Bowering has commented on his specific practice in *Caprice* in terms that echo Prætorius's account:

> In order to create a Canadian western you had to do something that was not an American western. I had to have all the signs of an American western but there had to be irony—you had to turn them upside down. Put it this way: you had to have (a) sign and (b) difference. So that's what I did all the way through. It's filled with signs, but it's filled with difference.[46]

This novel has—as the genre of the western expects—its cowboys and Indians, and its tale of revenge, set in a westernmost outpost of colonial progress that is dwarfed by the vast and inhospitable natural landscape that surrounds it. Outlaw Frank Spencer has killed fellow farmhand Pete Foster over a bottle of whisky. Pete's dying words are to name the sibling who will pursue Spencer in a quest for revenge. The sibling answers the call and sets out in hot pursuit. So far, so conventionally western. The signs are plain for all to see.

So, immediately, are the differences, for the sibling on whom Peter calls is his sister, and her name is Caprice. The novel's title, at a single stroke, turns upside down both gender roles and genre rules. The differences proliferate. In the predominantly Anglophone setting of British Columbia—and of the western—Caprice is from Quebec, a 'Frenchie', as her name implies. (So is her brother: his real name is Pierre.) Six feet tall, red-headed, Caprice totes a bullwhip rather than pistols. She has a peace-loving and baseball-playing lover—a schoolteacher by the name of Roy Smith—and she possesses a vocation for poetry. She puts both lover and vocation on hold in her solitary pursuit of justice for her murdered brother. In a genre that normally relegates women to the subordinate roles of moll or mother, Caprice is 'outlaw incarnate', as the Canadian writer and critic Aritha van Herk has put it.[47] More than just the heroine of the novel, Caprice embodies its spirit of pure caprice, its determination to bend the rules of the western, even as it meets them, and to explore new territory.

The novel displays its capriciousness at all levels of the work. It thematizes its displacement of the western from the United States to Canada by having Caprice cross the 'medicine line' (the border between the two countries) and ride all the way to Arizona, where Spencer flees after murdering her brother, before tracking him and his sidekick Loup Groulx back across the border and all the way to the scene of the murder, near Kamloops in the Thompson Valley of British Columbia. A group of rich and powerful British and Irish landholders have seized from the native so-called 'Indian' population, and now command, large tracts of the Thompson Valley, into which there have come migrant settlers from many places, including some—Caprice among them—from Francophone Quebec. As both a member of a subordinate minority French-speaking population in British Columbia and a woman, Caprice subverts the dominant power structures of the Anglophone North American West and its social and cultural modes, including the western. The Indians of the novel lend her a hand in this subversion. They are just two in number, not swarming hordes, and they refuse to play the noble savage or to become pistol fodder for cowboys. Instead, they observe the main action of the novel in the guise of a chorus, commenting with wry irony on the peculiar ways of the white settlers. The Indians provide a connection between the novel's capriciousness of theme—its deviation from the conventional treatment of their people—and the capriciousness of form whereby it introduces new modes of focalization and narration into the western.[48]

The narrator finds several means of alerting the reader to this process. These make *Caprice* an exercise in what Bowering called, in a 1982 essay, 'post-realist fiction'. In that essay, the novelist defines fiction as post-realist when it 'draws the reader's attention to the surface', rather than allowing the reader to drift 'into the softness of representation'. Its reflections of its own surface make post-realist or (as he also calls it) post-modern fiction akin to abstract painting, Bowering says, the one difference being that the surface of the fiction is a 'verbal' one. The novelist, in truly capricious fashion, is keen to disrupt the straight line of a literary history that presented reflective 'post-modern' as following on from representational 'modern' literature. 'It can be seen as one of many swellings of another (and older) tradition', he insists, mentioning the eccentric wit of Sterne. How apt it would have been had Bowering chosen to connect this 'swelling' with the capricious tradition across the arts which, as I have already suggested, moves in skips and starts—as far as the novel is concerned—from Rabelais to Sterne and Diderot and beyond. Bowering does not mention that tradition but clearly feels at home in it.[49]

Caprice suggests that connection by drawing the reader's attention to its capricious verbal surface in several ways. To tell its story, it deploys the conventional novelistic device of a narrator external to the events of the novel, writing about its protagonists in the third person. It lays bare its recourse to that device, however, by pointing to its use of the historic present of conventional narration: 'So this afternoon, or rather that one . . .', the narrator says on one occasion, and on another: 'Now, or rather, then . . .'.[50] Restless as to form, it sometimes switches out of the mode of the novel altogether, crossing into poetry and the essay.

It even blurs the distinction between the creator of its verbal surface and the creatures that people it. On one prominent occasion, for example, it suggests that Caprice herself is to be found at the centre of its web of words. The novel starts as it means to go on—arrestingly—by offering us a focalization of a scene from a classic western while varying the subject of the focalization: 'If you had ordinary English eyes, you would have seen late-morning sunlight flooding the light brown of the wide grassy valley [. . .]. But if you had those famous Indian eyes you could look down into the wide valley and see something moving.' That something turns out to be the figure of Caprice on horseback, and so our story begins, with Caprice at its centre.[51]

But who is the story's author? Some way in, the novel interrupts its narration to offer us what appear to be fragments of the poetry Caprice has written on the hoof, and these include a meditation on what different eyes are capable of seeing in the valleys of the Interior Plateau:

> How quiet
> the morning breaks
> my concentration
> on the target.
>
> Ordinary English eyes
> would see a flood of light
> coursing down the valley
> like a ghost of ice.
>
> Famous hunter eyes
> penetrate the shadows under rocks,
> behind the sage
> a fear not yet dried
> by the rising fire.[52]

That the sentences (quoted above) with which the narrator opens *Caprice* echo these lines of poetry so closely, in thought and phrasing, should give the novel's readers pause for thought.

Neither English nor Indian, Caprice asserts her right to elude binary oppositions, and to become a famous hunter with a difference. Ordinary English eyes might not view it this way, we surmise, but others will see that Caprice herself has written the novel that bears her name.

Migrants in Our Midst

HOW FAR WE have travelled since we first met an émigré in the company of A. A. Milne's old grey donkey, Eeyore, as he took an unlikely turn, in French, around the mulberry bush. I wanted to write about migrant words that first settled in English centuries ago and yet remain of markedly foreign, specifically French, derivation. Their histories are part of a linguistic and cultural process that has been going on at least since the Normans first crossed the English Channel. I introduced a conceptual model—creolization—able, with due modification, to account for that long and complex process. I started my account *in medias res*, by exploring the Frenchification of English in Restoration England, before surveying the long prehistory of that moment. I identified and analysed the emergence in Restoration English of particular émigrés, whose later course in various parts of the Anglophone world I traced, rather as an ornithologist might track migrating birds in flight.

Such choices have enabled me to perform an experiment in a cosmopolitan cultural criticism that is sensitive to language, to the social and cultural questions that language raises, and to the dialogue between the arts. I recognize that the book is, in many ways, a caprice. I will leave it to others to judge whether or not it is also a naïveté. Perhaps my greatest hope is that the book has not caused too much ennui.

I have written not so much in defence as in illumination of émigré words. The best defence of such words I know is a short 1959 essay, 'Wörter aus der Fremde' ('Words from Abroad'), by the German-Jewish philosopher Theodor Adorno (1903–69). Adorno wrote the essay in response to letters he received from listeners to his radio broadcasts on Proust, protesting against his allegedly excessive use of French foreignisms in German. His essay is a counterblast. Adorno claims that this is 'a case of sour grapes: outrage over foreign words is to be explained in terms of the psychic state of the one who is angry, for whom some grapes are hanging too high up'. He offers various causes for the elevation of the said grapes. The first of these is love of the foreign as an 'escape' from the 'spell of what one is and knows anyway': this love, he claims, is what lends foreign words the 'fecund and dangerous quality' that, while seductive to some, is hated by others. A second cause is educational privilege: Adorno observes that foreign words are accused of 'excluding those who did not have the opportunity to learn them early in life'. His defence of foreign words against this accusation is as nuanced as his defence of them against hatred is simple. He recognizes the fact of educational privilege, which he views as socially divisive, and concedes that foreign words are indeed 'components of a language of initiates'. He maintains, however, that such words 'are certainly not the only guilty parties and hardly the most important'. He observes that the 'criterion of intelligibility "for everyone"', which is pressed into action against foreign words from an apparently socially progressive position, is dominated by an 'ideal of manipulation' that seeks the means 'to degrade those to whom it is addressed to mere objects' and 'to harness them for purposes'—commercial or political—'that are not their own'. That manipulative ideal poses a much greater threat to German culture and society, he asserts, than foreign words do.[1]

It is to foreign words, indeed, that Adorno looks for a source of obstinate resistance to that manipulative ideal. Such words undermine the ideal, he claims, by the unassimilated relation they maintain to the language that surrounds them. This relation confirms an overlooked truth about language as a whole, which is that it cannot achieve the immediate equivalence of what is said to what is meant, an equivalence that the manipulative ideal deceptively offers human beings in treating them as mere objects. As Adorno claims, 'every foreign word contains the explosive material of enlightenment, contains in its controlled use the knowledge that what is immediate cannot be said in unmediated form but only expressed in and through reflection and mediation'. For this reason, he claims that foreign words can still 'shock with their obstinacy', observing that 'shock may now be the only way to reach human beings through language'. This observation brings Adorno to a summative statement of what he thinks foreign words can achieve:

Like Greeks in Imperial Rome, foreign words, used correctly and responsibly, should lend support to the lost cause of a flexibility, elegance, and refinement of formulation that has been lost and that people do not want to be reminded of. Foreign words should confront people with something that would be possible only if educational privilege ceased to exist, even in its most recent incarnation, the levelling of all people to a schooled half-culture. In this way foreign words could preserve something of the utopia of language, a language without earth, without subjection to the spell of historical existence, a utopia that lives on unawarely in the childlike use of language. Hopelessly, like death's-heads, foreign words await their resurrection in a better order of things.

This is wonderfully put. And it seems to me to hold good, largely, in the case of French and other foreign words in English.[2]

Adorno, it is true, teaches us to be wary of extrapolating from one case (German) to another (English). He offers no abstract defence of foreign words, but a concrete one, drawing examples from his radio broadcasts on Proust and analysing these with specific reference to the state of the German language and the attitudes of German speakers towards words of foreign, particularly French, derivation. He points out what he perceives as salient changes, to the historical situation of foreign words in German, that have taken place in the course of his lifetime. When, as a child, he was upbraided for incorporating foreign words into his German, he explains, this was because 'foreign words constituted little cells of resistance to the nationalism of World War I'. Some four decades on—at the time he was writing—Adorno sees the situation as having evolved, insofar as he considers that 'foreign words no longer have the function of protesting [against] nationalism, which in the era of the great power blocs no longer coincides with the individual languages of individual nations'. This change does not, however, prevent foreign words from continuing to shock in German, by means of what Adorno perceives as their unassimilated foreignness. He contrasts this situation with the one he claims to pertain in English. There, he claims, 'a tendency to linguistic doubling' may have been produced by the superimposition upon one another of Saxon and Norman elements, 'but the latter are too widespread and too much the marks of a historical victory to be experienced as foreign by anyone but an intransigent romantic'. The Norman elements have for this reason, Adorno suggests, been organically fused with the rest of the English language in a way that German has never achieved.[3]

I am comfortable enough to be ranked among the intransigent romantics (and have been called worse things). I would want nonetheless to maintain that in its use of foreign-derived words, particularly French ones, English has more in common with German than Adorno here allows. I have pointed out, from the very first sentence of this book, that the French words which turn English exist within—and over time, in some cases, move around—a spectrum of adaptation to their new linguistic environment. Adorno describes the situation of English in terms of the French words that have wholly adapted to their new setting. He forgets those that have only partly adapted or that remain unadapted. These words, by their wholly or partly unassimilated presence in the language, mark the continuing discomfort of the historical victory—of Norman over Saxon—to which he alludes. I have wanted to show in this book that these words, while certainly less in number than those that have wholly adapted, are a stable feature of English and that the controversy they stir has something to tell us about the situation of the language and its users.

It reveals, to my mind, a painful internal contradiction in that situation, at least as it obtains in the culture and society of modern England, the setting about which I have had most to say in this book. This is that, while the English language needs and has always needed émigrés to achieve elegance and completeness of self-expression, the English as a people have never yet learned to celebrate this fact about their language. We might say that, unlike the Anglophone artists at the heart of this book, English culture has on the whole failed to come to terms with its part in a creolizing process that started on either side of the English Channel and that continues to this day. It struggles in particular to appreciate the benefits of its mutual entanglement with French culture. It has never entirely shaken off the suspicion that this entanglement amounts to a humiliating foreign takeover. That suspicion is as old as the hills of England, and was certainly alive in the period of the Restoration, when the émigrés at the heart of this book first turned English. It seems to me to be reappearing at a time when—by contrast, perhaps, with the era in which Adorno wrote his essay—individual nations are minded to break away from the great power blocs of world politics and to go their own sweet self-sufficient way. If I am right, then we are once again living at a time when words from abroad may function as little cells of resistance to the resurgent nationalism of the day, serving as everyday reminders that the foreign is indeed, as Yasemin Yildiz suggests, 'lodged right in the mother tongue'.[4]

This book seemed to me to take on a new revelance as I was writing it. During that time, the newly elected president of the United States of America, Donald Trump, signed an executive order banning all citizens of certain Muslim-majority countries from travelling to the USA, prepared to build a wall separating that country from its southern neighbour Mexico, and took various opportunities to reduce immigration to the USA; the member states of the European Union differed sharply in their response to the biggest influx of migrants and refugees into Europe since the Second World War; and politicians negotiated, in the wake of the 2016 Brexit referendum, the withdrawal of the UK from the EU and its implications for citizens of EU countries living in the UK and for their UK counterparts resident elsewhere in the EU. The words that both connect and divide the British from their nearest continental European neighbour were drawn into the public debate surrounding the Brexit negotiations. It is true that I have yet to hear anyone echo the radical nationalist proposal of John Hare in the 1640s, who—as we saw earlier—advocated to his fellow English speakers in Britain 'that our Language be cleared of the Normane and French invasion upon it'.[5] Yet the same suggestion was made from the other side, as it were. A cabaret piece called 'The French Brexit Song', performed by Amanda Palmer, Sarah-Louise Young, and Maxim Melton, circulated widely on the internet in late 2019. It features two floridly Frenchified singers exacting revenge on the perfidious British by announcing to them: 'We're taking all our French words back.' The singers point out that the British will be the losers, reduced among other things to eating nothing but baked beans, since—as the song puts it—'You can't eat à la mode without le français.'[6]

This book was conceived long before the developments sketched above took place. Yet they have undoubtedly shaped its writing. They have caused me, in particular, to think more carefully about the metaphor of the émigré that I have used to describe the words that are my subject. We have already encountered this metaphor in the passage I quoted from Adorno's 1959 essay, which imagines words from abroad as if they were Greeks in imperial Rome, supporting an enlightenment that people do not want to be reminded of. The metaphor of words as people occurs frequently in the primary material on which this book is based. We might recall, for example, the terms John Evelyn used in 1665—as we saw in chapter 1 above—when he suggested to the Royal Society's committee for improving the English language, of which he was a member, that, since 'we have hardly any words that do so fully expresse' the meanings of French words like *naïveté* and *ennui* and Italian words like *svelto*, we should '(as the Romans did the Greeke) make as many of those do homage, as are like to prove good citizens'. Evelyn, like Adorno after him, uses the metaphor of words as people to place the influx of borrowings from one modern language to another in the prestigious classical setting of an imperial Rome that offered citizenship to enlightened and enlightening Greeks.

This underlying metaphor had, by the time Evelyn chose to classicize it, long characterized discussions of English language contact and change. In his 1531 work on education, *The Governor*, Sir Thomas Elyot advocated (and practised in his own style) the importation of words into English from Latin as well as modern foreign languages. About one Latin word (*maturitie*) he treats in this way, he says that once it has been used enough to be 'brought in custome', it will be 'as facile to understande as other wordes late commen out of Italy and Fraunce and made deinzins [denizens] amonge us'. By *denizen* Elyot here means a person who, while not a native, is at home in England. We know Elyot to have been writing at a time when many French and other foreigners who had settled in England sought to take out letters of denization, receipt of which meant that holders enjoyed many of the privileges of native inhabitants, although they remained subject to special taxation and marked out as non-natives by the letters themselves.[7]

The metaphorical transfer is easily made from the situation of such people to that of the French words they brought to England, some of which settled and prospered there without ever being fully naturalized, their foreign provenance marked by the manner of their pronunciation and the letters that spelled them. The metaphor points to similarities between these words and people migrating from France in respect of the treatment both have received in the Anglophone world. We have seen how such words meet now with admiration, now with hostility, symptoms of an unresolved ambivalence. A similar reception awaited the people who, in course of the sixteenth and seventeenth centuries alone, migrated in large numbers from France to England.

These settlers, despite the letters of denization many of them had received and the contribution they made to the culture and society of England, remained prey to a xenophobia that sometimes led to violence on the streets. Travelling foreign traders were the chief targets of rioting, such as that which took place in London on what became known as Evil May Day, in 1517. But no non-native was safe. The riot was imaginatively reconstructed at the end of the sixteenth century in a co-authored play, *Sir Thomas More*, in whose writing Shakespeare lent a hand. In this play a leader of the uprising states as its chief complaint 'that aliens and strangers eat the bread from the fatherless children, and take the living from all the artificers, and the intercourse from all merchants, whereby poverty is so much increased that every man bewaileth the misery of [an]other'. He urges the English to unite and 'not suffer the said aliens in their wealth'.[8] A member of the uprising, Clown Betts, speaks for many of them as they prepare to drag the strangers from their houses:

> Now Mars for thy honour,
> Dutch or French,
> So it be a wench,
> I'll upon her.

The rapid transition from seething resentment of non-natives to actual violence against them, sexual and other, is sketched here in the simplest of English rhymes.[9]

The play's co-authors have the young Thomas More (1478–1535), then a sheriff of London and later England's lord chancellor, quell the crowds gathered in St Martin's with the moving force of the arguments he addresses to them. More reverses the perspective by inviting the crowds to imagine a future situation in which they have rioted and the king has chosen to banish the rioters from England. He asks them:

> Whither would you go?
> What country, by the nature of your error,
> Should give you harbour? Go you to France or Flanders,
> To any German province, Spain or Portugal,
> Nay, anywhere that not adheres to England:
> Why, you must needs be strangers. Would you be pleased
> To find a nation of such barbarous temper
> That, breaking out in hideous violence,
> Would not afford you an abode on earth,
> Whet their detested knives against your throats,
> Spurn you like dogs, and like as if that God
> Owed not nor made not you, nor that the elements

Were not all appropriate to your comforts
But chartered unto them? What would you think
To be thus used? This is the strangers' case,
And this your mountainish inhumanity.[10]

More's speech is part of the contribution that Shakespeare made, by hand, to the co-authored play of *Sir Thomas More*. In that contribution, which happens to be his only surviving literary manuscript, Shakespeare has More make the case for tolerance on the part of the English towards the migrants in their midst by inviting his fellow Londoners to prove, by their future actions, that theirs is no nation of barbarous temper and mountainish inhumanity. Shakespeare's More leaves them in no doubt that the future starts here and now.[11]

So it does. This is not a book about the treatment of migrant peoples. Nonetheless, it seems to me that we would do well to recall 'the strangers' case' made by Shakespeare's More, at times such as these, when slogans proclaim, to wide assent, that in the US it is time to put 'America first' and, in Brexiting Britain, to 'take back control'. These slogans will rapidly become things of the past. Our ways of talking about our common life will go rolling on. Yet it will remain important for us to go on asking, at each moment of the history we make for ourselves, how we wish to conceive of, and relate to, that which to us seems alien and strange. We would do well to remember at such moments that, for many of us, the foreign starts—but does not end—with the French migrant words in our midst; to recognize that these are a part of us and the vocabulary we use; and to reflect, as we turn to that vocabulary for more enlightening ways of talking about the central processes of our common life, that we have been here before.

31 January 2020
Oxford—West Cork—Durham

ACKNOWLEDGEMENTS

THE ORIGINS OF this book may be traced back to my under-graduate training at Oxford in English and French. Its conception owes more than might be imagined to a 2005 Diary piece in the *London Review of Books* by Jenny Diski, in which she responded to my first book, *The* Je-Ne-Sais-Quoi *in Early Modern Europe*. Diski wrote about the *je-ne-sais-quoi* she had first encountered as a young woman in the London of the 1960s. Her piece brilliantly demonstrated, in a way I could not have anticipated, that the *je-ne-sais-quoi* was a modern 'keyword' of a kind that Raymond Williams—whose work in this area I was then discovering with enthusiasm—seemed to me to have left underinvestigated. A second source of inspiration to me were Aimé Césaire, Patrick Chamoiseau, and Jean-Luc de Laguarigue, whom I met in Martinique in 2005 in the company of and in conversation with Guillaume Pigeard de Gurbert. I am grateful to all four for exposing me to a 'creolizing imaginary', as Stuart Hall calls it, which has had a decisive influence on the conception of this book.

Perhaps less immediately plain to see in its influence has been the creolizing imaginary of an island much closer to home, Ireland, which Ita Mac Carthy introduced me to even as she was sharing with me the insights of her work on the *grazia* of the Italian Renaissance. Yet no one has more creolized my keywords than Ita. For all that this book owes her, as a scholar and a fellow traveller in the study of complex words, I here offer her my thanks.

I started writing the book while a tutorial fellow of Oriel College, University of Oxford, and finished it after moving to Durham University to take up a chair in French. I benefitted, during that time, from invaluable periods of research leave (including one spent in West Cork) and other forms of institutional support from Oxford and Durham. I have often had occasion, at both institutions, to appreciate the commitment of my colleagues in and beyond modern languages to the ideals of intellectual community, scholarly debate, and mutual support. The same ideals have characterized various research groups in which I have participated during the writing of this book. I would like to single out the Early Modern Keywords research network, the Cambridge-based ERC project 'Genius before Romanticism: Ingenuity in Early Modern Art and Science', and the Oxford Montaigne reading group. I thank each and every member of these groups for their collegial participation in many a lively debate. I have presented aspects of my work on this book in various other settings: these include All Souls College, Oxford; Durham University; King's College London; the School of Advanced Studies in the Russian Presidential Academy of National Economy and Public Administration (RANEPA [РАНХиГС]); and the Centre d'Études Interdisciplinaires sur Pascal, Port-Royal et l'Époque Moderne (CEIPPREM) of the Université de Sorbonne Nouvelle—Paris 3. I am grateful to the colleagues—Neil Kenny (All Souls), Amaleena Damlé (Durham), Patrick ffrench (King's), Maria Neklyudova (RANEPA), and Alain Cantillon (CEIPPREM)— who invited me to speak to audiences in these institutions. I thank the members of those audiences for their responses to my work. Thanks, also, to the staff of the Bodleian and Taylorian Libraries, where I did most of my research, and to Ben Tate and his colleagues at Princeton University Press. Ben's enthusiasm for the project and his commitment to serious play have nourished the book at every stage.

Without the help of many other individuals, too numerous to name in full here, I would not have brought this book to fruition. I have already referred collectively to my colleagues and friends at Oxford and Durham and in the groups listed above. I limit myself, in addition, to singling out Jerry Brotton, Ben Cairns, Julia Cairns, Marie-Claude Canova-Green, Maddy Chalmers, Catherine Clarke, Sara-Louise Cooper, Rachael Dann, Kathy Eden, Santiago Fouz Hernández, John Gallagher, Beth Goldsmith, Tom Hamilton, Karina Healy, Alice Hunt, Roland John, Roman Krznaric, Francesco Manzini, Charlie Marshall, Missa Marshall, James McConnachie, Michael Montgomery, Neela Montgomery, Michael Moriarty, Deirdre Mundow, Maria Neklyudova, John O'Brien, Ann O'Sullivan, Richard Parish, Roger Pearson, Deana Rankin, Kate Raworth, Todd Reeser, Nigel Saint, Cha Scott, Noel Sugimura, Annette Volfing, Bill Warrell, Penny Warrell, Boris Wiseman, and Serena Yagoub. These are people who listened to my ideas; offered wise counsel; gave me expert help; read parts or all of the book in draft; pointed out all but its remaining errors (which I acknowledge mine); suggested new sources and avenues for me to explore; helped me to do the rest of my job; looked after the children; took me in; took me out; took me for a drink (or 1933 of them); took me for a run. It is extraordinary to think that there are people in the list who did pretty much all of the above.

I also found support of all these kinds, and more besides, from the extended clan: the Scholars of Oxford and London and the Mac Carthys (however spelt) of Bawnahow and Bishopsland and beyond; but also from Altimaris, Calverts, Crowleys, Lattins, Neils, Sweets, *et j'en passe*, though I do so while offering a word of thanks, also, to those who so warmly accepted our invitation to join the clan: Sara Ros Gonzáles, Ana Isabel Furquet Santamaría, Giulia Ganugi, Claire and Sinead Hegarty, and Clodagh O'Neill.

Special mention must go, finally, to my three Graces. To Ita, *a ghillie bàn*, I say: take it as read. Alexander and Beatrice have really entered the spirit of this book as I have been writing it. I will always remember little Sandy—who had just been listening to the Velvet Underground song with Bea—trotting up, one fine day in Reenroe (West Cork), to ask me to confirm the truth of his sister's suggestion that '*femme fatale* is Irish for a tease'. And many is the morning when Bea, who is now learning French at school, skips in and out of the language to greet me with a trilling *Bonjour, monsieur!* To them I say: thank you for the music.

Note on the Text

All translations are mine (unless otherwise stated). Quotations from A. L. Hendriks, *To Speak Simply: Selected Poems 1961–1986*, are reproduced with the permission of Hippopotamus Press. In three sections of this book, each of them amounting to 500 words or less, I draw on previously published material of mine: in chapter 2, on 'Aesthetics: Ancients and Moderns', in *The Cambridge History of French Thought*, ed. Michael Moriarty and Jeremy Jennings, pp. 183–89, © Cambridge University Press 2019, reproduced with permission of the Press through PLSclear; in chapter 3, on 'The New Philologists', in Ita Mac Carthy (ed.), *Renaissance Keywords* (Legenda, 2013), pp. 1–9; and, in chapter 4, on my *Montaigne and the Art of Free-Thinking*, © Peter Lang Ltd 2010, reproduced with permission conveyed through Copyright Clearance Center, Inc.

Here We Go Round the Mulberry Bush

1. Milne, *World of Pooh*, 76–77. Throughout, I italicize words when referring to them as words, while adopting in all other situations the type face—either roman or italic—standardly used for the word (as per *OED*).

2. Mikkelson, 'Bush and French Word'.

3. On the global spread of modern English, see Mugglestone, *History of English*, 334–413. Lexical borrowings from English in contemporary European languages (including French) are the subject of Görlach's *Dictionary of European Anglicisms*. On the place of French in the long history of loanwords in English, see Durkin, *Borrowed Words*, esp. 21–34, 227–80, 305–49. Durkin (ibid., 18n), who bases his survey on evidence from *OED*, rejects, for his purposes, the distinction in German philology between fully naturalized loanwords (*Lehnwörter*) and foreignisms (*Fremdwörter*).

4. Important studies of the medieval period include Wogan-Browne, *Language and Culture*; Butterfield, *Familiar Enemy*; those of the early modern period include Lambley, *Teaching and Cultivation*; Jones, *Triumph of English*; Gallagher, *Learning Languages*. Williams, *French Fetish*, straddles the two periods.

5. I follow Kerrigan (*Archipelagic English*, 10–11) in using the term *English* as both 'a linguistic term broad enough to encompass Hiberno-English and Scots', and one that 'points to the mutual implication of English as a language with English ethnicity, nationhood, and the related beliefs and social practices that spread through seventeenth-century Britain and Ireland' and beyond.

6. Important studies of these processes include Bakhtin, 'Discourse in the Novel'; Kellman, *Translingual Imagination*; Yildiz, *Mother Tongue*; and Helgesson and Kullberg, 'Translingual Events'.

Chapter 1: French À la Mode

1. On the reputation of French fashion worldwide, see DeJean, *Essence of Style*.

2. On *à la mode* in languages other than English, see *OED*, s.v. 'à la mode'. On French foreignisms in German, see Kenny, *Curiosity*, 93–101; Kenny, *Uses of Curiosity*, 229–30.

3. Phillips, *New World of Words*, s.v. 'French-man'. For an analysis of the fas-

cination and fear in eighteenth-century English attitudes towards French, see Newman, *Rise of English Nationalism*.

4. Quoted in *OED*, s.v. 'à la mode', which surveys the North American usage of the phrase.

5. Jones, 'Printing Stage', 150.

6. See Lambley, *Teaching and Cultivation*; Stedman, *Cultural Exchange*; Gallagher, *Learning Languages*.

7. In addition to the studies cited in the previous note, see, on Huguenot immigration to England, Ireland, and Scotland, Gwynn, *Huguenot Heritage*, 26–41; Yardeni, *Refuge protestant*, 73–76.

8. On *Marriage À-la-Mode*, see Stedman, *Cultural Exchange*, 139–59. Durkin (*Borrowed Words*, 320) observes of Restoration England that 'the numbers of new French loanwords recorded in this period show no particular fluctuation', suggesting that 'the Gallicisms that attracted negative comment were emblematic ones representative of the usage of a small group, against a background of continued borrowing in a wide range of social and cultural contexts'.

9. Dryden, *Marriage À-la-Mode*, Act 2 Scene 1, lines 39–48. This and all further references to the play are to Dryden, *Works*, vol. 11.

10. Dryden, *Marriage À-la-Mode*, 2.1, 66–67; Etherege, *Man of Mode*, Act 1 Scene 1, lines 326–27; ibid., 3.2, 130.

11. Dryden, *Marriage À-la-Mode*, 1.1, 181–84; ibid., 2.1, 51. Cf. Etherege, *Man of Mode*, 3.2, 181.

12. On French commodities, see DeJean, *Essence of Style*. For Sir Fopling's song about champagne, see Etherege, *Man of Mode*, 4.1, 370–91.

13. Ibid., 4.1, 294–99; *Marriage À-la-Mode*, 4.1, 150–79. On French imports, see Gwynn, *Huguenot Heritage*, 60–90; Stedman, *Cultural Exchange*, 63–107, 159–89. On the 'foundational foreignness' of early printing in England, see Coldiron, 'Public Sphere/Contact Zone', 211–16.

14. On these and other French sources for Dryden's play, see the editorial commentary to *Marriage À-la-Mode*, 467–72. A *cit* was a derogatory term in seventeenth-century English for a citizen of the City of London (who was not a member of the gentry).

15. See Huchon, *Histoire*, 175–76.

16. Dryden, *Works*, 8:98; Evelyn, *Letterbooks*, 2:895–916 (915). On the early modern history of proposals to found an English equivalent to the Académie française, see Monroe, 'English Academy'; Emerson, 'Dryden'; Freeman, 'Proposal'.

17. Dryden, *Works*, 13:223–24; ibid., 4:86.

18. See Hunt, *Evelyn*.

19. Evelyn, *Letterbooks*, 1:370–74. Evelyn returned to this topic, years later, in two letters of 1689 to Samuel Pepys (ibid., 2:895–916 (915); 2:920–21). It is not clear to me what Evelyn means by *croopo* in his phrase *Svelto croopo*. It may be that *croopo* is a misspelling of *corpo* ('body'), and that he means 'slim figure', al-

though one would expect the adjective (*svelto*) to follow the noun (*corpo*) in Italian. Evelyn's editors are silent on this question.

20. Speroni's use of the metaphor of language as a garden, in his 1542 *Dialogo delle lingue*, is transplanted by Du Bellay into his 1549 *Defence* of the French language; for both passages see Du Bellay, *Deffence*, 80–81, 235–37.

21. Evelyn, *Letterbooks*, 1:373.

22. Ibid.

23. On French *galanterie*, see Viala's twin studies, *La France galante* and *La Galanterie*; on the English context, see Thomas, *In Pursuit of Civility*.

24. See, e.g., Scudéry, 'De l'air galant', 53.

25. Etherege, *Man of Mode*, 4.1, 219–23.

26. See Viala, *La France galante*, 203–25.

27. Dryden, *Marriage À-la-Mode*, 2.1, 29; Anon., *Gallantry À-la-Mode*; Vincent and Dekker, *Young Gallant's Academy*, 45; Etherege, *Man of Mode*, 3.2, 210–11; Pepys, *Diary*, 3:188 (quoted in *OED*, s.v. 'gallant'). See Lambley, *Teaching and Cultivation*, 361–80.

28. *OED*, s.v. 'galanterie'; Viala, *La Galanterie*, 331–50.

29. *OED*, s.v. 'gentleman'. On *politesse* and gallantry in the English context, see Thomas, *In Pursuit of Civility*, 28–31. On *The Gentleman's Journal*, see Tadié, 'English Prose'.

30. Anon., *Remarques*, 36, 2, 97. On this controversy see Novak, 'Restoration Comedy'.

31. Etherege, *Man of Mode*, 1.1, 330–31; ibid., 1.1, 117.

32. Ibid., 3.3, 318–19.

33. Ibid., pp. 157–58 ('Epilogue').

Chapter 2: Modes of English

1. On imitation in this context, see Stedman, *Cultural Exchange*, 108–59. On the English fetishization of French cultural objects, see Williams, *French Fetish*. On mimicry and ambivalence, see Bhabha, 'Of Mimicry and Man'. Bhabha has in mind the ambivalent mimicry of Englishness by the colonial subject of the British empire. For reasons made clear in the next chapter, I view in similar terms the mimicry of Frenchness by the foppish subjects of a former Norman colony, England.

2. I thank Kathryn Murphy for sharing with me *hogo* and *kickshaw*, among others, from her abundant supply of such mingled borrowings.

3. Etherege, *Man of Mode*, 4.1, 343. See Stedman, *Cultural Exchange*, 246–54. For a defence of the fop, see Staves, 'Kind Words'.

4. Etherege, *Man of Mode*, 1.1, 336–37. The mode for libertine gallantry *à la* Dorimant also attracted condemnation, of course, in the period. See, e.g., Sir Philip Wodehouse's poem 'A Satirical Flash' (in Hammond, *Restoration Literature*, 109–10).

5. See Rankin, *Between Spenser and Swift*, 164–73.

6. Evelyn, *Tyrannus*, 6, 11–12; ibid., 24–25. On this text, see Stedman, *Cultural Exchange*, 189–96.

7. Evelyn, *Tyrannus*, 6; ibid., 30. Evelyn's diary entry is quoted by Nevinson in his Introduction to *Tyrannus*, v–vi.

8. Evelyn, *Tyrannus*, 'To Him that Reades', [2]; ibid., 29.

9. Ibid., 30.

10. Ibid., 14–15; compare Montaigne, *Essais*, I.43:268–69.

11. Evelyn, *Tyrannus*, 'To Him that Reades', [1]; Boyle, *Works*, 1:303.

12. Hammond, *Dryden*, 25–68 (40).

13. Dryden, *Marriage À-la-Mode*, 4.3, 127–59.

14. Canova-Green, 'Molière', analyses in similar fashion the unacknowledged or semi-acknowledged debts to Molière of a range of Restoration English playwrights, including Etherege in *The Man of Mode* and Dryden in several plays, though these do not include *Marriage À-la-Mode*.

15. Dryden, *Essay*, 'To the Reader', 7. This and all further references to the *Essay* are to Dryden, *Works*, vol. 17.

16. On the Quarrel in France, see DeJean, *Ancients against Moderns*; Norman, *Shock of the Ancient*. On the Quarrel in Europe, see Bullard and Tadié, *Ancients and Moderns*.

17. Dryden, *Essay*, 54; ibid., 45.

18. On Renaissance theories of imitation, see Cave, *Cornucopian Text*; Greene, *Light in Troy*.

19. See Huchon, *Histoire*, 167–68.

20. On Dryden and the 'imperial imagination', see Brown, 'Dryden'. On the growing international prestige of French, see Gimelli Martin and Melehy, *French Connections*, 2–5; Lambley, *Teaching and Cultivation*, 292–93, 390–93.

21. See DeJean, *Essence of Style*, 107–11.

22. Callières, *Mots à la mode*, 104; Boursault, *Mots à la mode*, 273; Académie française, *Dictionnaire*, s.v. 'mode'.

23. For Rochester's poem, 'A Letter from Artemisa in the Town to Chloe in the Country', see Hammond, *Restoration Literature*, 101–8 (103 and 106 for the quotations; 101 for Hammond's dating of the poem).

24. Dryden, *Marriage À-la-Mode*, 221.

25. See the editorial commentary in ibid., 464–67.

26. See Cock, '*À la Mode* Disease'.

27. For a brief survey of this revival, see Payne Fisk, *English Restoration Theatre*, xv–xvii.

28. See John Barnard's Introduction in Etherege, *Man of Mode*, xxxvii–xlv, xlvii–li.

29. On these forms, see *OED*, s.vv. 'à la mode', 'à la', 'à la modality', 'alamodic', 'à-la-modeness'.

30. https://www.youtube.com/watch?v=7_0HIUCp_TY [last accessed 10 February 2020].

Chapter 3: Creolizing Keywords

1. Williams, *Keywords*, 14.

2. Ibid., 22, 24–25.

3. Ibid., 20.

4. Kenny, *Uses of Curiosity*; Marr et al., *Logodaedalus*; Mac Carthy, *Renaissance Keywords*; Greene, *Five Words*, 6; ibid., 12. Masten, *Queer Philologies*, is a keywords-inflected study of sex and gender in early modern England (see esp. 32).

5. Apter, *Against World Literature*, 34–35; ibid., 117–90 (117–18 for the reference to Williams). See also Cassin, *Dictionary of Untranslatables*, vii.

6. I would contend the same of MacCabe and Yanacek's *Keywords for Today*, which updates and extends Williams's *Keywords* in significant ways, but from which émigrés are conspicuous by their absence.

7. See Glissant, *Traité*, esp. 27; *Cohée du Lamentin*, esp. 50, 74–77. See also Enwezor et al., *Créolité and Creolization*.

8. DeGraff, 'Against Creole Exceptionalism', esp. 402–4. For the continuation of the controversy, see Bickerton, 'Reconsidering Creole Exceptionalism'; De-Graff, 'Against Creole Exceptionalism (Redux)'. For a judicious account of the longer history of creole linguistics, which assesses the controversial reception of Bickerton's work and subsequent trends, see Bachmann, 'Creoles', esp. 426–36.

9. DeGraff, 'Against Creole Exceptionalism', 391.

10. Hall, 'Créolité and Creolization', 13. (Hall's essay first appeared in Enwezor et al., *Créolité and Creolization*, 27–41.)

11. Hall, 'Créolité and Creolization', 13–15.

12. Ibid., 15–16. Hall refers to Brathwaite, *Development of Creole Society*; Pratt, *Imperial Eyes*.

13. Hall, 'Créolité and Creolization', 23.

14. Ibid., 25.

15. The essays gathered in Gutiérrez Rodríguez and Tate, *Creolizing Europe*, make the most sustained attempt to date in this area. While some of its contributors offer pregnant remarks about pre-modern European culture—Hall ('Créolité and Creolization') and Spivak ('World Systems'), for example, both present Dante as a creolizing writer—the volume's focus is nonetheless on contemporary transformations of European societies. Coldiron ('Public Sphere/Contact Zone', 214) and Williams (*French Fetish*, 15–17) both argue persuasively for the pertinence of reading early modern English literature in a postcolonial perspective. Neither, however, makes creolization central to that perspective.

16. See Brown, *Normans*; Winder, *Bloody Foreigners*, 22–30; Butterfield, *Familiar Enemy*, 11–17.

17. Gaunt, '*Roland*', 100. See also Bergin, *History of France*, 1–20, 46–54.

18. On the Hundred Years' War, see Butterfield, *Familiar Enemy*, 17–23. On Shakespeare's history plays, see Williams, *French Fetish*, 181–226.

19. Hill, 'Norman Yoke', 64–65.

20. Hare, *St. Edwards Ghost*, 20; quoted in Jones, *Triumph of English*, 249–50. On this see Hill, 'Norman Yoke', 79–80.

21. Jones, *Triumph of English*, 317–18.

22. Hill, 'Norman Yoke', 124n.; Johnson, 'Resignation Letter'. See also O'Toole, *Heroic Failure*, 153–74.

23. Kerrigan, *Archipelagic English*; Colley, 'Britishness and Otherness', 311, 316.

24. Colley, 'Britishness and Otherness', 327; Hare, *St. Edwards Ghost*, 23. See also Palmer, *Language and Conquest*, 108–47; Canny, *Making Ireland British*; Newman, *Rise of English Nationalism*, 74–80.

25. Gikandi, *Maps of Englishness*, xii. See also Stoler and Cooper, 'Between Metropole and Colony'.

26. See Gaunt, 'French Literature Abroad'.

27. On early English bilingual and polyglot dictionaries, see Cowie, *English Lexicography*, 1:41–85. On early French monolingual dictionaries, see Quemada, *Dictionnaires du français moderne*, 205–18; Matoré, *Histoire des dictionnaires français*, 70–87.

28. On early monolingual English dictionaries, see Cowie, *English Lexicography*, 1:131–81. On the *OED*, see ibid., 230–79, 378–410.

29. On national and regional dictionaries of English, see ibid., 1:279–301, 1:353–77. On the controversy that surrounded *Webster's Third*, see Morton, *Story*.

30. Howell, *Dictionary*, 'To the Nobility and Gentry of Great Britain', [A3ʳ]; Miège, *New Dictionary*, 'Preface to the Reader', [unpaginated]. On their rivalry, see Gallagher, *Learning Languages*, 49–50.

31. This quotation and all of the preceding ones in this paragraph are taken from Johnson's unpaginated preface to his *Dictionary*.

32. Callières, *Du bon et du mauvais usage*, 105–6. Eden (*Friends Hold All Things*, 14–23) traces from Augustine to Erasmus the idea of language and learning as 'spoils of war'.

33. 'Copier ses modes, son langage, / Et même à ses défauts rendre un parfait hommage' (Callières, *Mots à la mode*, 124).

34. Johnson, *Dictionary*, s.vv. 'alamode', 'Gallicism'. For Evelyn's view, see chapter 1 above, 29–31.

35. Mendies, *Abridgment of Johnson's Dictionary*, 388–89 (388).

Chapter 4: Naïveté

1. Dryden, *Marriage À-la-Mode*, 3.1, 209–11.

2. Ibid., 5.1, 86–90; 5.1, 92–93; 503.

3. 'Vray, sincere, ressemblant'; 'NAIF signifie aussi, ingenu, simple, qui dit les choses sans en prevoir les consequences'. Furetière, *Dictionnaire*, s.v. 'naif'. See also Richelet, *Dictionnaire*, s.v. 'naïveté'; Castor, *Pléiade Poetics*, 77–85.

4. Montaigne, *Works*, 186. 'Ces nations me semblent donq ainsi barbares, pour avoir receu fort peu de façon de l'esprit humain, et estre encore fort voisines de leur naifveté originelle' (*Essais*, I.31:206).

5. See Lestringant, 'Montaigne, le Brésil'.

6. Montaigne, *Works*, 196. 'Ils n'ont peu imaginer une nayfveté si pure et simple, comme nous la voyons par experience; ny n'ont peu croire que nostre societé se peut maintenir avec si peu d'artifice et de soudeure humaine' (*Essais*, I.31:206).

7. Montaigne, *Works*, 2. 'Je veus qu'on m'y voie en ma façon simple, naturelle et ordinaire, sans contention et artifice: car c'est moy que je peins. Mes defauts s'y liront au vif, et ma forme naïfve, autant que la reverence publique me l'a permis. Que si j'eusse esté entre ces nations qu'on dict vivre encore sous la douce liberté des premieres loix de nature, je t'asseure que je m'y fusse tres-volontiers peint tout entier, et tout nud' (*Essais*, 'Au lecteur', I:3).

8. See Atkinson, 'Montaigne and *Naïveté*'.

9. 'Il rejette donc bien loin cette vertu stoïque qu'on peint avec une mine sévère [. . .]. La sienne est naïve, familière, plaisante, enjouée, et pour ainsi dire folâtre' (*Entretien avec M. de Sacy*, par. 42, in Pascal, *Provinciales*, 733–34.

10. 'La naïveté avec laquelle le pauvre homme mandoit ces nouvelles la fit rire. *Le Comte de Bussi*. Elle dit des naïvetez à faire crever de rire' (Richelet, *Dictionnaire*, s.v. 'naïveté').

11. Butterfield, *Fowler's Concise Dictionary*, s.v. 'naive'.

12. Schiller, *Naive and Sentimental*, 21.

13. Ibid., 34.

14. *OED*, s.v. 'sentimental'; Schiller, *Naive and Sentimental*, 35.

15. Ibid., 39–42 (39).

16. Ibid., 43–66 (43).

17. Ibid., 41, 97n. See Robertson, 'Ancients, Moderns', 270–75.

18. Schiller, *Naive and Sentimental*, 40–41.

19. Ibid., 49–50.

20. Ibid., 80.

21. See the editorial Introduction, ibid., 9–14 (12–13).

22. Ibid., 56; ibid., 97n.

23. Ibid., 81–90 (81–82, 90).

24. In Plimpton, 'Le Carré', 53.

25. Le Carré, *Naive and Sentimental Lover*, 51–52, 55.

26. Ibid., 72–73.

27. Ibid., 63, 62.

28. Ibid., 5–6, 148, 58.

29. Ibid., 203.

30. Ibid., 368–69, 381, 388, 390.

31. Ibid., 526, 531, 533–34.

32. In Plimpton, 'Le Carré', 54.

33. Le Carré, *Legacy of Spies*, 262.

34. Kennaway, *Some Gorgeous Accident*, 194.

35. See the negative reviews of the novel cited in Edwards, 'Great Tradition,'

64; and Monaghan, *Novels*, ix. A defence along these lines is mounted in Edwards, 'Great Tradition', 65. Monaghan (*Novels*, 1–41) finds in Schiller's opposition the source of what he describes as the 'unity' of Le Carré's fiction.

36. Le Carré, *Naive and Sentimental Lover*, 257.

37. Examples include John Adams's 1999 symphonic work *Naive and Sentimental Music*, and a 2010 essay by Orhan Pamuk, *Naive and Sentimental Novelist*.

Chapter 5: Ennui

1. Quoted in *OED*, s.v. 'ennui, *n*.'. For a literary history of boredom, see Spacks, *Boredom*.

2. 'Non timebis a [. . .] daemonio meridiano' (Pss 90:5–6 [Vulg.]). I quote the 1610 English Douay-Rheims translation of the Vulgate. Both are found at http://vulgate.org/ot/psalms_90.htm [last accessed 10 February 2020].

3. Kuhn, *Demon of Noontide*, 42–46; *OED*, s.v. 'ennui, *n*.'.

4. Roy, *Utmost Happiness*, 346. The relationship between ennui and art as a 'creative act' is central to Kuhn, *Demon of Noontide* (see esp. 375–78).

5. Estienne, *Dictionaire francoislatin*, s.v. 'Ennuy *et fascherie*'; Furetière, *Dictionnaire*, s.v. 'ennui'. Ménage (*Dictionnaire étymologique*, s.v. 'Ennuy, ennuyer'), suggests that French *ennui* is an adaptation of Spanish *enojo* and that both, like the Italian *noia*, are formed from the Latin *noxa* ('harm, injury').

6. 'Lassitude d'esprit, causée par une chose qui deplaist par elle-mesme ou par sa durée'; 'le temps dure, [. . .] l'on trouve le temps long' (Académie française, *Dictionnaire*, s.v. 'ennuy').

7. 'Le malheur d'être trop heureux' (Jankélévitch, *Aventure*, 873); 'passionner le temps pour qu'en lui la conscience retrouve intensité et plénitude' (ibid., 956).

8. 'Pour les personnes de mon Sexe qui n'ont nulle occupation, le moyen de ne s'ennuyer pas souvent?' (Scudéry, *Conversations nouvelles*, 2:468).

9. Ibid., 2:479–502 (479, 502).

10. Goldsmith, *Exclusive Conversations*, 60.

11. Pascal, *Pensées*, S169. 'Un roi sans divertissement est un homme plein de misères.' This and all further references to the *Pensées* are to their numbering in Sellier's edition (which Ariew follows in his English translation).

12. Ibid., S33. 'Sans cela nous serions dans l'ennui, et cet ennui nous pousserait à chercher un moyen plus solide d'en sortir, mais le divertissement nous amuse et nous fait arriver insensiblement à la mort.'

13. Ibid., S749 (translation modified). 'Cet abandon dans l'horreur de la nuit'; 'Jésus dans l'ennui.' See also Bossuet, *Œuvres oratoires*, 3:70–7; 6:683. On ennui in Bossuet, Pascal, and their contemporaries, see Kuhn, *Demon of Noontide*, 101–27.

14. Hammond, *Playing with Truth*, 115–16.

15. See Kuhn, *Demon of Noontide*, 221–329.

16. Pearson, *Unacknowledged Legislators*, 94.

17. Ibid., 100, 128. See also Kuhn, *Demon of Noontide*, 198–218.

18. Chateaubriand, *René*, 81 (translation modified). 'Ce dégoût de la vie que j'avois ressenti dès mon enfance'; 'un profond sentiment d'ennui' (*René*, 408). Cited in Pearson, *Unacknowledged Legislators*, 128.

19. Pearson, *Unacknowledged Legislators*, 233–37.

20. Staël, *Corinne, or Italy*, 247 (translation modified). 'Une collection d'ennuis tout à la fois divers et monotones' (*Corinne ou l'Italie*, 367).

21. Staël, *Corinne, or Italy*, 251. 'L'on n'aime pas s'amuser une fois, pour découvrir que l'on s'ennuie tous les jours' (*Corinne ou l'Italie*, 373).

22. Staël, *Corinne, or Italy*, 255. 'Mener une vie indépendante, tout entière consacrée aux arts' (*Corinne ou l'Italie*, 379).

23. Pearson, *Unacknowledged Legislators*, 252.

24. Kuhn, *Demon of Noontide*, 256.

25. According to Étienne Dumont in his letter to Edgeworth of 1 November 1813, quoted in Butler, *Maria Edgeworth*, 223.

26. Edgeworth, *Ennui*, 144. This and all further references to this text are to Butler's Penguin edition (which includes Edgeworth's *Castle Rackrent*). For a psychoanalytical approach to the 'great ennui of childhood', see Phillips, *On Kissing*, 71–82 (71).

27. Cheyne, *English Malady*, ai (preface); ibid., 347; see *Trésor*, s.v. 'spleen'.

28. Baudelaire, *Flowers*, 17. 'Les ennuis et les vastes chagrins / Qui chargent de leur poids l'existence brumeuse' (ibid., 16).

29. Ibid., 147. 'J'ai plus de souvenirs que si j'avais mille ans'; 'un immense caveau, / Qui contient plus de morts que la fosse commune'; 'L'ennui, fruit de la morne incuriosité, / Prend les proportions de l'immortalité' (ibid., 146).

30. Ibid., 148. 'L'esprit gémissant en proie aux longs ennuis' (ibid., 149).

31. Ibid., 152–55.

32. Kuhn, *Demon of Noontide*, 314.

33. Baudelaire, *Flowers*, 7 (translation modified). 'Tu le connais, lecteur, ce monstre délicat, /—Hypocrite lecteur,—mon semblable,—mon frère!' (ibid., 6).

34. Ibid., 11. 'Ce monde ennuyé' (ibid., 10).

35. Edgeworth, *Ennui*, 305.

36. Ibid., 152; ibid., 290.

37. Ibid., 304.

38. Ibid., 323.

39. Myers, 'Completing the Union', 47. I also draw, in what follows, on Butler's Introduction to Edgeworth, *Novels and Selected Works*, 1:XLVII–LII.

40. Edgeworth, *Irish Bulls*, 123.

41. Edgeworth, *Ennui*, 273.

42. Ibid., 225. See Brundan, 'Cosmopolitan Complexities', 129–32.

43. Hendriks, *To Speak Simply*, 96n. On the painting, see Moorby, 'Sickert, *Ennui*'.

44. Quoted in Moorby, 'Sickert, *Ennui*'. On Sickert's French reading, see Robins's editorial Introduction to Sickert, *Complete Writings*, xxvii–xxxvi.

45. Sickert, *Complete Writings*, 252–55 (252); see also 60–61.

46. Ibid., 300; ibid., 97.

47. Ibid., 264, 267.

48. Woolf, *Sickert*, 22, 26, 13.

49. Ibid., 13–14.

50. Ibid., 15, 21.

51. Ibid., 22, 11, 25.

52. Ibid., 21, 25–27.

53. Hendriks, *To Speak Simply*, 96n (emphasis mine).

54. Ibid., 49–66. For a brief account of Hendriks's life and works, see Noel-Tod, *Modern Poetry*, 260–61.

55. Hendriks, *To Speak Simply*, 11.

56. Ibid., 96.

Chapter 6: Caprice

1. Dryden, *Marriage À-la-Mode*, 4.3, 89–104.

2. Cotgrave, *Dictionary*, s.v. 'caprice'.

3. *OED* (s.v. 'caprice') notes that around 1700 the stress fell on the word's first syllable and that Pope rhymed *caprice* with English *vice*.

4. Johnson, *Dictionary*, s.v. 'caprichio'.

5. Phillips, *New World*, s.v. '*caprichio* or *caprice*'; Bailey, *English Dictionary*, s.v. 'caprice'.

6. *OED*, s.v. 'caprice'.

7. 'Le mot de *caprice* étoit nouveau du temps d'Henry Estienne, et il luy sembloit fort étrange' (Furetière, *Dictionnaire*, s.v. 'caprice'). See Estienne, *Deux Dialogues*, 80, 141–43.

8. Gracián, *Homme de cour*, maxim ccxviii, 302–3.

9. 'Déreglement d'esprit' (Furetière, *Dictionnaire*, s.v. 'caprice'). On capricious children see, e.g., *Trésor*, s.v. 'caprice', B.5.b.

10. 'Il peut se prendre en bonne part' (Academie française, *Dictionnaire*, s.v. 'caprice').

11. Furetière, *Dictionnaire*, s.v. 'capricieux'; Cresswell, *Word Origins*, s.v. 'caprice'. See also Estienne, *Deux Dialogues*, 141–42.

12. Huarte de San Juan, *Tryal of Wits*, 153. The source of this quotation is the 1698 translation of Huarte de San Juan's work by Bellamy, not the 1594 one by Carew (*Examination of Mens Wits*, 67), *pace OED* (s.v. 'capricious').

13. Marr et al., *Logodaedalus*, 114.

14. 'caprice, se dit aussi des pieces de Poësie, de Musique, et de Peinture, qui reüssissent plûtost par la force du genie, que par l'observation des regles de l'art, et qui n'ont aucun nom certain. St. Amant a intitulé quelques pieces, *Caprice*. Les *caprices*, ou postures de Calot Graveur. [C]aprices de Musique' (Furetière, *Dictionnaire*, s.v. 'caprice'). On *caprice* and the arts, see Peureux, *Caprice*.

15. Rosand, 'Antic Line', 300.

16. Ibid., 308.

17. Ibid., 300. See also Kanz, *Kunst des Capriccio*; Auclair, 'Callot dessinateur'.

18. Marin, 'Capriccio', 9–11. On the fan in French literary culture of this period, see Ibbett, *Fans*.

19. See Rosand, 'Antic Line', 300–27.

20. See Montaigne, *Essais*, I.21:103; Peureux, *Caprice*, 17–18.

21. Corneille, *Theatrical Illusion*, 200. 'Qu'on en nomme l'invention bizarre et extravagante tant qu'on voudra, elle est nouvelle [. . .] et j'ose dire que la représentation de cette pièce capricieuse ne vous a point déplu' (*Théâtre*, 627).

22. Saint-Amant, *Œuvres*, 2:141–229; 3:1–92, 285–337. See Peureux, 'Caprice dans la poésie française', 116–25.

23. Saint-Amant, *Œuvres*, 2:155–98.

24. 'Et le Caprice, avecques sa peinture, / Qui fait bouquer et l'Art, et la Nature, / Ce Fou divin, riche en inventions, / Bizarre en mots, vif des descriptions' ('La Pétarrade aux rondeaux: Caprice', ibid., 2:201–7 (202)).

25. 'Le caprice est la Poésie même, folie divine, coup de force du génie [. . .] où par "impétuosité du génie" et "ardeur d'esprit", la représentation s'excède elle-même dans les artifices du langage' (Marin, 'Capriccio', 7).

26. On *Capriccio*, see Del Mar, *Richard Strauss*, 3:179–245; Wilhelm, *Fürs Wort*.

27. Strauss and Krauss, *Capriccio*, 6–7 (translation modified).

28. Darlow, *Dissidence*, 46–51.

29. Strauss and Krauss, *Capriccio*, 7; ibid., 37.

30. Ibid., 37 (translation modified).

31. See Tenschert, 'Sonnet in Strauss's *Capriccio*'.

32. Strauss and Krauss, *Capriccio*, 23–28.

33. Ibid., 53, 57.

34. Ibid., 67–68.

35. See Del Mar, *Richard Strauss*, 3:44–51; Wilhelm, *Strauss*, 228–30, 253–57. Both quote excerpts from Strauss's letter to Zweig.

36. See Del Mar, *Richard Strauss*, 3:245.

37. See Johnson, *Dictionary*, s.vv. 'maggot', 'maggotty'; *OED*, s.v. 'maggot'.

38. Nuttall, *Shakespeare the Thinker*, 8.

39. Shakespeare, *All's Well*, Act 1 Scene 1, line 157.

40. Ibid., 2.3, 287–89.

41. https://www.capricebourret.com [last accessed 10 February 2020].

42. Edgeworth, *Belinda*, 69; ibid., 36.

43. Ibid., Appendix, 482.

44. See Bowering, 'Home Away'.

45. Grace, 'Afterword', 258. See also Langston, 'Burning History'.

46. Quoted in Miki, *Record of Writing*, A48.

47. Van Herk, '*Caprice* Dreams a Western', VII.

48. See, e.g., Bowering, *Caprice*, 198–202.

49. Bowering, 'Painted Window', 120–22. On home as a place where 'without consideration one participates in the tradition', see Bowering, 'Home Away', 34.

50. Bowering, *Caprice*, 167, 212.

51. Ibid., 1.

52. Ibid., 88; compare ibid., 1.

Migrants in Our Midst

1. Adorno, 'Words from Abroad', 186–87; ibid., 190–191. See Yildiz, *Mother Tongue*, 67–108.

2. Adorno, 'Words from Abroad'; 190; ibid., 192.

3. Ibid., 186, 191–92, 187.

4. Yildiz, *Mother Tongue*, 67.

5. See chapter 3, n. 20 above.

6. Palmer et al., 'French Brexit Song'.

7. Elyot, *Governor*, fol. 85ᵛ; quoted in Jones, *Triumph of English*, 79. On denization, see Winder, *Bloody Foreigners*, 43–44.

8. Munday and Chettle, *Sir Thomas More*, Act 1, lines 123–34.

9. Ibid., 4.53–56.

10. Ibid., 6.141–56.

11. See ibid., Appendix 2, 344–94 (esp. 378–83).

Académie française. *Le Dictionnaire de l'Académie françoise dedié au Roy*. Paris: Veuve Jean-Baptiste Coignard, 1694. Online in *Dictionnaires*.

Adorno, Theodor W. 'Words from Abroad'. In *Notes to Literature*, 1:185–99. 2 vols. Edited by Rolf Tiedemann; translated by Shierry Weber Nicholsen. New York: Columbia University Press, 1991–92.

Anonymous. *Gallantry À-la-Mode: A Satyrical, in III Parts, Representing the Vanities of Several Humours of this Present Age*. Early English Books Online. London: T. R. and N. T., 1674.

———. *Remarks upon Remarques, or, A Vindication of the Conversations of the Town, in Another Letter Directed to the Same Sir T.L.* London: William Hensman, 1673.

———. *Remarques on the Humours and Conversation of the Town. Written in a Letter to Sir T.L.* London: Allen Banks, 1673.

Apter, Emily. *Against World Literature: On the Politics of Untranslatability*. London: Verso, 2013.

Atkinson, James. 'Montaigne and *Naïveté*'. *Romanic Review* 64 (1973): 245–57.

Auclair, Valérie. 'Les *Capricci di varie figure*, ou Callot dessinateur'. In Peureux, *Caprice*, 81–99.

Bachmann, Iris. 'Creoles'. In *The Cambridge History of the Romance Languages*, 2:400–44. 2 vols. Edited by Martin Maiden, John Charles Smith, and Adam Ledgeway. Cambridge: Cambridge University Press, 2011–13.

Bailey, Nathan. *The Universal Etymological English Dictionary*. 3rd edn. London: Thomas Cox, 1737. Online in *Lexicons*.

Bakhtin, Mikhail M. 'Discourse in the Novel'. In *The Dialogic Imagination: Four Essays*, 259–422. Edited by Michael Holquist; translated by Caryl Emerson and Michael Holquist. Austin, TX: University of Texas Press, 1981.

Baudelaire, Charles. *The Flowers of Evil*. Translated with notes by James McGowan. Includes parallel French text. Oxford: Oxford University Press, 1993.

Benítez-Rojo, Antonio. *The Repeating Island: The Caribbean and the Postmodern Perspective*. Translated by James E. Maraniss. Durham, NC: Duke University Press, 1992.

Bergin, Joseph. *A History of France*. London: Palgrave, 2015.

Bernabé, Jean, Patrick Chamoiseau, and Raphaël Confiant. *Éloge de la créolité/ In Praise of Creoleness*. Bilingual French–English edition. English translation by M. B. Taleb-Khyar. Paris: Gallimard, 1993.

Bhabha, Homi. 'Of Mimicry and Man: The Ambivalence of Colonial Discourse'. In *Tensions of Empire: Colonial Cultures in a Bourgeois World*, 152–60.

Edited by Frederick Cooper and Ann Laura Stoler. Berkeley and Los Angeles: University of California Press, 1997.

Bickerton, Derek. 'Reconsidering Creole Exceptionalism'. *Language* 80 (2004): 828–33.

Bold, Alan, ed. *The Quest for Le Carré*. London: Vision, 1988.

Bond, Edward. *Restoration: A Pastoral*. London: Methuen, 2000.

Bossuet, Jacques Bénigne. *Œuvres oratoires*. 7 vols. Edited by J. Lebarq, Ch. Urbain, and E. Levesque. Paris: Librairie Hachette, 1914–26.

Boursault, Edmé. *Les Mots à la mode*. In *Petites comédies rares et curieuses du XVIIᵉ siècle*, 1. Edited by Victor Fournel. Paris: A. Quantin, 1884.

Bowering, George. *Burning Water*. Vancouver: New Star Books, 2007.

———. *Caprice*. Vancouver: New Star Books, 2010.

———. 'Home Away: A Thematic Study of Some British Columbian Novels'. *Imaginary Hand: Essays*, 23–41. Edmonton: NeWest Press, 1988.

———. 'The Painted Window: Notes on Post-Realist Fiction'. In *The Mask in Place: Essays on Fiction in North America*, 113–27. Winnipeg: Turnstone Press, 1982.

———. *Shoot!* Vancouver: New Star Books, 2008.

Boyle, Robert. *The Works*. 6 vols. Edited by Thomas Birch. Hildesheim: Georg Olas, 1965–66.

Brathwaite, Edward. *The Development of Creole Society in Jamaica 1770–1820*. Oxford: Clarendon Press, 1978 (repr.).

Brown, Laura. 'Dryden and the Imperial Imagination'. In *The Cambridge Companion to John Dryden*, 59–74. Edited by Steven N. Zwicker. Cambridge: Cambridge University Press, 2004.

Brown, R. Allen. *The Normans and the Norman Conquest*. London: Constable, 1969.

Brundan, Katy. 'Cosmopolitan Complexities in Maria Edgeworth's *Ennui*'. *Studies in the Novel* 37 (2005): 123–40.

Bullard, Paddy, and Alexis Tadié, eds. *Ancients and Moderns in Europe: Comparative Perspectives*. Oxford: Voltaire Foundation, 2016.

Bussy, Roger de Rabutin. *The Amorous History of the Gauls*. London: S. Illidge, 1725.

———. *Histoire amoureuse des Gaules*. Edited by Roger Duchêne in collaboration with Jacqueline Duchêne. Paris: Gallimard, 1993.

Butler, Marilyn. *Maria Edgeworth: A Literary Biography*. Oxford: Clarendon Press, 1972.

Butterfield, Ardis. *The Familiar Enemy: Chaucer, Language, and Nation in the Hundred Years War*. Oxford: Oxford University Press, 2009.

Butterfield, Jeremy. *Fowler's Concise Dictionary of Modern English Usage*. 3rd edn. Oxford: Oxford University Press, 2016.

Callières, François de. *Des mots à la mode (1692)*; *Du bon et du mauvais usage dans les manières de s'exprimer (1693)*. Geneva: Slatkine reprints, 1972.

Callot, Jacques. *Capricci di varie figure*. Rome: Calisto Ferrante, [1617].

Canny, Nicholas P. *Making Ireland British, 1580–1650*. Oxford: Oxford University Press, 2001.

Canova-Green, Marie-Claude. 'Molière ou comment ne pas reconnaître sa dette: le théâtre de la Restauration en Angleterre'. In *La France et l'Europe du Nord au XVIIe siècle: de l'Irlande à la Russie*, 109–19. Edited by Richard G. Maber. Tübingen: Narr/Francke/Attempto, 2017.

Cassin, Barbara, ed. *Dictionary of Untranslatables: A Philosophical Lexicon*. Translated by Steven Rendall, Christian Hubert, Jeffrey Mehlman, Nathanael Stein, and Michael Syrotinksi. Translation edited by Emily Apter, Jacques Lezra, and Michael Wood. Princeton, NJ: Princeton University Press, 2014.

Castor, Grahame. *Pléiade Poetics: A Study in Sixteenth-Century Thought and Terminology*. Cambridge: Cambridge University Press, 1964.

Cave, Terence. *The Cornucopian Text: Problems of Writing in the French Renaissance*. Oxford: Clarendon Press, 1979.

Chateaubriand, François-René de. *Atala*; *René*. Translated by Rayner Heppenstall. London: Oxford University Press, 1963.

———. *Atala*; *René*; *Les Aventures du dernier Abencérage*. *Œuvres complètes*, vol. 16. Edited by Béatrice Didier. Paris: Honoré Champion, 2008.

Cheyne, George. *The English Malady (1733)*. Edited by Roy Porter. London: Tavistock/Routledge, 1990.

Cibber, Colly *The Comical Lovers: A Comedy*. Dublin: Augustus Long, n.d.

Cock, Emily. 'The *À la Mode* Disease: Syphilis and Temporality'. In *Disease and Death in Eighteenth-Century Literature and Culture: Fashioning the Unfashionable*, 57–75. Edited by Allan Ingram and Leigh Wetherall Dickson. Basingstoke: Palgrave Macmillan, 2016.

Coldiron, A. E. B. 'Public Sphere/Contact Zone: Habermas, Early Print, and Verse Translation'. *Criticism* 46 (2004): 207–22.

Colley, Linda. 'Britishness and Otherness: An Argument'. *Journal of British Studies* 31 (1992): 309–29.

Corneille, Pierre. *The Cid*; *Cinna*; *The Theatrical Illusion*. Translated by John Cairncross. Harmondsworth: Penguin, 1975.

———. *Théâtre complet*. Edited by Georges Couton. Paris: Garnier, 1971.

Cotgrave, Randle. *A Dictionarie of the French and English Tongues*. London: Adam Islip, 1611. Online in *Lexicons*.

Cowie, A. P., ed. *The Oxford History of English Lexicography*. 2 vols. Oxford: Clarendon Press, 2009.

Cresswell, Julia. *The Oxford Dictionary of Word Origins*. Oxford: Oxford University Press, 2009.

Darlow, Mark. *Dissonance in the Republic of Letters: The Querelle des Gluckistes et des Piccinnistes*. Oxford: Legenda, 2013.

DeGraff, Michel. 'Against Creole Exceptionalism'. *Language* 79 (2003): 391–410.

———. 'Against Creole Exceptionalism (Redux)'. *Language* 80 (2004): 834–39.

DeJean, Jean. *Ancients against Moderns: Culture Wars and the Making of a Fin de Siècle*. Chicago: University of Chicago Press, 1997.

———. *The Essence of Style: How the French Invented High Fashion, Fine Food, Chic Cafés, Style, Sophistication, and Glamour*. New York: Free Press, 2005.

Dell, Henry. *The Frenchify'd Lady Never in Paris*. Dublin: Sarah Cotter, 1761.

Del Mar, Norman. *Richard Strauss: A Critical Commentary of His Life and Works*. 3 vols. London: Barrie and Jenkins, 1978.

Dictionnaires des XVIe et XVIIe siècles. Paris: Classiques Garnier, 2018. Online database.

Dryden, John. *The Works of John Dryden*. General editor: H. T. Swedenberg Jr; textual editor: Vinton A. Dearing. 20 vols. Berkeley and Los Angeles: University of California Press, 1956–2000.

Du Bellay, Joachim. *Deffence et illustration de la langue françoyse*. Edited by Jean-Charles Monferran. Geneva: Droz, 2001.

Durkin, Philip. *Borrowed Words: A History of Loanwords in English*. Oxford: Oxford University Press, 2014.

Eden, Kathy. *Friends Hold All Things in Common: Tradition, Intellectual Property, and the* Adages *of Erasmus*. New Haven, CT: Yale University Press, 2001.

Edgeworth, Maria. *Belinda*. Edited by Kathryn J. Kirkpatrick. Oxford: Oxford University Press, 1994.

———. *Castle Rackrent*; *Ennui*. Edited by Marilyn Butler. London: Penguin, 1992.

———. *An Essay on Irish Bulls*. Edited by Jane Desmarais and Marilyn Butler. Dublin: University College Dublin Press, 2006.

———. *The Novels and Selected Works of Maria Edgeworth*. 12 vols. Edited by Marilyn Butler and Mitzi Myers. London: Pickering and Chatto, 1999–2003.

Edwards, Owen Dudley. 'The Clues of the Great Tradition'. In Bold, *Quest for Le Carré*, 41–68.

Elyot, Thomas. *The Book Named The Governor*. Menston, UK: The Scolar Press, 1970.

Emerson, Oliver Farrar. 'John Dryden and a British Academy'. In *Essential Articles for the Study of John Dryden*, 263–80. Edited by H. T. Swedenberg Jr. London: Frank Cass, 1966.

Enwezor, Okwui, Carlos Basualdo, Ute Meta Bauer, Susanne Ghez, Sarat Maharaj, Mark Nash, and Octavio Zaya, eds. *Créolité and Creolization: Documenta 11 Platform 3*. Ostfildern-Ruit: Hatje Cantz, 2003.

Estienne, Henri. *Deux Dialogues du nouveau langage françois italianizé et autrement desguizé, principalement entre les courtisans de ce temps*. Edited by Pauline M. Smith. Paris: Classiques Garnier, 2007.

Estienne, Robert. *Dictionaire francoislatin*. Geneva: Slatkine, 1972. Online in *Dictionnaires*.

Etherege, George. *The Man of Mode*. Edited by John Barnard. London: Bloomsbury, 2007.

Evelyn, John. *The Letterbooks of John Evelyn.* 2 vols. Edited by Douglas D. C. Chambers and David Galbraith. Toronto: University of Toronto Press, 2014.

———. *Tyrannus, or The Mode: In a Discourse of Sumptuary Lawes.* Edited from the edition of 1661 by J. L. Nevinson. Oxford: Luttrell Society/Blackwell, 1951.

Freeman, Edmund. 'A Proposal for an English Academy in 1660'. *Modern Language Review* 19 (1924): 291–300.

Furetière, Antoine. *Dictionaire universel.* Geneva: Slatkine, 1970. Online in *Dictionnaires.*

Gallagher, John. *Learning Languages in Early Modern England.* Oxford: Oxford University Press, 2019.

Gaunt, Simon. 'The *Chanson de Roland* and the Invention of France'. In *Rethinking Heritage: Cultures and Politics in Europe,* 90–101. Edited by Robert Shannan Peckham. London: Tauris, 2003.

———. 'French Literature Abroad: Towards an Alternative History of French Literature'. *Interfaces* 1 (2015): 25–61.

Gikandi, Simon. *Maps of Englishness: Writing Identity in the Culture of Colonialism.* New York: Columbia University Press, 1996.

Gimelli Martin, Catherine, and Hassan Melehy, eds. *French Connections in the English Renaissance.* Farnham, UK: Ashgate, 2013.

Glissant, Édouard. *La Cohée du Lamentin: Poétique V.* Paris: Gallimard, 2005.

———. *Traité du Tout-monde: Poétique IV.* Paris: Gallimard, 1997.

Goldsmith, Elizabeth C. *Exclusive Conversations: The Art of Interaction in Seventeenth-Century France.* Philadelphia: University of Pennsylvania Press, 1988.

Görlach, Manfred. *A Dictionary of European Anglicisms: A Usage Dictionary of Anglicisms in Selected European Languages.* Oxford: Oxford University Press, 2001.

Grace, Sherrill. 'Afterword'. In Bowering, *Shoot!,* 254–60.

Gracián, Baltasar. *L'Homme de cour.* Translated by Amelot de la Houssaye. 3rd edn. The Hague: Abraham Troyel, 1692.

Greene, Roland. *Five Words: Critical Semantics in the Age of Shakespeare and Cervantes.* Chicago: University of Chicago Press, 2013.

Greene, Thomas M. *The Light in Troy: Imitation and Discovery in Renaissance Poetry.* New Haven, CT: Yale University Press, 1982.

Gutiérrez Rodríguez, Encarnación, and Shirley Anne Tate, eds. *Creolizing Europe: Legacies and Transformations.* Liverpool: Liverpool University Press, 2015.

Gwynn, Robin D. *Huguenot Heritage: The History and Contribution of the Huguenots in Britain.* London: Routledge, 1985.

Hall, Stuart. 'Créolité and the Process of Creolization'. In Gutiérrez and Tate, *Creolizing Europe,* 12–25.

Hammond, Nicholas. *Playing with Truth: Language and the Human Condition in Pascal's Pensées.* Oxford: Clarendon Press, 1994.

Hammond, Paul. *Dryden and the Traces of Classical Rome.* Oxford: Oxford University Press, 1999.

———, ed. *Restoration Literature: An Anthology.* Oxford: Oxford University Press, 2002.

Hare, John. *St. Edwards Ghost: Or, Anti-Normanisme.* London: Richard Wodenothe, 1647.

Helgesson, Stefan, and Christina Kullberg. 'Translingual Events'. *Journal of World Literature* 3 (2018): 136–52.

Hendriks, A. L. *To Speak Simply: Selected Poems 1961–1986.* Sutton, UK: Hippopotamus Press, 1988.

Hill, Christopher. 'The Norman Yoke'. In *Puritanism and Revolution: Studies in Interpretation of the English Revolution of the Seventeenth Century*, 58–125. Harmondsworth: Penguin, 1986.

Howard, James. *The English Mounsieur: A Comedy.* London: James Magnes, 1674.

Howell, James. *A French and English Dictionary, Composed by Mr. Randle Cotgrave: With Another in English and French.* London: Anthony Dolle, 1673. Online in *Lexicons*.

Huarte de San Juan, Juan. *The Examination of Mens Wits: in Which by Discouering the Varietie of Natures is Shewed for What Profession Each One is Apt, and How Far He Shall Profit Therein.* Translated by Richard Carew from the Italian version of Camillo Camilli. Early English Books Online. London: Adam Islip, 1594.

———. *The Tryal of Wits: Discovering the Great Difference of Wits among Men, and What Sort of Learning Suits Best with Each Genius.* Translated by Edward Bellamy. Early English Books Online. London: Richard Sare, 1698.

Huchon, Mireille. *Histoire de la langue française.* Paris: LGF, 2002.

Hunt, John Dixon. *John Evelyn: A Life of Domesticity.* London: Reaktion, 2017.

Ibbett, Katherine, ed. *Fans. Seventeenth-Century French Studies* 36 (2014). Special issue.

Jankélévitch, Vladimir. *L'Aventure, l'Ennui, le Sérieux.* In *Philosophie morale*, 825–990. Edited by Françoise Schwab. Paris: Flammarion, 1998.

Johnson, Boris, and Theresa May. 'Boris Johnson's Resignation Letter and May's Reply in Full'. https://www.bbc.com/news/uk-politics-44772804 [last accessed 10 February 2020].

Johnson, Samuel. *A Dictionary of the English Language.* London: W. Strahan, 1755. Online in *Lexicons*.

Jones, Richard Foster. *The Triumph of the English Language: A Survey of Opinions Concerning the Vernacular from the Introduction of Printing to the Restoration.* Stanford, CA: Stanford University Press, 1953.

Jones, Suzanne. 'Printing Stage: Relationships between Performance, Print, and Translation in Early English Editions of Molière'. *Early Modern French Studies* 40 (2018): 146–65.

Kanz, Roland. *Die Kunst des Capriccio: kreativer Eigensinn in Renaissance und Barock*. Munich: Deutscher Kunstverlag, 2002.

Kellman, Steven G. *The Translingual Imagination*. Lincoln, NE: University of Nebraska Press, 2000.

Kennaway, James. *Some Gorgeous Accident*. Edinburgh: Mainstream Publishing, 1981.

Kenny, Neil. *Curiosity in Early Modern Europe: Word Histories*. Wiesbaden: Harrassowitz, 1998.

———. *The Uses of Curiosity in Early Modern France and Germany*. Oxford: Oxford University Press, 2004.

Kerrigan, John. *Archipelagic English: Literature, History, and Politics 1603-1707*. Oxford: Oxford University Press, 2008.

Kuhn, Reinhard Clifford. *The Demon of Noontide: Ennui in Western Literature*. Princeton, NJ: Princeton University Press, 1976.

La Fontaine, Jean de. *The Complete Fables*. Translated by Norman R. Shapiro; introduction by John Hollander; illustrations by David Schorr. Urbana, IL: University of Illinois Press, 2007.

———. *The Complete Tales in Verse: An Illustrated and Annotated Translation*. Translated by Randolph Runyon. Jefferson, NC: McFarland, 2009.

———. *Contes et nouvelles en vers*. Edited by Georges Couton. Paris: Classiques Garnier, 1961.

———. *Fables*. Edited by Marc Fumaroli. Paris: Livre de Poche, 1985.

Lambley, Katherine. *The Teaching and Cultivation of the French Language during Tudor and Stuart Times*. Manchester: Manchester University Press, 1920.

Langston, Jessica. 'Burning History: George Bowering's Disruption and Demythologizing of the Canadian Exploration Narrative'. *Open Letter* 14 (2010): 105–22.

Le Carré, John. *Agent Running in the Field*. London: Penguin, 2019.

———. *A Legacy of Spies*. London: Penguin, 2017.

———. *The Naive and Sentimental Lover*. London: Hodder and Stoughton, 2011.

———. *A Perfect Spy*. London: Hodder and Stoughton, 2011.

Lestringant, Frank. 'Montaigne, le Brésil et l'unité du genre humain'. *Montaigne Studies* 22 (2010): 9–21.

Lexicons of Early Modern English. Edited by Ian Lancashire. https://leme.library.utoronto.ca. Online database.

MacCabe, Colin, and Holly Yanacek, eds. *Keywords for Today: A 21st Century Vocabulary*. Oxford: Oxford University Press, 2018.

Mac Carthy, Ita, ed. *Renaissance Keywords*. Oxford: Legenda, 2013.

Marin, Louis. 'Il capriccio à partir des Caprices de Saint-Amant et de Jacques Callot'. In *Il capriccio nell'incisione francese del Seicento e del Settecento*, 5–12. Edited by Philippe Morel and Cesare Nissirio. Rome: Carte Segrete, 1983.

Marr, Alexander, Raphaële Garrod, José Ramòn Marcaida, and Richard J. Oosterhoff. *Logodaedalus: Word Histories of Ingenuity in Early Modern Europe*. Pittsburgh, PA: University of Pittsburgh Press, 2018.

Masten, Jeffrey. *Queer Philologies: Sex, Language, and Affect in Shakespeare's Time*. Philadelphia: University of Pennsylvania Press, 2016.

Matoré, Georges. *Histoire des dictionnaires français*. Paris: Larousse, 1968.

Ménage, Gilles. *Dictionnaire étymologique ou Les Origines de la langue françoise*. 1694. Online in *Dictionnaires*.

Mendies, John, *Abridgment of Johnson's Dictionary, English and Bengali: Peculiarly Calculated for the Use of European and Native Students, to Which Are Subjoined Abbreviations Commonly Used in Writing and Printing, and a Short List of French and Latin Words and Phrases in Common Use among English Authors*. 2nd edn. Calcutta: Baptist Mission Press, 1851.

Miège, Guy. *A New Dictionary, French and English, With another English and French*. London: Thomas Basset, 1677. Online in *Lexicons*.

Miki, Roy. *A Record of Writing: An Annotated and Illustrated Bibliography of George Bowering*. Vancouver: Talonbooks, 1989.

Mikkelson, David. 'Bush and French Word For Entrepreneur'. https://www.snopes.com/fact-check/french-lesson [last accessed 10 February 2020].

Milne, A. A. *The World of Pooh*. London: Methuen, 1958.

Molière. *Comedies*. 2 vols. Translated by Henry Baker and James Miller. London: Dent, 1929–51.

———. *Œuvres complètes*. 2 vols. Edited by Georges Forestier, Claude Bourqui, Alain Riffaud, Anne Piéjus, and David Chataignier. Paris: Gallimard, 2010.

Monaghan, David. *The Novels of John le Carré: The Art of Survival*. Oxford: Blackwell, 1985.

Monroe, B. S. 'An English Academy'. *Modern Philology* 8 (1910): 107–22.

Montaigne, Michel de. *Complete Works*. Translated by Donald Frame. London: Everyman, 2003.

———. *Les Essais*. Edited by Pierre Villey and V.-L. Saulnier. Paris: Presses Universitaires de France, 1992.

Moorby, Nicola. 'Walter Richard Sickert, *Ennui*, c. 1914'. https://www.tate.org.uk/art/research-publications/camden-town-group/walter-richard-sickert-ennui-r1133434 [last accessed 10 February 2020].

Morton, Herbert C. *The Story of* Webster's Third: *Philip Gove's Controversial Dictionary and Its Critics*. Cambridge: Cambridge University Press, 1995.

Motteux, Peter Anthony, ed. *The Gentleman's Journal: or The Monthly Miscellany. By Way of Letter to a Gentleman in the Country*. 3 vols. London: R. Baldwin, 1692–94.

Mugglestone, Lynda, ed. *The Oxford History of English*. Oxford: Oxford University Press, 2006.

Munday, Anthony, and Henry Chettle. *Sir Thomas More*. Revised by Henry Chettle, Thomas Dekker, Thomas Heywood, and William Shakespeare. Edited by John Jowett. London: Bloomsbury Arden Shakespeare, 2011.

Myers, Mitzi. '"Completing the Union": Critical *Ennui*, the Politics of Narrative, and the Reformation of Irish Cultural Identity'. *Prose Studies* 18 (1995): 41–77.

Newman, Gerald. *The Rise of English Nationalism: A Cultural History 1740–1830*. London: Weidenfeld and Nicolson, 1987.

Noel-Tod, Jeremy, ed. *The Oxford Companion to Modern Poetry*. 2nd edn. Oxford: Oxford University Press, 2013.

Norman, Larry F. *The Shock of the Ancient: Literature and History in Early Modern France*. Chicago: University of Chicago Press, 2011.

Novak, Maximilian. 'Margery Pinchwife's "London Disease": Restoration Comedy and the Libertine Offensive of the 1670s'. *Studies in the Literary Imagination* 10 (1977): 1–24.

Nuttall, A. D. *Shakespeare the Thinker*. New Haven, CT: Yale University Press, 2007.

O'Toole, Fintan. *Heroic Failure: Brexit and the Politics of Pain*. London: Head of Zeus, 2018.

The Oxford English Dictionary [*OED*]. 3rd edn (in progress). Edited by J. A. Simpson. http://www.oed.com. Oxford: Oxford University Press, 2000–. Online database.

Palmer, Amanda, Sarah-Louise Young, and Maxim Melton. 'French Brexit Song'. https://www.youtube.com/watch?v=uPLe9qhpBF8 [last accessed 10 February 2020].

Palmer, Patricia. *Language and Conquest in Early Modern Ireland: English Renaissance Literature and Elizabethan Imperial Expansion*. Cambridge: Cambridge University Press, 2001.

Pamuk, Orhan. *The Naive and the Sentimental Novelist*. Translated by Nazim Dikbaş. Cambridge, MA: Harvard University Press, 2010.

Pascal, Blaise. *Pensées*. Edited and translated by Roger Ariew. Indianapolis: Hackett, 2005.

———. *Les Provinciales, Pensées et opuscules divers*. Edited by Gérard Ferreyrolles and Philippe Sellier. Paris: Pochothèque, 2004.

Payne Fisk, Deborah, ed. *The Cambridge Companion to English Restoration Theatre*. Cambridge: Cambridge University Press, 2000.

Pearson, Roger. *Unacknowledged Legislators: The Poet as Lawgiver in Post-Revolutionary France*. Oxford: Oxford University Press, 2016.

Pepys, Samuel. *The Diary of Samuel Pepys: A New and Complete Transcription*. Edited by Robert Latham and William Matthews. 11 vols. London: G. Bell, 1970–83.

Peureux, Guillaume. 'Le Caprice dans la poésie française du XVIIe siècle: un panorama'. In Peureux, *Caprice*, 113–31.

———, ed. *Le Caprice. La Licorne* 69 (2004). Special issue.

Phillips, Adam. *On Kissing, Tickling, and Being Bored: Psychoanalytical Essays on the Unexamined Life*. London: Faber and Faber, 1993.

Phillips, Edward. *The New World of Words: or, Universal English Dictionary*. 6th edn. London: J. Phillips, 1706.

Plimpton, George. 'John le Carré: The Art of Fiction CXLIX'. *Paris Review* 39 (1997): 50–74.

Pratt, Mary Louise. *Imperial Eyes: Travel Writing and Transculturation*. London: Routledge, 1992.

Quemada, Bernard. *Les Dictionnaires du français moderne 1539–1863. Étude sur leur histoire, leurs types, leurs méthodes*. Paris: Didier, 1967.

Rankin, Deana. *Between Spenser and Swift: English Writing in Seventeenth-Century Ireland*. Cambridge: Cambridge University Press, 2005.

Richelet, Pierre. *Dictionnaire françois*. Geneva: Slatkine, 1994. Online in *Dictionnaires*.

Robertson, Ritchie. 'Ancients, Moderns, and the Future: The *Querelle* in Germany from Winckelmann to Schiller'. In Bullard and Tadié, *Ancients and Moderns*, 257–75.

Rosand, David. 'The Antic Line'. In *Drawing Acts: Studies in Graphic Expression and Representation*, 265–327. Cambridge: Cambridge University Press, 2002.

Roy, Arundhati. *The Ministry of Utmost Happiness*. London: Penguin, 2018.

Saint-Amant, Marc Antoine de Gérard, sieur de. *Œuvres*. 5 vols. Edited by Jacques Bailbé and Jean Lagny. Paris: Didier, 1967–79.

Schiller, Friedrich. *On the Naïve and Sentimental in Literature*. Translated and introduced by Helen Watanabe-O'Kelly. Manchester: Carcanet New Press, 1981.

Scudéry, Madeleine de. *'De l'air galant' et autres conversations: pour une étude de l'archive galante*. Edited by Delphine Denis. Paris: Champion, 1998.

———. *Artamène, ou Le Grand Cyrus*. 10 vols. Paris: Augustin Courbé, 1649–53.

———. *Artamenes, or The Grand Cyrus: An Excellent New Romance*. Translated by F. G. London: Humphrey Moseley, 1653.

———. *Conversations nouvelles sur divers sujets*. 2 vols. Paris: Claude Barbin, 1684.

Shakespeare, William. *All's Well That Ends Well*. Edited by G. K. Hunter. London: Arden Shakespeare, 2000.

Sickert, Walter. *The Complete Writings on Art*. Edited by Anna Gruetzner Robins. Oxford: Oxford University Press, 2000.

Spacks, Patricia Meyer. *Boredom: The Literary History of a State of Mind*. Chicago: University of Chicago Press, 1995.

Spivak, Gayatri Chakravorty. 'World Systems and the Creole, Rethought'. In Gutiérrez and Tate, *Creolizing Europe*, 26–37.

Staël, Madame (Anne-Louise-Germaine) de. *Corinne, or Italy*. Translated by Sylvia Raphael. Oxford: Oxford University Press, 1998.

———. *Corinne ou l'Italie*. Edited by Simone Balayé. Paris: Gallimard, 1985.

Staves, Susan. 'A Few Kind Words for the Fop'. *Studies in English Literature* 22 (1982): 413–28.

Stedman, Gesa. *Cultural Exchange in Seventeenth-Century France and England*. Farnham, UK: Ashgate, 2013.

Stoler, Ann Laura, and Frederick Cooper. 'Between Metropole and Colony: Rethinking a Research Agenda'. In *Tensions of Empire: Colonial Cultures in a Bourgeois World*, 1–56. Edited by Frederick Cooper and Ann Laura Stoler. Berkeley and Los Angeles: University of California Press, 1997.

Strauss, Richard, and Clemens Krauss. *Capriccio: A Conversation Piece for Music*. Libretto in English translation by Maria Massey. London: Boosey and Hawkes, 1963.

Tadié, Alexis. 'English Prose in a European Context'. In *The Oxford Handbook of Seventeenth-Century Prose*. Oxford: Oxford University Press, forthcoming in 2020.

Tenschert, Roland. 'The Sonnet in Richard Strauss's Opera *Capriccio*: A Study in the Relation between the Metre and the Musical Phrase'. *Tempo* 47 (1958): 7–11.

Thomas, Keith. *In Pursuit of Civility: Manners and Civilization in Early Modern England*. New Haven, CT: Yale University Press, 2018.

Trésor de la langue française informatisé: dictionnaire de la langue du XIXᵉ et du XXᵉ siècle (1789–1960). http://atilf.atilf.fr/tlf.htm. Online database.

Van Herk, Aritha. ' "A Lot of Beautiful Things Are Dangerous": *Caprice* Dreams a Western'. In Bowering, *Caprice*, v–xi.

Viala, Alain. *La France galante: essai historique sur une catégorie culturelle, de ses origines jusqu'à la Révolution*. Paris: PUF, 2008.

———. *La Galanterie: une mythologie française*. Paris: Seuil, 2019.

Vincent, Samuel, and Thomas Dekker. *The Young Gallant's Academy, Or, Directions How He Should Behave Himself in All Places and Company: As in an Ordinary, in a Play-house, in a Tavern, as He Passes along the Street All Hours of the Night, and How to Avoid Constables Interrogatories: To Which Is Added, the Character of a Town-Huff: Together with the Character of a Right Generous and Well-bred Gentleman*. London: R. Mills, 1674.

Walcott, Derek. *Omeros*. London: Faber and Faber, 1990.

Wilhelm, Kurt. *Fürs Wort brauche ich Hilfe: die Geburt der Oper* Capriccio *von Richard Strauss und Clemens Krauss*. Munich: Nymphenburger, 1988.

———. *Richard Strauss: An Intimate Portrait*. Translated by Mary Whittall. London: Thames and Hudson, 1989.

Williams, Deanne. *The French Fetish from Chaucer to Shakespeare*. Cambridge: Cambridge University Press, 2004.

Williams, Raymond. *Keywords: A Vocabulary of Culture and Society*. London: Fontana Press, 1988.

Winder, Robert. *Bloody Foreigners: The Story of Immigration to Britain*. London: Little, Brown, 2004.

Wogan-Browne, Jocelyn, ed. *Language and Culture in Medieval Britain: The French of England, c. 1100–c. 1500*. With the assistance of Carolyn Collette and others. Woodbridge, UK: York Medieval Press/Boydell and Brewer, 2009.

Woolf, Virginia. *Walter Sickert: A Conversation*. London: Tate Publishing, 2005.

Yardeni, Myriam. *Le Refuge protestant*. Paris: Presses Universitaires de France, 1985.

Yildiz, Yasemin. *Beyond the Mother Tongue: The Postmonolingual Condition*. New York: Fordham University Press, 2012.

As elsewhere in the book, I italicize in this index words that are discussed primarily as words, while adopting in all other situations the type face—either roman or italic—standardly used for the word in English (as per *OED*). Some entries list instances where the main entry word is treated as a word alongside instances where it is treated in other ways. In such cases, the main entry word is set in the type face—either roman or italic—standardly used for that word, and subentries are used to distinguish the various treatments it receives.

A NOTE ON THE TYPE

THIS BOOK has been composed in Miller, a Scotch Roman typeface designed by Matthew Carter and first released by Font Bureau in 1997. It resembles Monticello, the typeface developed for The Papers of Thomas Jefferson in the 1940s by C. H. Griffith and P. J. Conkwright and reinterpreted in digital form by Carter in 2003.

Pleasant Jefferson ("P. J.") Conkwright (1905–1986) was Typographer at Princeton University Press from 1939 to 1970. He was an acclaimed book designer and AIGA Medalist.

The ornament used throughout this book was designed by Pierre Simon Fournier (1712–1768) and was a favorite of Conkwright's, used in his design of the *Princeton University Library Chronicle*.